Parallel Developments

A Geophysical / Paleontological Timeline from Big Bang to 3000BC

BERNHARD R. TEICHER

Copyright

Parallel Developments

Edited by H.B.Teicher, BIOCOMM PRESS
Cover design by BIOCOMM PRESS

CONTENTS

A Introduction

An attempt has been made to reconcile the sometimes contradictory information from the source references (3rd col. in the timeline) into a consolidated scheme, by super-imposing later published information over data published earlier, but considering the reliability of sources as well (e.g. National Geographic would supersede anonymous newspaper accounts). This, however, has been restricted to clear cases of availability of a more recent dating with (almost) identical details. Earlier datings have sometimes been left to indicate the progress made in recent years.

The source references are listed at the end of the listing (see INDEX).

Subject references (2nd col. in the timelines), listed in the INDEX, page 3, identify groups of data for detailed scrutiny by specialists.

Times are quoted as **BP** = Before Present, truncated to 5 000 BP
Ga = Giga years = billions of years ago
Ma = Mega years = millions of years ago
ka = kilo years = thousands of years ago

The 5 000 BP cut-off is arbitrary but was chosen to incorporate the end of the major migrations of the Amerindians as well as the start of the Indo-European peoples.
The G, M, k abbreviations are used for Billions, Millions, and Thousands.

All dates, obviously, are tentative and some are merely speculative. Timing of, particularly, the Quaternary (Lower Paleolithic to Neolithic Age) varies greatly as to locality, even within a continent/subcontinent
It should be understood, that some of the quoted points-in-time are not actually given by the references, but have been inter- or extrapolated by myself to enable me to place the various data in sequence. It is here, where mistakes are most likely to have been made by me.

The tectonic data up to 200 Ma, end of the Triassic Period and final break-up of Pangaea, is anecdotal at best, because whole shields and even continents have been swallowed up by the earth's crust or mantle before this time. Data since this point seems to be more realistic and reliable.

I am not a scientist but an amateur who is interested in the inter-linked relationship between geological, paleontological and environmental developments. Any criticism and additions (preferably with stated sources) are most welcome, and to facilitate this, I have provided in sections E and F (see INDEX page 3) extracts for each of the subjects.

B.R.Teicher
btteicher@gmail.com

Margate/South Africa
15-04-2012

B Geological Timeline from 5000 BP(= 3000 BC)

This is a summary in the conventional mode, e.g. the oldest layers at the bottom of the pile (as found in rock formations), while the following Integrated Timeline uses the "upside down" structure.

The Geological Timeline is generally based on information obtained from Bishop et al., Philips Minerals, Rocks etc. (source 9), Stanley, Earth and Life through Time (source H) and the Time Scale of the Geological Society of America, 1999, but with adjustments from various other sources to allow for a global application instead of a North American bias. The "promotion" of the Ediacaran Period has been incorporated.

All these classifications are based on present-day (more or less) generally accepted conventions, but they are, of course, very approximate and subject to alterations based on new data or changed interpretations.

5,0 ka to 543 Ma ***PHANEROZOIC EON***
= fossil yielding times

5,0 ka to 65 Ma **Cenozoic Era**

5,0 ka to 1,8 Ma QUATERNARY PERIOD

5,0 to 10,0 ka Holocene Epoch
5,0 to 7,0 Neolithic Age
7,0 to 10,0 Mesolithic (Eurasia)/Archaic (Americas) Age

10,0 ka to 1,8 Ma Pleistocene Epoch
10,0 ka to 42,0 ka Upper Paleolithic Age
42,0 ka to 1,8 Ma Lower Paleolithic Age

1,8 to 65,0 Ma **Tertiary Sub-Era**

1,8 to 23,8 Ma NEOGENE PERIOD = LATE TERTIARY

1,8 to 5,3 Ma Pliocene Epoch
1,8 Ma to 2,6 Ma Oldowan Sub-Epoch (Africa)
5,3 to 23,8 Ma Miocene Epoch

23,8 to 65,0 Ma PALEOGENE PERIOD = EARLY TERTIARY

23,8 to 33,7 Ma Oligocene Epoch
33,7 to 54,8 Eocene Epoch
54,8 to 65,0 Paleocene Epoch

65,0 to 248,2 Ma **Mesozoic Era**

65,0 to 144,0 Ma Cretaceous Period
144,0 to 205,7 Jurassic Period
205,7 to 248,2 Triassic Period

248 to 543 Ma **Paleozoic Era**

248 to 290 Ma Permian Period
290 to 354 Carboniferous Period
354 to 417 Devonian Period
417 to 443 Silurian Period
443 to 490 Ordovician Period
490 to 543 Cambrian Period

543 Ma to 4,7 Ga ***PRE-CAMBRIAN EON***

also known as ***CRYPTOZOIC EON*** or ***Hadaicum*** *= times prior to known fossils, now recognized as a misnomer, as much older fossils have been found*

543 Ma to 2,5 Ga **Proterozoic Era**

543 to 600 Ma Ediacaran Period
600 to 650 Ma Vendian Period
650 Ma to 1,6 Ga Riphean Period
1,6 to 2,5 Ga Early Proterozoic Period

2,5 to 3,8 Ga **Archean Era**

3,8 to 4,6 Ga **Priscoan or Hadean Era**

4,6 Ga to Big Bang 13,7 Ga ***COSMIC EON***
(my choice of term)
= time from the BIG BANG to the formation of the Earth

Figure 1: 1999 Geological Timescale by the Geological Society of America

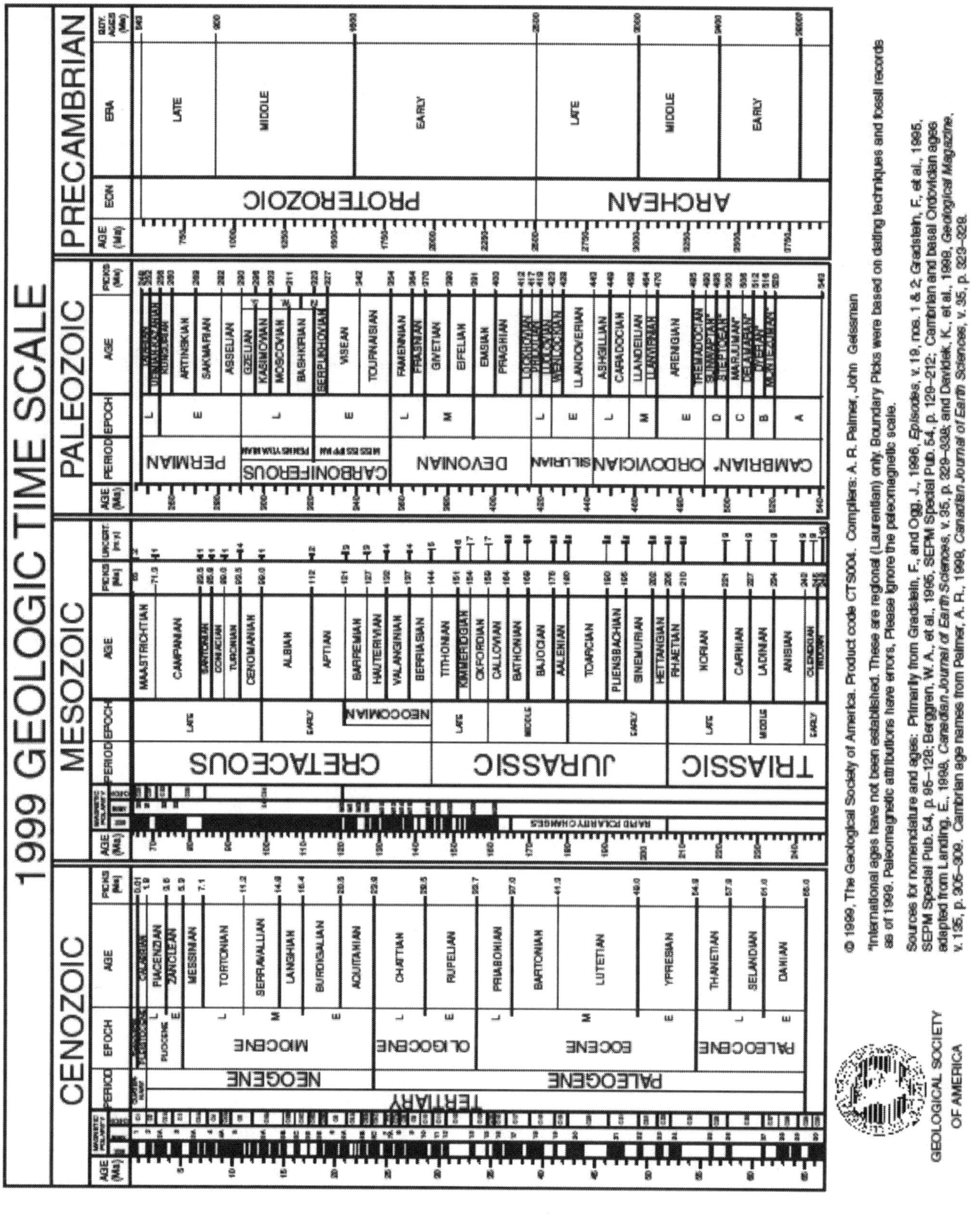

GEO TIMES

Time	Subdivision		Division	Major division
13,7/ 4,6 Ga				COSMIC EON
4,6/ 3,8 Ga		**1**	Priscoan Era	PRECAMBRIAN EON
3,8/ 2,5 Ga			Archean Era	
2,5/ 1,6 Ga	Early Proterozoic P.		Proterozoic Era	
1,6/ 650 Ma	Riphean Period			
650/ 600 Ma	Vendian Period			
600/ 543 Ma	Ediacaran Period			
543/ 490 Ma	Cambrian Period		Lw.Paleozoic Era	PHANEROZOIC EON
490/ 443 Ma	Ordovician Period			
443/ 417 Ma	Silurian Period			
417/ 354 Ma	Devonian Period		Up.Paleozoic Era	
354/ 290 Ma	Carboniferous Period			
290/ 248 Ma	Permian Period			
248,2/ 205,7 Ma	Triassic Period	**2**	Mesozoic Era	
205,7/ 144,0 Ma	Jurassic Period			
144,0/ 65,0 Ma	Cretaceous Period			
65,0/ 54,8 Ma	Paleocene Epoch	**3**	Paleogene Period	Cenozoic Era
54,8/ 33,7 Ma	Eocene Epoch			
33,7/ 23,8 Ma	Oligocene Epoch			
23,8/ 5,3 Ma	Miocene Epoch		Neogene Period	
5,3/ 1,8 Ma	Pliocene Epoch			
1,8/ 42,0 ka	L.Paleolithic Age	**4**	Pleistocene Epoch	Quartenary P.
42,0/ 10,0 ka	Upper Paleolithic Age			
10,0/ 7,0 ka	Mesolithic Age		Holocene Epoch	
7,0/ 5,0 ka	Neolithic Age			

C Integrated Geophysical/Paleontological Timeline to 5000BP

(following the historical sequences, starting with the earliest events)

Part 1 Big Bang to End of Mesozoic = KT Boundary

13,7 Ga to 4,6 Ga — C O S M I C   E O N

(my choice of term)

	Subject Ref.	Source Ref.	
13,7 **Ga**	c	K	Big Bang creating universe, eventually consisting of >100G galaxies each with 200G stars, 4% "normal" atoms, 23% "dark matter" and 73% "dark (anti-gravity) energy" (see Notes at end of this section)
13,7±100My	c	P	Big Bang (NASA microwave project 2003)
$13,7-10^{-44}$s	c	AD	Natural Laws start to operate (see 13,7 Ga -1s)
$13,7-10^{-32}$s	c	W	Temperature of universe dropped to only 11G°C (see 13,7 Ga -1min)
13,7-10,5s	c	AD	Universe cooled enough that quarks cannot exist any longer independently, 3 each cluster to form protons and neutrons, but not atoms yet (see 13,7 Ga -380ky)
13,7-0,01s	c	W	Universe in quark-gluon-plasma condition (13,7-380ky)
13,7-1s	c	AD	Neutrinos stop reacting with matter ($13,7-10^{-44}$s Ga)
13,7-1s	c	T	Gravity, strong and weak nuclear forces and the other physical forces appear (see 13,7Ga -10^{-44}s)
13,7-1s	c	AE	10G°C = temperature in H-bomb, mostly photons, electrons and neutrinos and their anti-particles with some protons and neutrons (13,7-100s Ga)
13,7-1min	c	T	Universe now 1,6 trillion km across, appearance of H and He, 98% of all universal matter now in existence (see 13,7 Ga-10^{-32}s)
13,7-100s	c	AE	1G°C = temperature inside hottest stars, protons and neutrons combine to atomic nuclei, 1 proton and neutron each = nucleus of deuterium (heavy hydrogen), then 2 protons and neutrons each = helium nucleus (see 13,7 Ga -380ky)
13,7-10ky	c	AD	Rate of expansion of universe dominated by energy up to now, from then on by matter
13,7-380ky	c	AD	Energy of photons insufficient to separate electrons from protons = recombination, end of plasma oscillation, echo horizon 220k Ly = extent of universe then, size increase since then 1 100x, temperature 3 000°K (see 13,7 Ga -0,01s and 13,7-380ky)
13,7-380ky	c	Q	Separation of energy and matter

	Subject Ref.	Source Ref.	
13,7 **Ga** -380ky	c	AB	H appears as 1st element by adding an electron to the nucleus, universe is now "transparent" for electro-magnetic radiation, there are no gravitational waves (see 13,7 Ga -10^{-5}s)
13,7 -1My	c	Q	Universe <0,1% of present size
13,6	c	AG	1st short-lived stars appear (see 13,45 Ga)
13,5	c	I	Universe plunged in darkness (see 13,2 and 12,8 Ga)
13,45	c	AG	Last of short-lived stars appear (see 13,6 Ga)
13,3	c	K	Primordial structure of universe now established
13,2	c	I	1st short-lived (< 1My) star produces hydrogen and helium, nuclear fusion of hydrogen atoms creates light, becomes supernova, creating heavier atoms (oxygen, carbon) (see 13,6 and 13,5 Ga)
13,1	c	AF	Age of small proto-galaxies seen by Hubble, blue light
13,07	c	AG	Supernova of short-lived star 13,1G Ly away
>13,0	c	AG	UDFy-38 135 539, the most distant galaxy found
12,8	c	P	1st stars, end of "Dark Age" (Sir Martin Rees) (13,5)
12,7	c	Q	Oldest planet found in Globular Cluster M4
12,0	c	W	Milky Way started (see details at end of subject)
12,0 ±1Gy	c	AD	Average age of star clusters in the Milky Way halo (Hertzsprung/Russell diagrams)
11,7	c	K	2 000 galaxies already in existence
11,0	c	W	Supernova explosion is source of almost mass-less neutrinos, which can transverse planets, forming electrons, myons, tauons (see 5,0 Ga)
10,7	c	W	Very old spiral galaxy seen when very young, 30 gas accumulations 200M Ly across, no stars
7,0	c	AD	Expansion of universe until now braked by gravitation (see 6,0 and 5,0 Ga)
6,0	c	AD	Expansion of universe linear (see 7,0 and 5,0 Ga)
6,0	c	K	Number of red (dying) stars begins to exceed the number of blue (new) stars
5,5	c	W	Start of accelerating expansion of universe (5,0 Ga)
5,0	c	I	Supernova explosion creates natural atoms heavier than uranium (92 protons), e.g. a plutonium isotope of 94 protons, a component of rare earth bastnasite
5,0	c	AD	Expansion of universe starts to accelerate (see 7,0, 6,0 and 5,0 Ga)
*5,0	c	AE	Solar system is formed from supernova debris (4,7 Ga)
*4,7	c	Q	99,9% of a gas/dust cloud 24G km across became our Sun, 0,1% formed the planets, comets, meteorites (see 4,587 Ga)
*4,7	c	H	Formation of the solar system: planets and oldest meteoroids from debris of imploding star and subsequent exploding supernova (see 5,0 and 4,55 Ga)

	Subject Ref.	Source Ref.	
*4,7 **Ga**	c	Q	Sun temperatures: photosphere 5,7k°C, chromosphere 10k°C, corona 2M°C
*4,7 -20My	c	AB	Water exists in solar system, but source unclear (volcanic eruptions, proto-planet, asteroids ?), but inner planets Mercury to Mars lost all water (see 4,25 Ga)

4,6 Ga to 543 Ma **P R E - C A M B R I A N E O N**

4,6 Ma to 3,8 Ga **P r i s c o a n E r a**

4,6	c	P	Small baby (new) galaxies formed 100Ly away
*4,6	c	3,H	Bombardment of Earth and Moon starts, meteorites/ comets bring carbon and its compounds as carbonaceous chondrites (see 3,9 Ga)
*4,6	c	I	Moon forms from primeval solar nebula (4,53 Ga,700 Ma)
*4,6	c	I	Probable Moon temperatures: 90km outer crust at 440°K, intermediate zone 800km at 800°K, central core 900km radius at 1 100°K, assuming mostly olivine interior
*4,6	c	I	Probable configuration of the Moon: outer 6km "loose material", next 16km basalt, next 38km eclogite or anorthosite rocks
*4,6	c	I	"Genesis Bean", glass fragment ex drilling core, Moon
*4,6	c	K	Mt.Olympus crater, 24km high walls, 600km diameter, Valles Marineris canyon 7km deep, 4 000km long, Mars
*4,6	g	F	Earth a ball of igneous molten rocks (see 4,4 Ga)
*4,59	g	U	Earth has 65% of present size, largely segregated into core and mantle
*4,587	c	W	Interstellar 5 000°C molecular cloud 100's of Ly across, debris of dead stars, for 10My gravity draws particles together (see 4,7 Ga)
*4,57±30My	c	AD	Oldest solar system rocks and meteorites

***Note:** *in the light of the newest information, all entries regarding the solar system prior to 4,567 Ga have to be re-dated, but I have left the original dates given by the references unchanged, pending confirmation*

4,567	c	AM	A supernova causes collapse of a gas/dust cloud, rotation flattens the cloud into a disk shape, with the proto sun in the center, radiometric dating from meteorites (see 4,55 Ga)
4,55±70My	c	T	Age of solar system rocks (C.Patterson) (see 4,57 Ga)
4,55	c	T	Sun has 75% of present brightness

	Subject Ref.	Source Ref.	
4,55 **Ga**	c	W	Mass of solar system contracts, spin increases and superheats, forming ±20 planets, during following 30My these start to collide (see 4,7 and 4,53 Ga)
4,55	c,g	AM	Start of planet formation(see 4,567 and 4,4 Ga)
4,54	g	AM	Best estimate of Earth's age
4,53	c	W	Moon was 15x closer than now (see 4,6 Ga and 700 Ma)
4,53	c,g e	U F,Q	Earth struck a glancing blow by a Mars-sized object, which is mostly thrown into Earth's orbit, part falls back, vaporizing part of the mantle, rest forming Moon surface, tilted Earth's axis, now spins in a conical path for 26My, creating seasons and tides, increased revolutions, rotating NiFe nucleus creates magnetosphere, protecting atmosphere from solar wind (see 4,55 Ga)
4,5	c	W	Huge floods and glaciers formed 2 500km long, 3km deep and up to 500km wide Kasei Valles, Mars
4,5	c	7	Mars surface "active" but solid, no plate tectonics, plenty of water 200m below the poles, kept liquid due to overlay pressure (see 3,8 Ga)
4,5	c	W	CO_2 ice sublimes to gas from the bottom, carrying dust fountains to surface which causes dark areas, Mars
4,5	c	AG	New theory: ice covering a huge moon crashing into Saturn was stripped off, forming the rings, which are 95% ice("Nature")
4,5	c,b	P,W	Carbonaceous chondrite meteor contains 74 types of amino acids (8 used by Earthly proteins), strings of polyols sugar unknown on Earth, components of Earth life (left-handed amino, di-amino acids) came from space, maybe forming proteins, molecules, Murchison, Australia (see 4,0 Ga)
4,404	g,e	W AM	Oldest zircon crystal in globally oldest sandstone deposits, proof of presence of water, Pilbara, Western Australia (see 4,252 and 3,0 Ga)
4,4	c	AM	Sun nuclear fusion starts, solar wind removes remainders of the gas/dust cloud (see 4,55 Ga)
4,4	c	Q	Planets have about ⅓ of present size
4,4	g,e	7,F	Rocky islands in magma ocean, crust probably has present average thickness of 35km, first water (see 4,6 and 3,9 Ga)
4,3	g	7	Melting of the interior of the Earth, NIFE core
4,3	e	7	Water etc. expelled, this photo-dissociated to oxygen and hydrogen (see 4see 4,0 Ga)
4,28	g	AB	Nuvvuagittuq volcanic greenstone belt, Quebec, Canada
4,252	g	W	Oldest diamond inclusions in zircon crystals, Pilbara, Western Australia (see 4,406 Ga)

	Subject Ref.	Source Ref.	
4,25 **Ga**	c,e	W	Impactor space craft (2005) proves much ice in meteorites, but water differs from ours, oceans are green (iron content), denser atmosphere reddish, now believed water reached Earth from outer asteroid belt meteorites, deflected into Earth orbit by Jupiter (see 4,7 Ga -20My)
4,1	g	F	Grano-diorite rocks of Acasta, Canada (see 4,03 Ga)
4,03	g	AB	Acasta gneiss, Northern Territory, Canada (4,1 + 3,9)
4,0	c	I	Mare Imbrium result of meteorite impact, Moon (3,3 Ga)
4,0	e	Q	A day is less than 10 hours long (see 3,3 Ga)
4,0	e	3,U	1st atmosphere, O_2 level <0,1% of present, mainly CO_2 and some N_2 (see 4,3 Ga)
4,0	e	W	Moderate temperatures of ±90°C and absence of acids allow H and CO_2 to form methane (see 3,9 and 2,5 Ga)
4,0	e	P	Sun radiation only 70% of present, balanced by CO_2 greenhouse effect, temperature 50 - 80°C, atmospheric pressure 30 - 50 bar, today about 1 bar (see 2,5 Ga)
4,0	b	W	1st life forms prokaryotes: B.archaea, anaerobic, from hydrothermal vents such as at the mid-Atlantic ridge (see 3,9, and 3,5 Ga)
4,0	b	U	4 self-replicating molecules, precursors to RNA, DNA, all life evolves from LUCA (see 3,5 Ga)
4,0	b	U	Amino acids, nucleotides, sugars in left- and right-handed form, all life uses left-handed amino acids and right-handed nucleotides and sugars (see 4,5 Ga)
3,9	c	7,H	Great Bombardment of Earth and Moon ends (4,6 and 3,8)
3,9	g	T	Earth crust completely solidified (see 4,4 Ga)
3,9	g	G,3	Greenland gneisses, metamorphic greenstone, possibly part of vanished north-western continent, Huronian orogeny, Arctic Canada (see 4,03 Ga)
3,9	g,e	U	Oldest sedimentary banded iron rocks, indication of surface water, Amitsoq terrane, Isua Group, Greenland (see 4,4 and 2,0 Ga)
3,9	e,b	3,U	Laminated slime mats and proto-stromatolites formed by blue-green prokaryotes cyano-bacteria photo-synthesize CO_2 into C and O_2, reacted to $CaCO_3$, further reducing the CO_2 content of the atmosphere, Barberton, South Africa (see 4,0, 3,5 and 3,0 Ga)
3,85	g	P	Quartz/clinopyroxene rocks, Isua Group, Greenland
3,85	b	F,P	1st life forms develop in shallow water, carbonates, fossils of single-cell thermophilic bacteria, Isua Group, Greenland (see 4,0 Ga)

3,8 Ga to 2,5 Ga **A r c h e a n E r a**

	Subject Ref.	Source Ref.	
3,8 **Ga**	c	AF	2 asteroid storms hit Earth and Moon (see 3,9 Ga)
3,8	c	I	Age of Moon surface soil (see 3,7 Ga)
3,8	c	P	1st volcanic eruptions, Mars (see 4,0 Ma)
3,8	c	P	Phyllosilicate clays, result of basalt immersed in water for very long times, Mars (see 4,5 Ga)
3,8	g	5	Swaziland shield, oldest rocks of Africa, South Africa
3,8	e	T,W	Oceans are acidic and shallow and contain almost the present volume of water
3,7	c	I	Minimum age of Moon rocks (see 3,8 Ga)
3,7	c	I	Lava eruptions on Moon start (see 3,3 Ga)
3,644	g	AH U	Intrusion of 1st granites, , grano-diorite, high Na content, Komatiite basalt part of ancient continental and oceanic crusts, Kaapvaal craton, Barberton, South Africa (see 3,3 Ga)(
3,6	g	1	Siberian shield formed (see 2,5 and 1,5 Ga)
3,6	b	H	Proposed anaerobic bacteria operating chemosynthesis, changing SO_4 to SO_3 structures, emitting O_2
3,553	g	AH	Basement granites, Pongola, South Africa
3,5	e,b	T,W S	Proto-stromatolites produce O_2 by photosynthesis, Sebakwia, Zimbabwe, Warrawoona, Western Australia and Pilbara, Australia (see 3,9 Ga)
3,5	b	AG	Stromatolite-like structures indicate live, Mars
3,5	b	V	LUCA (Last Universal Common Ancestor) (see 4,0 Ga)
3,5	b	P,6	Dividing B.archaea and proto-stromatolites, greenstone belt, Barberton, South Africa (see 4,0 Ga)
3,5	b	K	T4 virus, a bacteriophage virus eating the E.coli (Escherichia) bacterium
3,465	c	U,D	1st recorded 20km diameter super-meteorite impact, melting rocks to glass spherules, crater across Gondwana, Barberton, S.Africa, Pilbara, W.Australia
3,45	g	AH	Start of formation of Barberton etc. greenstone belts, South Africa (see 3,0 Ga)
3,45	e	AG	Earth's magnetic field exists, Barberton, S.Africa
3,4	c	I	10 layers of asphalt at Hadley Rille (= gorge), Moon
3,4	g	U	Oldest island arc by subduction of oceanic crust with associated batholiths, eroded sediments fill ocean trench, Barberton, South Africa (3,3 and 3,2 Ga)
3,3	c	I	Lava filling Mare Imbrium at Hadley Rille, Moon (4,0)
3,3	c	I	Lava eruptions on Moon end (see 3,7 Ga)
3,3	g	U	Oldest island arc eroded, Barberton, S.Africa (3,4 Ga)
3,3	g	AH	End of formation of Barberton etc. greenstone belts, start of post-greenstone granite intrusions, South Africa (see 3,644 and 3,0 Ga)

	Subject Ref.	Source Ref.	
3,3 **Ga**	e	AM	Probably 14 hrs/d (see 4,0 and 3,1 Ga)
3,2	g	U	Ripple marks in oceanic sandstones, Barberton, S.Afr.
3,2	g	U	Island arcs amalgamate, form oldest micro-continent, Kaapvaal craton, South Africa (see 3,3 and 3,4 Ga)
3,1	c	U	Indication of 18 day lunar month
3,1	g	U	Granites, high K content, Kaapvaal craton stabilized, South Africa (see 3,074 Ga)
3,1	g	1	Baltic/Ukrainian shields exist
3,1	e	U	Earth rotating faster, days shorter, more days per year (see 3,3 and 2,45 Ga)
3,074	g	U	Rifting and thinning of Kaapvaal craton, eruption of rhyolites, South Africa (see 3,1 and 2,97 Ga)
3,0	g	U	UR super-continent starts to assemble: parts of southern Africa, Madagascar, India, western Australia, eastern Antarctica (see 1,5 Ga)
3,0	g	AH	End of post-greenstone granite intrusions, South Africa (see 3,3 Ga)
3,0	g	U AF	Oldest diamonds formed 100-200km below at 900-1 300 C, ejected by explosive volcanic eruptions at 10-30km/h (Eggler, 1989), last few km probably at several 100km/h, otherwise they would have turned into carbon, Southern Africa (see 2,0 Ga)
3,0	g	H	Pongola super group astride greenstone belt, South Africa (see 3,45 Ga)
3,0	g	AB	Globally oldest sand deposits, Jack Hills, Western Australia (see 4,406 Ga)
3,0	g	P	Northern Scandinavian orogeny, Kola peninsula, Russia (see 1,9 Ga)
3,0	b	I	Probable age of photosynthesis (see 3,9 Ga)
2,97	g	U	Rifts subside, Kaapvaal craton submerged, start of Witwatersrand Supergroup (see 3,074 and 2,714 Ga)
2,95	e	U	Possibly 1st glaciation, South Africa
2,914	g	AH U	Granitic crust sags, formation of large Witwatersrand Basin (inland sea), alluvial gold deposits laid down, Witwatersrand and Zululand, South Africa
2,9	g,b	S	Carbonaceous kerogen (bitumen) of biological origin (Hallbauer), Witwatersrand, South Africa
2,9	b	AB	Proto-stromatolite fossils, Ulundi, South Africa
2,8	g	H	Start of Witwatersrand deposits of up to 8km thick and 400 000km^2 of mixed lava and sediment (conglomerates), South Africa (see 2,5 Ga)
2,8	g	R	Basement granite/gneiss laid down, Zimbabwe
2,8	g	S	Extensive volcanic activity, Southern Africa

	Subject Ref.	Source Ref.	
2,714 **Ga**	g	AH	Zimbabwe craton collides with and fractures Kaapvaal craton, Ventersdorp flood lavas cover the Witwatersrand Basin, 100 000km^2 magma outpours, 2km thick, creates 6km high mountain ridge (Limpopo Belt), now completely eroded, South Africa (see 2,97 Ga)
2,7	e	H	Huron, first known global glaciation (see 2,4 Ga)
2,7	e	W	Underwater volcanoes absorb most O_2, enriching oxygen-rich seabed minerals
2,7	b	I	$CaCO_3$ produced by organisms similar to present blue-green algae (see 2,65 and 2,0 Ga)
2,65	g	U	Kaapvaal craton again flooded, South Africa (2,714 Ga)
2,65	b	U	Cyano-bacteria cause precipitation of $CaC0_3$ (limestone), later changed to dolostone, South Africa (see 2,7 Ga)
2,6	g	B	Black Reef, overlaying Schagen paleosols on Archean basement = oldest terrestrial ecosystem, Swaziland
2,6	g,e b	AH	Start of Transvaal stromatolitic dolostones, free oxygen generation, South Africa (see 2,4 Ga)
2,6	e	H	Heat production of the Earth only 37% of original, but double the present value
2,6	e	B	Earth has an ozone shield
2,5	g	H	End of Witwatersrand deposits of up to 8km thick and 400 000km^2 of mixed lava and sediment (conglomerates), South Africa (see 2,8 Ga)

2,5 Ga to 543 Ma — P r o t e r o z o i c E r a

2,5 Ga to 1,6 Ga — Early Proterozoic Period

2,5	g	H	Start of massive banded ironstone formation (1,8 Ga)
2,5	g	W	Granulite facies start to metamorph Archean granites into Charnockite group of gneissose rocks, but only in former Gondwana continents, Madras, India (550 Ma)
2,5	g	AH	Billions of tons of dolomitic limestone deposits, Transvaal/Griqualand West basin, South Africa
2,5	g	U	Start of Arctica super-continent: parts of northern Canada, eastern Siberia, Greenland (3,6 and 1,5 Ga)
2,5	e	U	Evidence of global freezing (Snowball Earth theory, Kirschvink) except near underwater volcanoes (see 2,2 and 1,5 Ga)
2,5	e	AF	"Oxygen Revolution", some life starts to depend on oxygen
2,5	e	H	Global heat production double of present, leading to unstable crust

	Subject Ref.	Source Ref.	
2,5 **Ga**	e	U	CO_2 atmosphere changes to one dominated by N_2, methane production partly compensates for this change, pressure near present
2,5	b	U	Cyano-bacteria reach peak
2,45	e	AM	19 hrs/d, 457 d/a, 14,5 lunar months (see 3,1 Ga, 620 Ma)
2,45	e	AM	Moon's recession from Earth was 1,24cm/a, now 3,82
2,4	c	X	16km diameter impact crater, Suavjaervi, Russia
2,4	g,e	AH	End of Transvaal stromatolitic dolostones, free oxygen generation, South Africa (see 2,6 Ga)
2,4	e	H	End of global Huron glaciation (see 2,7 Ga)
2,3	g	H	Start of extensive marine sedimentation (see 1,8 Ga)
2,3	e,b	H	Start of period of abundant stromatolites, free oxygen (see 1,5 Ga and 580 Ma)
2,2	g	AH	Transvaal iron formations deposited, South Africa
2,2	e	W	Global ice age, oceans frozen 800m deep (see 2,5 and 1,5 Ga, 900 Ma)
2,2	e	H	Apparent global glaciation, Canada, South Africa etc.
2,2	b	S	Possibly trace fossils of metazoans, Witwatersrand dolostones (dolomites), South Africa (see 1,0 Ga)
2,1	g	H	Australia has only half of present area, eastern Australia (Adelaide and Tasman orogenies) added later in conjunction with Samfrau orogeny (see 400 Ma)
2,1	b	AG	250 metazoans, similar to small jellyfish, Gabon
2,061	g	U,5	Bushveld complex developed, globally largest Cr, Pt and V deposits, Merensky and UG2 reefs, largest igneous lopolith, 65 000km², 8km thick, South Africa (see 2,054 Ga)
2,054	g	AH	End of Bushveld complex intrusion, S.Africa (2,061)
2,049	g	U	Volcanic pipe carrying copper and apatite (phosphor mineral), Phalaborwa complex, South Africa
2,023	c	U,X	Vredefort Dome, result of 10 - 15km diameter asteroid impact with 300km diameter crater, 5km deep, world's largest, now eroded, South Africa
2,023	c,g	U	New theory of combination of Vredefort Dome meteorite impact with hot spot mantle plume, South Africa
2,0	c	X	30km diameter meteorite impact crater, Yarrabubba, Western Australia
2,0	c	P,W	Copernicus crater 93km diameter, 3,76km deep, 1,2km high cone, Moon
2,0	g	U	Atlantica super-continent starts: parts of South America and West Africa (see 1,5 Ga)
2,0	g	K	Formation of diamonds, Kimberley, South Africa (see 3,0 and 1,6 Ga)
2,0	g	H W,T	Wopmay orogeny, gunflint cherts, metamorphosed quartzite rocks form mountains, Lake Superior, Canada

	Subject Ref.	Source Ref.	
2,0 **Ga**	g	W AJ	Great Unconformity, sedimentary base formed then, later overlaid by younger sandstones, from Arizona, USA to Alberta, Canada, sediments start to form Grand Canyon area, USA (see 1,7 Ga)
2,0	g	H	Tectonic rift formations look like at present, Canada
2,0	g,e	3,6 W	Banded Fe formation ends = free oxygen ±2% of present values (see 3,9 and 1,9 Ga, 580 Ma)
2,0	g,e	W	Continents and oceans similar to present appearance but in different shapes and positions
2,0	b	I	About a dozen types of proto-bacteria similar to present blue-green algae, Lake Superior, Canada (2,7)
2,0	b	U	Symbiotic relationship between anaerobic cyano-bacteria and the mitochondrial-bearing respiring purple bacteria created chloroplasts within cells, ancestors of plants, fungi and animals
2,0	b	3	Aerobic eukaryotes depending on oxygen: single/multi-celled with nucleus, DNA, RNA, ATP, organelles (mito-chondria, chloro plasts, captured prokaryotes such as cyano-phyta (blue-green algae)
2,0	b	3	Grypania fossil plants
1,9	g	Q	Ocean crust subducted under African plate, creating rift along Richtersveld coast, Namibia (see 1,6 Ga)
1,9	g	P	Svekofennian orogeny, Southern Scandinavia (3,0 + 1,8)
1,9	g	H	Begin of consolidation of several cratons to North American continent (see 850 Ma)
1,9	g	AC	Formation of Columbia or Nuna (Nena ?) super-continent (see 1,8 and 1,6 Ga)
1,9	g	H	Canadian craton grows by accretion of Baltica
1,9	g,e	U	Sedimentary rocks stained red by iron oxide, proof of significant free O_2, Kaapvaal craton, South Africa (see 2,0 Ga)
1,9	b	H	Appearance of varied bacteria and cyano-bacteria, Gunflint Cherts, Canada (see >1,4 Ga)
1,9	b	H	Stromatolites evolve, only complex life form until 1,5 Ga (see 1,5 Ga)
1,85 ±3My	c	X	200km x 100km oval meteorite impact crater, 10-19km diameter exploding meteorite, equivalent to 10bn Hiroshima bombs, Sudbury, Ont./Canada
1,85	g	H	North America/Greenland nucleus of Laurentia, added Northern Ireland/Scotland, Scandinavia, Siberia
1,8	c	X	30km diameter impact crater, Keurusselkae, Finland
1,8	c	X	10km diameter impact crater, Paasselka, Finland
1,8	g	U	Start of Columbia, a speculative super-continent of unspecified components (see 1,9 and 1,5 Ga)
1,8	g	H	End of extensive marine sedimentation (see 2,3 Ga)
1,8	g	H	End of massive banded ironstone formation (2,5 Ga)
1,8	g	W	Ocean is covering Southern Natal to Cape, South Africa

	Subject Ref.	Source Ref.	
1,8 **Ga**	g	U	Collision of Congo craton with Kaapvaal/Zimbabwe craton, Ubendian Belt, Southern Africa
1,8	g	P	Gothic orogeny, Southern Scandinavia (see 1,9 Ga)
1,7	g	P	Filipstad granite strip and Dalarna volcanoes, Sweden
1,7	g	AJ W	Sandstones of the Great Unconformity are metamorphosed by magma intrusions to schist, Grand Canyon area, USA (see 2,0 Ga and 500 Ma)
1,64	c	X	20km diameter impact crater, Amelia Creek, Australia
1,63 ±5My	c	X	30km diameter meteorite impact crater, Shoemaker (formerly Teague), Western Australia

1,6 Ga to 650 Ma Riphean Period

1,6	g	Q	Richtersveld rift closed again, causing orogeny parallel to coast, Namibia (see 1,9 Ga)
1,6	g	U	Kimberlite pipes, Postmasburg, S.Afr. (2,0 + 1,2 Ga)
1,6	g	U	Nena super-continent of Arctica, Baltica, Ukraine, western N.America, eastern Antarctica (see 2,5 + 1,9 + 1,3 Ga)
1,6	g	H	Probable rifting of Angara (= Siberia) from North American plate, later drifting towards Baltica (= Europe), forming Ural
1,5	g	U	Formation of Ur, Arctica and Atlantica super-continents complete (see 3,0 + 2,5 + 2,0 Ga)
1,5	g	U	End of Columbia speculative super-continent (1,8 Ga)
1,5	e	U	Renewed global freeze (Snowball Earth theory) (2,5 Ga)
1,5	b	3	Stromatolites form 100m high reefs which are still alive, Shark Bay, Australia (see 1,9 Ga, 10,0 ka)
1,5	b	AB	Start of sexual propagation to pass on and to advance the genetic information
>1,4	b	H	1st eukaryotic life forms (see 1,9 Ga)
1,4	c	X	3km diameter meteorite impact crater, Goyder, Northern Territory, Australia
1,4	b	W	Tappania fossil fungi, China/Australia (see 850 Ga)
1,3	g	U	End of Nena super-continent (see 1,6 Ga)
1,3	g	Q	Basement granites/gneisses, Namibia
1,3	g	W	Antarctica drifts over and eliminates ocean, joins Africa, forming Namaqua-Natal Mobile Belt (see 1,1 Ga and 450 Ma)
1,2	g	AH	Cullinan, globally oldest kimberlite pipe, yielding largest diamond ever found, South Africa (see 1,6 Ga)
1,2	g	U AG	Nepheline syenite = alkaline (K and Na) volcanoes, Pilanesberg, South Africa, Kola peninsula, Siberia and in Greenland
1,2	b	B	Terrestrial microfossils, Arizona
1,1	g	U	Rodinia super-continent formed by collision of Nena, Ur and Atlantica super-continents (see 700 Ma)

	Subject Ref.	Source Ref.	
1,1 **Ga**	g	H,U	Grenville orogeny, due to collision of Canadian shield with super-continent Rodinia, surrounded by the Panthalassan Ocean (see 1,0 Ga, 700 Ma)
1,1	g	AH	Start of Namaqua-Natal mountains S.Africa (1,1 + 1,0)
1,1	g	H	"Geo Catastrophe", an aborted continental rift, 100m wide, 1 500km long, USA
1,1	g	K	Porongurups Range appears, Australia
1,067	g	AB	Margate suite of metamorphic rocks laid down, S.Afr.
1,025	g	AB	Granite intrusions, Marble Delta, Natal, South Africa
1,0	c	X	3km diameter impact crater, Iso-Naakkima, Finland
1,0	c	X	4km diameter impact crater, Suvasvesi N, Finland
1,0	c	X	9km diameter meteorite impact crater, Lumparn, Finland
1,0	g	AH	End of Namaqua-Natal mountain building, South Africa (see 1,1 Ga)
1,0	g	W	Southern edge of Kaapvaal craton subducted, forming Natal Metamorphic Province and mountain range of metamorphosed rocks and granites 1 000's of km long Natal/Cape Province, South Africa (see 490 Ma)
1,0	g	P	"Augen"-porphyry, Malmoe, Sweden
1,0	g	P	Dahlsland/Telemark orogeny, Scandinavia
1,0	g	P	A mountain has sunk to 5km depth, Copenhagen, Denmark
1,0	b	I	Blue-green and green algae, fungi (eukaryotes), Bitter Springs, Australia (see 440 Ma)
1,0	b	AB	Foraminifera have $CaCO_3$ shield with perforations for suction "feet" to adhere to sand particles
1,0	b	S	Trace fossils of metazoans, Katanga, Congo (2,2 Ga)
1,0	b	3	Chuaria, an eukaryote of 10mm diameter
900 **Ma**	e	H	Gnejsoe glaciation, global except Antarctica (see 2,2 and 1,5 Ga and 750 Ma)
850	g	H	Completion of consolidation of several cratons to North American continent (see 1,9 Ga)
850	e	H	Start of series of global or regional glaciations with tillite deposits (see 600 Ma)
850	b	P	Oldest fungus (previously oldest 380 Ma), no living order, Victoria Is., Canada (see 1,4 Ga)
850	b	H	Adaptive radiation of acritarchians (microscopic algae) (see 543 Ma)
835	g	I	Ultrabasic igneous rocks, St.Paul, Mid-Atlantic
800	g	H	Formation of rift (mobile) zones where later the continents would separate from Gondwana (see 182 Ma)
800	g	AG	Ayers Rock not a sandstone monolith, but also consists of shales, mudstones and conglomerates (see 100 Ma)
800	b	H	Oldest protozoan predators
750	g	AC	Rodinia super-continent breaks up into Proto-Laurasia and Proto-Gondwana super-continents, separated by *Proto-Tethys*, and Congo craton (1,1 Ga, 720, 700 Ma)

	Subject Ref.	Source Ref.	
750 **Ma**	g	AG	Eruptions of the chain of volcanoes south of the Massif Central, Cap d'Agde, France
750	e	1	Sturtian glaciation (see 900 Ma)
740	g	AH	Start of Pan-African mountain building (see 570 Ma)
720	g	AC	Proto-Laurasia split into Laurentia, Siberia (NE of Laurentia, separated by *Paleo-asian ocean)*, Baltica (east of Laurentia, separated by *Iapetus ocean)* (750)
720	e,b	L	Higher oxygen levels allow multi-cellular life (700)
700	c	I	Moon captured by Earth gravitational forces (4,53 Ga)
700 ±5	c	X	14km diameter impact crater, Jaenisjaervi, Russia
700	g	AB	During "Snowball Earth" drop stones transported by glaciers onto floating/melting ice sheets, Namibia
700	g	H,U	Rodinia super-continent breaking up into Ur with eastern Antarctica, Laurentia, Atlantica, Baltica (Europe), Siberia and dispersing globally, creating *Iapetus ocean* separating North America/Greenland, Gondwana and Baltica (Europe) (1,1 Ga, 700, 500, 380)
700	g	K	Seychelles granites rise, not as an island, but in the interior of Gondwana
700	b,z	U	Multi-cellular organisms with tissue differentiation (see 800 and 720 Ma)
670	b,z	S,U	Fauna and flora similar to Ediacaran, including shelly cloudina (animal) and skeletonized calcareous algae fossils, 1st hard shells by bio-mineralization, maybe to deter predators, Kuibis, Namibia, China (see 650 and 600 Ma)
670	z	L	Proto-jellyfish, segmented worms, arthropods, corals = all soft-bodied, generally NOT precursors of present phyla, global distribution, Ediacaran Hills, South Australia

650 Ma to 600 Ma . Vendian Period

650	b	I	Fossil maritime multi-cellular organisms (see 670 Ma)
650	z	U	Otavia, possibly proto-sponge, 1st animal fossil in Africa (see 600 and 550 Ma)
646 ±42	c	X	25km diameter meteorite impact crater, Strangways, Northern Territory, Australia
630	e	AB	CO_2 build-up globally, average temperature changes from -50° to +50°C (see 2,5 Ga, 850 Ma)
620	e	AM	21,9 hrs/d, 400 d/a, 13,1 lunar months (see 2,45 Ga, 400 Ma)
600	c	X	1,5km diameter impact crater, Saarijaervi, Finland
600	c	X	6,6km diameter impact crater, Soederfjaerden, Finland
600	c	X	60km diameter impact crater, Beaverhead, Mont./USA
600	g	H	Metamorphosis of banded iron stones ends

	Subject Ref.	Source Ref.	
600 **Ma**	e	H	End of a series of global or regional glaciations with tillite deposits (see 850 Ma)
600	b	H	Most acritarchians disappear (see 543 Ma)
600	b,z	V	Eukaryotes develop into metazoans, present-day choano-flagellants eukaryotes still produce proteins required for metazoans and animals (see 670 Ma)

600 Ma to 543 Ma **Ediacaran Period**

600	g	AC	Begin of Pannotia super-continent, largely around the poles, with a small strip near the equator connecting the polar masses (see 540 Ma)
600	g	U	Begin of formation of Gondwana by collision of Ur with eastern Atlantica super-continents (see 550, 520 Ma)
600	g	R,U	Malmesbury Sediments, Cape Province, South Africa
600	g	S	Otavi system, Namibia
600	g	S	Start of granite emplacements, which weakened the Gondwana plate, Cape, South Africa
600	z	U	Split of Ediacaran fauna and Cambrian true animals (see 670 Ma)
600	z	U	Sponge-like otavia, Otavi, Namibia (see 650, 550 Ma)
590	c	X	90km diameter impact crater, Acraman, South Australia
590	z	6	Soft-bodied 0,5m long multi-cell animals in deep seas
580	e	1	Oxygen ±7% of present value (see 2,0 Ga, 500, 360 Ma)
580	e	H	Sea levels lower than at any time during the Paleozoic, very low in regard to continents (see 440 Ma)
580	e	1,H	Tillites proof Varangian global glaciation except in South America
580	b	H	End of period of abundant stromatolites (see 2,3 Ga)
580	z	3	Fossils with bilateral symmetry, jellyfish with radial symmetry (floating but mostly anchored)
580	z	H	Marine arthropods, annelids (ring worms)
570	c	X	13km diameter impact crater, Spider, W.Australia
570	g	AH	End of Pan-African mountain building (see 740 Ma)
570	z	7	Multi-cellular animal embryos, China (see 500 Ma)
560	c	X	6km diameter impact crater, Saeaeksjaervi, Finland
550 ±100	c	X	2,35km diameter impact crater, Holleford, Ont./Canada
550	c	X	10km diameter meteorite impact crater, Kelly West, Northern Territory, Australia
550	g	U	Ur and Atlantica now welded together, Gondwana consolidated: Africa/South America/Australia/India Antarctica/Madagascar/Falkland Plateau (see 600 Ma)
550	g	W	End of Granulite facies metamorphing Archean granites into Charnockite group of gneissose rocks, but only in former Gondwana continents, Madras, India (2,5 Ga)

	Subject Ref.	Source Ref.	
550 **Ma**	b,z	H	Archaeo-cyathids, similar to but unrelated to sponges, involved in forming reefs by calcareous algae, Ediacaran Hills, Australia (see 650, 600 Ma)
545	c	X	6km diameter meteorite impact crater, Foelsche, Northern Territory, Australia
543	e	3,6	Ediacaran glaciation (see 530 Ma)
543	b,z	3,6	Ediacaran extinction, 70% of life extinct, especially single cell organisms, e.g. acritarchians (850 Ma)

543 Ma to 5,0 ka **P H A N E R O Z O I C E O N**

543 Ma to 248,2 Ma **P a l e o z o i c E r a**

543 Ma to 490 Ma **Cambrian Period**

	Subject Ref.	Source Ref.	
540 **Ma**	g	AC	End of Pannotia super-continent (see 600 Ma)
540	g	K	Granitic base of Table Mountain solidifies, Cape Town, South Africa (see 260 Ma)
540	b	AB	Life neither botanical nor zoological, consuming dissolved minerals via large surface
540	b,z	3	Sexual and food competition starts, "survival of the fittest", viruses (stripped-down cells) as parasites
530	e	7	Cambrian Warming (see 543 and 450 Ma)
530	b,z	7	"Cambrian explosion of life" (see 525 Ma)
530	z	3	Small shelly mollusk fossils, brachiopods, trilobites with eyes (the oldest visual system = thousands of calcite rods) and other arthropods, possibly from pre-Cambrian un-fossilized tiny shell-less animals (see 450 Ma)
530	z	G	Branching sponges, jellyfish, big arthropods, echinoderms: proto-crinoids (sea-lily), eleutherozoa (starfish, sea urchins), mollusks (see 500 and 290 Ma)
530	z	L	Pikaia, founder of chordata phyla (see 450 Ma)
525	g	H	Gondwana, Laurasia (N.America/Greenland/Scotland), Siberia, Baltica, Kazakh, China, all continents/cratons near equator, mostly flooded by shallow seas (see 520 Ma)
525	b,z	L	Possibly end of "Cambrian explosion of life", ±30 of present phyla found, no NEW body building plans since developed, all ecological niches occupied (530 Ma)
520	g	AC	Gondwana and Baltica are formed, formation of Laurentia near the equator, with the *Panthalassic ocean* to north and west, the *Iapetus ocean* in the south and the *Khanty ocean* in the east (600, 525 Ma)
520	z	3,6	Burgess shale: all major marine groups incl. predators exist, but only in northern hemisphere, Canada
520	z	AB	Anomalocaris.canadensis, 60cm to 2m long, largest predator amongst extinct invertebrates
515	c	X	18km diameter meteorite impact crater, Lawn Hill, Queensland, Australia
510	g	S	End of granite emplacement, Cape, S.Africa (600 Ma)
508	c	X	19km diameter impact crater, Glikson, Australia
505	c	X	6km diameter impact crater, Rock Elm, Wis./USA

	Subject Ref.	Source Ref.	
500 **Ma**	c	AA	Greater Magellanic Cloud, a distant galaxy, came close (70k Ly) to our Milky Way galaxy
500 ±10	c	X	5km diameter meteorite impact crater, Gardnos, Norway
500 ±20	c	X	5km diameter impact crater, Mizarai, Lithuania
500	c	X	8km diameter impact crater, Clover Bluff, Wis./USA
500	c	X	3,2km diameter impact crater, Newporte, N.D./USA
500	c	X	24km diameter impact crater, Presqu'ile, Que./Canada
500	g	U	Arabia added to Gondwana (see 380 Ma)
500	g	P	Start of formation of Natal Group sandstones, Natal, South Africa (see 350 Ma)
500	g	H	Micro-cratons of England and Scotland are separated for 100s of km by *Iapetus ocean*
500	g	H	North America/Greenland (Laurentia), Siberia (Angara), Scandinavia/Northern Europe (Baltica), *Iapetus* ocean development ends, separating these major plates (see 700, 460 Ma)
500	g	U	Rift between African and Falkland plates starts, forms Agulhas Sea between Africa and Antarctica (550 Ma)
500	g	W AJ	Great Unconformity: schists submerged by sea, covered by new sediments, Grand Canyon area, USA (see 1,7 Ga and 250 Ma)
500	g	Y	Chihuahuan desert, Mexico/Texas
500	e b,z	W	Ozone levels are now sufficient to protect terrestrial life incl. animals from UV radiation (see 580 Ma)
500	b	V	1st terrestrial plants, neither leaves nor roots (450)
500	z	G,Q	Star fish, 70kg, 2m long predators, sea-scorpions, sea-urchins, nautiloid cephalopods: catfish, octopus, cuttlefish, squid and nautilus (see 530 Ma)
500	z	Q	Nautilus (squid-like) now generally only 20cm long, but present Humbold squid up to 2m long (see 300 Ma)
500	z	W	Embryos of worm-like animals scanned by SRXTM tomography, yolk pyramids, Siberia/China (see 570 Ma)
490	z	H	Cambrian mass-extinction of marine fauna

490 Ma to 443 Ma Ordovician Period

490	g	W	1st sediments deposited on African continent, Cape/ Natal coast, South Africa (see 1,0 Ga)
480	g	U	Table Mountain sandstones deposited in Agulhas Sea, Cape Peninsula, South Africa
480	g	AC	Avalonia micro-continent breaks from Gondwana and drifts towards Laurentia, later forms US, Nova Scotia and England
474	c	Q	Age of Mars meteorite rocks
470	c	X	3km diameter meteorite impact crater, Granby, Sweden
470	c	X	8km diameter meteorite impact crater, Neugrund,Estonia

		Subject Ref.	Source Ref.	
470	±30 **Ma**	c	X	16km diameter meteorite impact crater, Ames, Okla./USA
470		g	H	Baltic Sea north of England (near N.Africa), Scotland near Greenland, separated by *Proto-Tethys* (380, 300)
470		g	H	1st Appalachian (Taconian) orogeny starts, creating base of Appalachians (see 420 and 395 Ma)
470		e	H	Equator dissects Canada and Angara (Siberia)
470		z	H	Brachiopods, crinoids, stromatolites: = timing fauna
460		g	H	*Iapetus* narrows, Laurentia, Baltica close (700, 440)
455		c	X	7km diameter meteorite impact crater, Kardia, Estonia
455		c	X	7,5km diameter meteorite impact crater, Lockne, Sweden
455		c	X	2km diameter meteorite impact crater, Tvaeren, Sweden
450	±10	c	X	8,5km diameter impact crater, Calvin, Mich./USA
450		c	X	30km diameter impact crater, State Islands, Ont/Canada
450		g	AC	Siberia close to Euramerica, with the *Khanty ocean* separating them
450		g	I	Melt water channel in Sahara sandstone by ice cap of South Pole (plate has wandered 8 000km) (see 1,3 Ga)
450		e	H	Temporary drop in sea levels due to global ice age (see 530 Ma)
450		b	I,S	Terrestrial multi-cellular plant fossils: when plants migrated to land they had to develop structures to hold them up, tubes to transport liquids and water-proof but breezing skin (see 500 Ma)
450		b	H	Early terrestrial plants, non-vascular, without roots, leaves, but horizontal stems and upright shoots (415)
450		b	7,H	Higher vegetation colonizes land, limited to marshes and moors (see 500 Ma)
450		b	W	Protein of 2 000 atoms reconstructed, belonging to gluco-corticoide group, active in present-day humans
445	±2	c	X	6km diameter impact crater, Pilot, N.W.T./Canada
443		z	3	Ordovician mass extinction: >½ marine species extinct

443 Ma to 417 Ma Silurian Period

440		g	AC	Baltica collided with Laurentia (see 460, 430 Ma)
440		e	S	Gondwana ice age, South Pole in central Africa, ice covering most of Africa and South America, but not Antarctica, Greenland tropical, sea levels low (see 580, 430, 360 Ma)
440		b	G	Chlorophyta (green algae) appear (see 1,0 Ga)
435		b	3	Liverwort early terrestrial plant, fossil spores (220)
435		z	4 G,H	Ostracoderms: small, armored jaw-less fish with outer carapace, cartilage internal skeleton North America (see 450, 420, 354 Ma)
430	±25	c	X	8km diameter impact crater, Couture, Que./Canada
430		c	X	4km diameter impact crater, Glasford, Ill./USA

	Subject Ref.	Source Ref.	
430 **Ma**	g	AC	Laurentia, Baltica and Avalonia merge to minor super-continent Euramerica or Laurussia, closing *Iapetus ocean* and North and South China crotons rift from Gondwana (see 440 Ma)
430	e	H	Melting of polar glaciers, sea levels high, warming South pole in southern Morocco (see 440, 380 Ma)
425	z	W	Shell crayfish with young in breeding chamber, Herefordshire, UK (see 400 Ma)
425	z	7	Tracks of arthropods = first terrestrial animals, Western Australia (see 420, 400 Ma)
420	g	H	Taconian orogeny ends (see 470 Ma)
420	z	K	"Pneumodesmus" oldest millipede fossil, Rhynie chert, Scotland (see 425, 410 Ma)
420	z	H	Appearance of acanthodiae, 1st jawed fish (435, 354 Ma)
418	e,b	Y	O_2 levels probably higher than now, plants grew only 3cm tall, oldest wildfire recorded, England

417 Ma to 354 Ma Devonian Period

415	g	P	Start of red gneiss, metamorphosed ex older granites, Spessart, Germany (see 325 Ma)
410	b	K,I H	Baragwanathia fossils, oldest vascular plants, dated by graptolites, still no roots but proto-leaves and spore receptacles, Yeo fossil site, Victoria, Australia (see 450 Ma)
410	z	W	Millipedes with up to 750 pairs of feet, 2m length, 50cm wide, largest arthropod ever, could kill animals up to deer-size (see 420, 400 Ma)
410	z	W	Eoactinistia.foreyi lung fish, Victoria, Australia (see 395 Ma)
409	z	K	Oldest shark skeleton, paired chest fin radii (until now unknown with cartilage fish), 20 My earlier than previously known, 50-75cm long, Canada (see 360 Ma)
>400	g	H	Samfrau orogeny along southern coast of Gondwana, adding the eastern part to Australia (see 2,1 Ga)
400 ±50	c	X	8km diameter impact crater, La Moinerie, Que./Canada
400	c	X	12,5km diameter impact crater, Nicholson, N.W.T.Canada
400	e	Q	Year has 400 days at 22 hours (see 620 and 120 Ma)
400	b	G	Psilophytales, early vascular terrestrial plants lacking roots, leaves, Rhynie cherts, Scotland (see 370 and 345 Ma)
400	b	U	Dutoitia, 1st terrestrial plant fossil, South Africa
400	z	AB	Arrow-tail crayfish fossils, they had blue blood (425)
400	z	V	Hax genes activated, reshaping fins into limbs in lobe-fin fish embryos, leading to fish with fingers on fins, later a fish walking on land (see 385 Ma)
400	z	AF	Wing-less insect eggs are round and smooth (300 Ma)

Ma		Subject Ref.	Source Ref.	
400 **Ma**		z	AB	Fish 1st vertebrates, develop facility to communicate by sounds using a neural regulating group of cells unchanged since than in all vertebrates
400		z	W	Dunkleosteus.terrelli, an 11m, 4t armor-plated fish with a 5 000kg force of its jaws, the greatest ever (see 380 Ma)
400		z	H,7 I	Terrestrial fossils: proto-scorpions, millipedes evolve, spider webs first as shelter, later to catch insects once these had developed wings, Rhynie chert, Scotland (see 410, 320 Ma)
397		z	AG	Fossilized footprints of 1st vertebrate tetrapod (365)
396	±20	c	X	3,8km diameter impact crater, Brent, Ont,/Canada
395	±25	c	X	8km diameter impact crater, Elbow, Sask./Canada
395		g	H	Caledonian orogeny Scotland and Scandinavia (350 Ma)
395		g	1	Canadian folding, intrusions
395		g	H	2nd Appalachian (Acadian) orogeny starts due to Laurentia, Greenland and Baltica fusing to Old Red Continent (=Laurasia), closing *Iapetus ocean* (see 500, 380 Ma)
395		z	5,H	Coelacanths (actinista), the most primitive species of proto-modern lung fish, thought to be extinct since 80 Ma, found living off South Africa and Indonesia, live birth, limb-like fins, jaws, 100kg (410, 375 Ma)
390		g	P	Cu, Zn, Pb ores deposited, Rammelsberg, Harz, Germany
385		g	H	Laurasia and Gondwana possibly temporarily connected
385		e	H	Devonian global warming (see 330 Ma)
385		z	V	Eusthenopteron lobe-fin fish had fins with 1 large and 2 smaller long bones, similar to present mammal limbs (see 400, 375 Ma)
385		z	H	Fringe-finned fish with limb-like fins, a sister group of lung fish (see 350 Ma)
380	±5	c	X	15km diameter meteorite impact crater, Kaluga, Russia
380		g	H	*Iapetus* closed, England/Scotland, Northern/Southern Ireland united (see 700, 470 and 460 Ma)
380		g	H	Proto-Andean orogeny starts (see 200 Ma)
380		g	H	*Proto-Tethys* separates Gondwana and Old Red Continent and China/Siberia (see 700 and 395 Ma)
380		g	AC	Southern Europe separates from Gondwana, heading towards Euramerica across new *Rheic Ocean* (340 Ma)
380		g	H	Turkey, Arabia are part of Gondwana, Florida attached to North Africa/South America (see 500 Ma)
380		e	H	South Pole in Parana basin, South America (440, 430)
380		b	G	Rhodophyta (red algae) appear
380		b,z	H	Tabulata/stromatopora reef communes prosper, Canning basin, Australia and Bighorn Canyon, Montana (360 Ma)

	Subject Ref.	Source Ref.	
380 **Ma**	z	AB	Materpiscis.attenboroughi, a 23cm placoderm armored fish, 1st live birth, sex with penetration, with fetus and umbilical cord, proving live births evolved as early as egg laying, 30 My earlier than previously known (see 400 Ma)
378 ±5	c	X	8,5km diameter impact crater, Ilyinets, Ukraine
375	g	H	Hunsrueck slates deposited, Germany
375	b	Z	Appearance of 1st pollen grains and seeds
375	z	V,W Z	Ichthyostegalia, "missing link" between actinista (lung fish) and tetrapod (amphibians): body of 2m long lobe-fin fish with scales and fins, 20cm long flat skull, distinct neck, bones within fins relating to legs, arms and wrists, but neck, ribs, bones in pectoral fins like tetrapod, sub-tropical climate, Tiktaalik, Arctic Canada (see 395, 385 Ma)
370	b	G	Psilophytales disappear (see 400 and 900 ka)
370	b	H	Continents partially covered by forests, higher plants: vascular stems, roots, seeds, leaves, photo-synthesis (see 360 Ma)
370	b	G	Lycopodiales appear: baerlap (lycopodium.clavatum) (see 350, 300 Ma) and club mosses (see 270, 210 Ma)
370	b	H	Appearance of seeds, obviating the need of terrestrial plants to live near water/moors
365	b	G	Phaeophyta (brown algae) appear
365	z	V	Tetrapod vertebrates have fully developed limbs including toes, despite being aquatic (397, 360 Ma)
364 ±8	c	X	40km diameter impact crater, Woodleigh, W.Australia
361 ±1,1	c	X	52km diameter meteorite impact crater, Siljan, Sweden
360	c	X	7km diameter impact crater, Piccaninny, W.Australia
360 ±20	c	X	3,8km diameter impact crater, Flynn Creek, Tenn./USA
360	e	H	Gondwana glaciation ends (see 440 Ma)
360	e b,z	S	O_2 levels 35% of atmosphere in Devonian/Carboniferous, allowing plants/animals to grow large quickly, South Africa (see 580 and 200 Ma)
360	b	H	1st large trees and forests (see 370 Ma)
360	b,z	H	Tabulata/stromatopora reef communes extinct, Canning basin, Australia and Bighorn Canyon, Montana (380 Ma)
360	z	W	Bothriolepis.africana, coelacanth, lamprey and a new placoderm fish species in fossil beds in marine sub-arctic shale, Grahamstown, S.Africa (see 345 Ma)
360	z	G,H	Predaceous mollusk-eating sharks (see 409, 300 Ma), 10m long placoderms (armored fish), rays, insect-like arthropods (see 300 Ma)
360	z	AF	Tetrapods, common ancestors of all vertebrates (see 365, 350 Ma)
354	z	G,H	Devonian mass extinction: 70% of marine species incl. jawless ostracoderms (435), jawed acanthodiae (420)

354 Ma to 290 Ma Carboniferous Period

	Subject Ref.	Source Ref.	
351 ±20 **Ma**	c	X	2,44km diameter impact crater, West Hawk, Man./Canada
350	g	P	End of formation of Natal Group sandstones, Natal, South Africa (see 500 Ma)
350	g	P	Le Piton de la Fournaise, oldest still active volcano, Isle de La Reunion, Indian Ocean (see 250 and 65 ka)
350	g	H	Acadian/Caledonian orogenies end, USA/Europe (395 Ma)
350	e,z	W	O_2 maximum of 30%, causing fish-like vertebrates to leave the oceans, developing into amphibians (tetrapods) (see 375, 360, 270 Ma)
350	b	K	Lichen, symbiosis of green/blue-green algae with fungi
350	b	U	Club mosses, lycopodiales, ancestral gymnosperms, South Africa (see 370, 300 Ma)
350	z	5	Rhipditia fish, relatives of the coelacanth, colonize land, developing tracheae/lungs, establishing 5-digit tetrapods ,developed into all subsequent vertebrates (see 360, 340 Ma)
350	z	H	Freshwater bivalves, New York State, USA
345	c	X	14km diameter meteor. impact crater, Gweni-Fada, Chad
345	b	3	Rhynie cherts yield fossilized ferns, Scotland (400)
342 ±15	c	X	54km diameter impact crater, Charlevoix, Que./Canada
340	g	AC	NW Africa collided with, South America moved north touching southeast Euramerica (see 380 Ma)
340	g	H	Limestone deposits ex fusulines, crinoids, bryozoan detritus creating 100m high reefs
340	e	H	Highest sea levels, shallow flooding of continents (see 580 Ma)
340	z	H	Amphibians the only terrestrial vertebrates, up to 6m long (see 350, 320 Ma)
340	z	AB	Thuringothyris.mahlendorffae, 30 skeletons, oldest terrestrial vertebrates, mostly <1m high, proto-saurians, 12 species, some previously unknown, including seymouria, previously only found in USA (proving existence of contemporary connection), Tambach, Thueringer Wald, Germany (see 287 Ma)
330	e	Q	Global warming (see 385, 240 Ma)
325	g	P	Variscan orogeny, end of granite metamorphosed to red gneiss, Spessart, Germany (see 415 and 320 Ma)
325	g	H	Siberia and China separate (see 260 Ma)
325	z	H	Mass extinction of marine fauna (crinoids, ammonoids)
320	c	X	8km diameter impact crater, Serpent Mound, Ohio/USA
320 ±80	c	X	7km diameter impact crater, Crooked Creek, Mo./USA
320	g	H	3rd Appalachian (Alleghenian/Variscan) orogeny starts in Laurasia by collision of Laurasia and North Africa, causes Mauritanean/Atlas orogeny in North Africa (see 280 Ma)

	Subject Ref.	Source Ref.	
320 **Ma**	e	P	Start of Permo-Carboniferous ice age, covering Central/South Africa, Antarctica, parts of South America, Australia (see 270 Ma)
320	z	H	Winged insects (see 400, 300 Ma)
320	z	H	Oldest reptiles with amniote eggs, independent from aquatic reproduction (see 340, 300 Ma)
312	g	P	Porphyry granite, Fichtelgebirge, Germany (290 Ma)
310	g	U	Subduction zone along southern margin of Gondwana creates Cape mountains and Karoo depression which later filled with Ecca sediments
310	b	H	Calcareous algae contribute to reefs
310	z	W	16 orders of reptiles start to evolve, turtles are 1 of 4 which survived to present (see 300 Ma)
300 ±50	c	X	2,5km diameter impact crater, Mishina Gora, Russia
300	c	X	6km diameter impact crater, Decaturville, Mo./USA
300	c	X	6km diameter impact crater, Middlesboro, Ky./USA
300	c	X	4km diameter impact crater, Ile Rouleau, Que./Canada
300	c	X	12km diameter impact crater, Serra da Cangalha, Brazil
300	g	U	Pangaea starts to form, most continents again consolidated (see 260 Ma)
300	g	A	Africa placed east-west, not north-south (see 80 Ma)
300	g	AC	North China craton collides with Siberia, closing most of the *Proto-Tethys* (see 470, 280 Ma)
300	g	AC	Kazakhstania and Baltica crotons collided, closing *Ural ocean* and starting the Uralian orogeny and completing Laurasia (see 260 Ma)
300	g	P	Hercynian orogeny: Harz, Massif Central, Pyrenees, Lake District, Western Europe (see 65 Ma)
300	g	U,5 R	Dwyka tillite, overlaid by sandstone (part of Karoo system), glacial striations when Gondwana drifted over South Pole, Nooitgedacht, South Africa (290 Ma)
300	g	1	Proto-Rocky Mountains start to rise (see 65 Ma)
300	e	W	Ice cap of Gondwana over Southeast Africa, Antarctica, South India, Northern Australia, Western South America (see 290 Ma)
300	b	H	Lycopodiales spore scale trees (sigillaria =vertical scales and lepidodendrales =rhombic scales) produced coal deposits, Europe, North America (370, 275 Ma)
300	b	H	Glossopteris, a seed fern in wet areas (see 270 Ma)
300	b	H	Cordaitales trees are gymnosperma in dry areas, producing coal deposits, Gondwana (see 350 Ma)
300	b	G	Charophyta (stoneworts)
300	b	W	10 000ha rain forest fossils in coalmine roof, tree-sized horsetails, 40m club mosses Illinois, USA (270)
300	z	3	Sea-lily forests, related to sea-urchins, 100s species
300	z	Q	Vampire squid, precursor to modern squids and octopuses, Monterey Canyon off California (500 Ma)

Ma	Subject Ref.	Source Ref.	
300 **Ma**	z	W	Sharks develop ability to rip apart prey larger than themselves (see 360 and 170 Ma)
300	z	AF	Insect eggs develop spikes and other means to anchor them on suitable bases (see 400, 290 Ma)
300	z	Q,Y	Odonates (dragonflies, damselflies) and cockroaches (see 320 Ma)
300	z	3	Reptiles with almost solid bone heads (see 310 Ma)
300	z	7	Synapsids = mammal-like large terrestrial reptiles (see 260 Ma)
290 ±20	c	X	26km/36km diameter meteorite impact crater, Clearwater East/West, Que./Canada
290 ±35	c	X	4,5km diameter meteorite impact crater, Dobele, Latvia
290	g	AB	European plate near equator
290	g,e	U	Drifting north of Gondwana ends glaciation, rivers form swamps creating coal deposits, South Afr. (300)
290	z	G	Most echinoderms disappear (see 530 Ma)

290 Ma to 248,2 Ma **Permian Period**

290	g	P	Margin granite, Fichtelgebirge, Germany (312, 288 Ma)
290	g	P	Rhyolite, volcanic quartzite porphyry, Spessart, Germany
290	e,b	AB	Sparse vegetation of mainly ferns and conifers, arid and warm climate, Central Europe
290	b	G	Sphenophyllales, oldest articulate plants, shrubs with triangular stems joined like bamboo (see 190 Ma)
290	b	G	Calamitales, like modern horsetails but tall trees (see 175 Ma)
290	b	G	Coenopteridales (spore ferns) (see 185 Ma)
290	b	G	Cordaitales, oldest gymnosperms (naked-seeded plants) high trees branched only at crown, fructification, lanceolate leaves (see 270, 185 Ma)
290	z	G	Pulmonata (air-breathing snails), spiders, 7 orders of winged insects up to 75cm wingspan, cockroaches (300)
290	z	G	Proto ray-finned fish (see 115 Ma)
290	z	AB	Gerobatrachus.hottoni missing link fossil between frog (200, 180 Ma) and salamander (100 Ma), fused ankle bones of salamander, wide skull of frog, backbone a mix of both
288	g	P	Central granite, Fichtelgebirge, Germany (290, 286 Ma)
287	z	W	Eudibamus.cursoris, 1st bi-pedal proto-saurians, male and female dimetrodon with 2m dorsal sails, 250 brachiosaurs, 80cm proto-saurus (oldest quadruped terrestrial vertebrates) Tambach, Thueringer Wald, Germany (see 340 and 270 Ma)
286	g	P	Tin granite, Fichtelgebirge, Germany (see 288 Ma)
285	e,z	Q	Marine animals in warm, shallow sea, Moab, Utah (150)

Ma	Subject Ref.	Source Ref.	
280 **Ma**	c	X	8km diameter impact crater, Des Plaines, Ill./USA
280 ±10	c	X	11km diameter impact crater, Ternovka, Ukraine
280	g	AC	The Cimerian craton starts to drift from Gondwana to Laurasia, closing the *Proto-Tethys* and opening the *Tethys* (see 300, 200 Ma)
280	g	AC	Australia at the South Pole
280	g	H	Alleghenian orogeny stops (see 320 and 80 Ma)
280	e	H	Sea levels rise again (see 250 Ma)
280	b	1	Protozoans changed dramatically (see 250 Ma)
280	z	3	Dragonflies as big as seagulls, millipedes 2m long
275	b	G	Lepidodendrales (scale trees),seed-like cones, thin wooden stele, fibrous periderm (see 300, 185 Ma)
275	b	G	Pteridospermales (seed ferns) (see 190 Ma)
270	e	P	End of Permo-Carboniferous ice age, Gondwana (320 Ma)
270	e,z	W	Saurians survived O_2 minimum of 15% by developing new breathing system, using air sacks hidden in hollow bones, inherited by present-day birds (see 350 Ma)
270	b	5,U	Coal forests, mostly glossopteris, cordaitales, ferns, horsetail, club mosses, Antarctica/New Guinea/ South Africa (see 300 Ma)
270	b,z	U	Start of most complete fossil record of Gondwana, Karoo, South Africa (see 180 Ma)
270	z	P	Locusts thrive in Richtersveld, Namibia
270	z	H,3	Therapsidae (mammal-like carnivorous reptiles) with advanced legs and jaws, able to tear apart their prey before swallowing, ectotherm (cold blooded), up to 3m: dimetrodon, anteosaur, pelycosaur with dorsal fins, possibly already endotherm (warm blooded) with a pelt (see 287 and 220 Ma)
265	e	H	Extreme climatic and sea-level variations
265	z	U	Mesosaurus, small aquatic 1st reptile fossil found in South Africa (see 250 Ma)
260	g	K	Table Mountain sandstone on granite base, was 3km high, now eroded to 1,5km, South Africa (see 540 Ma)
260	g	H	China, Siberia welded to Europe, create Ural mountain, completing Pangaea, 5km thick sediments (see 325, 300 and 205,2 Ma)
260	g	H	Cathay (=Southeast Asia) the only separate continent
260	g	H	"Zechstein Sea" up to 7 marine saline cycles from the North and evaporations, with 1km deep anhydrite, salt, copper shales and oil deposits Northern Germany/Baltic Sea/East Greenland (see 230 Ma)
260	g	7	Limestone (Karst) plateaux, started out as coral reefs in tropical sea, southern tip of Chile
260	z	U	Synapsid, anapsid, diapsid reptiles radiate, South Africa (see 300 Ma)

	Subject Ref.	Source Ref.	
260 **Ma**	z	AF	Mammal-like impala-sized saber-toothed therapsid Tiarajudens.eccentricus, similar to a South African species, oldest known example of closely related terrestrial vertebrates in Gondwana , Southern Brazil
250 ±80	c	X	6km diameter meteorite impact crater, Kursk, Russia
250	c	X	4km diameter meteorite impact crater, Gow Sask./Canada
250	g	5	Strong folding, Cape formations, South Africa
250	g	P,U	Karoo Sea largely silted up, Ecca and Beaufort shales and sandstones, Fraserburg, South Africa (see 190 Ma)
250	g	P	Oslo rift, similar to East African rift valley, Larvicite, rhombic porphyry, Oslo Fjord, Norway
250	g	W	Jutland covered by shallow warm ocean, precipitating salt deposits several km thick, overlaid by 4km thick loam/sand, then by a $CaCO_3$ cover, the top salt altered to gypsum, Moensted, Denmark (see 60 Ma)
250	g	7	Top layer of Grand Canyon, USA (see 500 and 5,5 Ma)
250	e	H	Extreme temperature gradation between poles/equator
250	e	6	Reduced salinity, lower temperatures (sea and land), drop in sea levels (see 280, 100 Ma)
250	e	H	Start of Michigan River as precursor to the Mississippi River, USA
250	b	7	Bacterial spores of this age found alive now
250	b	3	Protists several cm across (see 280 Ma)
250	b	G	Equisetales (horse-tails) (see 175 Ma
250	z	7,3	Brachiopods with "lids" (see 530 Ma)
250	z	3,G	Lung fish, many species, true bugs, beetles, stone-flies abundant
250	z	1	Reptiles spread, fish: large scales, cartilage skeletons, animated suspension since then
250	z	Q	Some reptiles returned to seas (see 265, 200 Ma)
250	z	G,7	Archosauria.lagosuchus, A.euparkeria, common ancestors of dinosaurs, crocodilians, flying reptiles, birds
250	z	AF	Start of ichthyosaur ("fish lizard") run (see 90 Ma)
250	z	3	Saurian egg with shell, Texas (see 300 Ma)
250	z	7	Cynodont (dog-toothed lizard), precursor to Gondwana mammals (see 210 Ma)
250	z	AM	Fossilized termite mounds, South Africa
248,2	g,e	3	Huge lavas in Siberia, plume volcanism rising 3 000km to surface, lava fields 3km thick, cause acid rain
248,2	b,z	U,6	Permian Extinction: major extinction of 96% of all species, 90% of maritime (trilobites, all corals etc.), 80% of terrestrial life extinct, including glossopteris, therapsids
248,2	e,z	H	Permian extinction not a single but continuous event over several My, probably caused by cooling and low sea levels

248,2 to 65,0 Ma — M e s o z o i c E r a

248,2 Ma to 205,7 Ma — Triassic Period

	Subject Ref.	Source Ref.	
244,4 **Ma**	c	X	40km diameter impact crater, Araguainha, Brazil
240	g	W	Oldest dolomite caves, Nelspruit, South Africa
240	e	1	Triassic global warming, arid dessert climate (see 330, 215 and 130 Ma)
240	z	W	Pig-sized mammal-like lystrosaurs herbivore reptile survived Permian extinction together with some carnivore species, Gondwana (see 210 Ma)
240	z	Z	Crocodilians spread
240	z	AF	Giant ichthyosaur raptor, Augusta Mtns., Nevada, USA
240	z	AG	1m high dinosaur-like Asilisaurus.kongwe, 10My older than previous dinosaur fossils, Tanzania
230	c	X	1,5km diameter impact crater, Karikkoselkae, Finland
230	g	H	Shallow "Muschelkalk Meer" (Shelly Limestone Sea), part of the Tethys, covers same area as "Zechstein Sea", flooding from the South, depositing shelly limestones, keuper and red sandstones, Central Europe (see 260 and 2,0 Ma)
230	z	H	Crocodilians as terrestrial reptiles (see 190 Ma)
225	g	3	*Tethys* covering 65% of Earth's surface (like now), between Laurasia (Eurasia, N.America) and Gondwana at equator, later mostly disappeared into crust (190 Ma)
225	g	AB	Pangaea breaks up: Laurasia (Eurasia, North America) separate from Gondwana (South America, Africa, Australia, Antarctica) (see 205,2 Ma)
225	b	G	Filicales appear, spore ferns (see 95 Ma)
225	b,z	3,H	Modern reef-building hexa-corals symbiotic with algae, phyto-plankton (dinoflagellates, nano-plankton)
225	z	7	Pro-sauropods, herbivore crocodiles, Madagascar (see 190, 170 Ma)
225	z	Q	Henodus.chelyops, a placodont marine reptile, wider than long, bony carapace, Europe (see 215 Ma)
225	z	I	Sinocondon, mammal-like, 1st modern jaw hinge evolved (see 210 Ma)
220 ±32	c	X	40km diameter impact crater, Saint Martin, Man./USA
220	c	AH	1,1km diameter impact crater, Tswaing, South Africa
220	b	G	Hepaticae (liverworts) (see 435 Ma)
220	b	G	Musci (mosses) (see 205 Ma)
220	b	G	Coniferales (conifers) appear (see 190 Ma)
220	z	7	Long-tailed pterosaurs evolve globally, 120 species, possibly warm-blooded with fur (= hair), first vertebrates to fly (see 270, 144 Ma)
215	g	H	Palisades formation in a sill, New York, US

	Subject Ref.	Source Ref.	
215 **Ma**	g	H	Petrified Forest, Arizona, USA
215	e	1	Warming of Gondwana reaches peak (see 240 Ma)
215	z	H	Hexa (=6-sided) corals appear, recent species built coral reefs
215	z	Q	Giant ichthyosaurs, largest ever marine reptile, gave birth to live young (240 Ma), plesiosaurs (200 Ma), nothosaurs, probably 1st reptiles to hunt in the sea, placosaurs, maritime saurians with lungs (225 Ma) North America
214 ±8	c	X	23km diameter impact crater, Rochechouart, France
214 ±1	c	D,X	Manicougan crater, 100km diameter, largest of 3 - 5 craters formed within a few hours by parts of a comet, Quebec, Canada
210	c	W	M32 galaxy crashes through the center of the Andromeda spiral galaxy, 65k Ly diameter
210	b	U	Riverine forest: seed ferns, cycads and ginkgos, wetlands: seed ferns, club mosses and horsetails, open woodland: cycadeoids, ginkgo, conifers, Gondwana
210	b	G	Ginkgoales, proto-leafed tree, 1 species left, China (see 60 Ma)
210	b	U	Early gymnosperms, Molteno formation, South Africa
210	z	Y	Efficia.okeefeae, a 2,5m ancestor of crocodiles, New Mexico, USA (see 250 Ma)
210	z	G	Fish-eating trematosaurs, rhynchosaurs, ponderous herbivores
210	z	I	Cpl. skeletons of cynodont (see 250 Ma) and lystrosaur (see 240 Ma), both therapsidae, Antarctica
210	z	H,I	Mammal-like reptiles develop to morganucodentids, shrew-sized 1st proto-mammals, larger cranium/brain, single lower jaw bone, molars more complicated, jaw bones in 1 piece, separate middle-ear bones, 1 set of permanent teeth, hence producing mother milk (see 225, 200, 195, 190 Ma)
206	b	G	Cycadales (modern cycads) appear (see 190 Ma)
206	b	AB	Numerous species of trees leave pollen traces (205 Ma)
205,7	e,b	AB	Release of 8 000 Gt CO_2, causes global warming, algae explosion absorbs most maritime O_2,resulting in extinction of 80% of maritime flora, mid-Atlantic
205,7	c b,z	7,H	Triassic extinction (by comet impact, indicated by iridium abundance and a "fern spike" ?), mass extinction of marine species, mammal-like reptiles extinct, seed ferns disappear (see 215, 210, 140 Ma)

205,7 Ma to 144,0 Ma Jurassic Period

	Subject Ref.	Source Ref.	
205,2 **Ma**	g	AB	1st signs of Pangaea break-up into Laurasia (Eurasia, North America) and Gondwana (South America, Africa, India, Australia, Antarctica) (see 260, 175, 150 Ma)
205,2	g	AB	Intensive volcanism starts, Southern Africa (183 Ma)
205	e,b	AB	Number of tree species much reduced due to acid rain (see 205,7 Ma), instead pollen of pioneer plants: ferns, horsetails, mosses containing toxic carbon C_2H_4 (see 220, 206 Ma)
205	z	I	Toothed monotremes, modified molars for modified diet (see 190, 175 Ma)
200 ±25	c	X	9km diameter impact crater, Red Wing, N.D./USA
200 ±100	c	X	12km diameter impact crater, Wells Creek, Tenn./USA
200	c	X	4,5km diameter impact crater, Riachao Ring, Brazil
200	g	AC	The Cimerian craton collided with Eurasia, closing the *Proto-Tethys* and opening the *Tethys* enclosed by Pangaea in the form of a "C" (see 280 Ma)
200	g	AB	Jura Sea, depositing huge sediments of shelly lime-stone, covers Central Europe (see 185 Ma)
200	g	V	Start of Gulf of Mexico, separating North and South America (see 160 Ma)
200	g	H	Andean orogeny starts by S.America subducting Nazca oceanic plate, crust 70km thick, still active (see 380, 50 and 16 Ma)
200	g	Q	Land surface completely covered by granite
200	e	Q	Earth radius speculated to be 38% smaller
200	e	A	Equator runs along West African coast between North and South America (see 40 Ma)
200	e	Y	O_2 levels 10 - 13% of present (see 360, 65 and 50 Ma)
200	b	P	Wollemi pine flourishes, Gondwana (see 2,0 Ma)
200	z	V	Frogs evolve (see 290, 180, 90 Ma)
200	z	3	Marine reptiles: ichthyosaurs, plesiosaurs (are not dinosaurs) return from land to sea, give birth there (see 250, 190 Ma)
200	z	1	Proto-mammals had 4 - 5x larger relative brains than reptiles, were 1st to have brain neo-cortex: higher cognitive functions (see 210, 195 Ma)
200	z	3	2 types of dinosaurs: saurischian (lizard-hipped) and ornithischian (bird-hipped) (see 80 Ma)
200	z	U	Shrew-sized 1st true mammals, alongside therapsid ancestors (140), South Africa (see 210, 190 Ma)
195	g,e	W	Start of clay deposits under Paris, London, Oxford and most of France and England by a warm tropical sea (see 140 Ma)
195	z	G	Chelonia (turtles, tortoises) of unknown ancestry

	Subject Ref.	Source Ref.	
195 **Ma**	z	I	Hadrocodium.wai, mouse-like proto-mammal with detached middle-ear bones, relatively large brain, China (see 190, 200 Ma)
190 ±30	c	X	7km diameter impact crater, Cloud Creek, Wyo./USA
190 ±20	c	X	2,5km diameter impact crater, Viewfield, Sask./Canada
190	g	H	Tethys separates Eurasia and Africa, leftovers are present Mediterranean, Black + Caspian Seas (225 Ma)
190	g	U	Karoo sand sea becomes sandstones, S.Africa (250 Ma)
190	b	1	Conifers, cycads abundant (see 220 and 206 Ma)
190	b	G	Pteridospermales (seed ferns) extinct (see 275 Ma)
190	b	G	Sphenophyllales extinct (see 290 Ma)
190	z	G	Cuttlefish, 600 genera of ammonoids
190	z	H	Crocodilians now also marine reptiles (see 230 Ma)
190	z	G	Ichthyosaurs, allosaurs (carnivores), enormous 4-pedal amphibious dinosaurs, pterosaurs (flying reptiles with 11m wing span), 1m long snake-like animals (200)
190	z	P	Massospondylus.carinatus, a pro-sauropod, 6 eggs (oldest ever) with embryos, Golden Gate, South Africa (see 225, 170 Ma)
190	z	K	Elephant shrew and golden mole do not belong to insectivore branch of mammals, but to afrotheria, together with elephant, aardvark and hyrax (DNA), ancestor a tiny paper-clip sized proto-mammal, China
190	z	S	Erythrotherium and megazostrodon the 1st true mammals (see 210, 195 Ma)
190	z	S	4 main mammal groups: monotremes (205, 175), multi-tuberculates (175), marsupials (167, 100), placentals (see 167, 125 Ma) (see also Notes for details)
187	z	AG	Arcusaurus, 2m long dinosaur, Senekal, South Africa
185	g	P	"Jurassic Coast" formed, Devon / Dorset, England (200)
185	b	G	Lepidodendrales (scale trees) disappear (see 275 Ma)
185	b	G	Calamitales (horse-tails) extinct (see 290, 175 Ma)
185	b	G	Cycadeoidales (cycads-like) appear (see 80 Ma)
185	b	G	Coenopteridales (spore ferns), cordaitales (oldest gymnosperms) extinct (see 290 Ma)
185	z	Q	Temnodontosaurus, an ichthyosaur, eyes 20cm diameter, could dive 650m deep, Europe
183	g	AH	Karoo dolerites intrude, 2M km^3 Drakensberg basalts erupt, 2km thick, now eroded to 1,8km covering Karoo sandstones, South Africa (see 205,2 Ma)
182	g	U	Begin of break-up of Gondwana (see 800, 140 Ma)
181	g	S	End of lava outpours, Drakensberge, South Africa
180	c	X	3,5km diameter impact crater, Kgagodi, Botswana
180	g	U	Mantle plumes cause Maluti Mountain to rise, S. Africa
180	g	7	Magma streams, Dry Valleys, Antarctic see 160 Ma)
180	g	Y	Massive dunes formed from eroding Appalachians turned into sandstone, Colorado Plateau, USA (see 160 Ma)

Ma	Subject Ref.	Source Ref.	
180 **Ma**	b,z	U	End of fossil record of Gondwana, Karoo, S.Afr. (270)
180	z	H	Proto-frog, Argentine (see 200, 90 Ma)
180	z	K	Dinosaurs look like rhinos, with long necks and tails, High Atlas, Morocco
175	g	AC	Start of rift of Pangaea, resulting in formation of Laurasia and Gondwana (see 205,2 and 150 Ma)
175	b	G	Neocalamitales (horse-tails) appear (185, 140 Ma)
175	b	G	Pleuromeiales, short un-branched shrub with needle-like leaves, rootlets (see 125 Ma)
175	b	G	Caytoniales (gymnosperms), fern-like foliage, pollen-bearing shoots appear (see 105 Ma)
175	z	W	Platypus, a monotreme mammal, 5 pairs of chromosomes determine its sex, most mammals only have 2 pairs, similarity to chromosomes of birds and mammals, which are thought to have evolved independently (205 Ma)
175	z	H,G	Herbivore multi-tuberculata mammals appear, the most abundant until their disappearance, developed independently from proto-mammals (see 190 and 60 Ma)
170	c	X	10km diameter impact crater, Upheaval Dome, Utah/USA
170	g	H	Start of shallow maritime calcareous deposits (aragonite needles), their great mass forcing sea bed to sink 10km, Bahamas Bank, West Atlantic
170	g	5	Limestones form south of Massif Central, France (130)
170	z	3	Modern sharks appear (see 300 Ma)
170	z	1	Brontosaurs (sauropoda) disappear (see 190, 225 Ma)
169 ±7	c	X	20km diameter meteorite impact crater, Obolon, Ukraine
167 ±3	c	X	80km diameter meteorite impact crater, Puchezh, Russia
167	z	I	Ancestor of marsupial and placental mammals with tribosphenic teeth, Gondwana (see 190 Ma)
165 ±5	c	X	3,2km diameter impact crater, Zapadnaya, Ukraine
165	g,e	Z	Start of violent period of breaking up of continents and climate changes (see 155 Ma)
165	z	G	Oldest sturgeons appear
165	z	G	Hymenoptera (ants, bees, wasps, true flies, earwigs) appear (see 148 and 100 Ma)
165	z	G	Stegosaurs (plated, 4-pedal) (see 160, 150 Ma)
164	z	W	Castorocauda.lutrasimilis, a fishotter-like mammal, 60cm long crane, China
161	z	Z	Tuojiangosaurus, herbivore with long, tapering spikes from each shoulder, China
160	c	W	2 huge asteroids collided at edge of solar system, breaking into 140k pieces of >1km, 3oo pieces of >10km diameter, one later hitting Yucatan, Mexico (see 64,98 Ma)
160 ±10	c	X	8km diameter impact crater, Vepriai, Lithuania
160	g	A,I	North America separates in the form of many islands from Laurasia, starting North Atlantic (100, 80, 55)

	Subject Ref.	Source Ref.	
160 **Ma**	g	A	New Guinea separates from Australia
160	g	1	Plateau lavas pour out, Antarctica (see 180, 120 Ma)
160	g	Y	Forests, rivers, swamps, inland seas with dinosaurs, crocodiles, giant seagoing lizards and huge sharks, Morrison Formation, Colorado Plateau, USA (180, 150)
160	g	I,V	Gulf of Mexico now established, near Cuba (see 200 Ma)
160	e,z	I	Marine plankton evolved, extracting CO_2 from atmosphere using C to form shells, releasing O_2
160	z	Q	Huge fish and flying reptiles, Svalbard, N.Atlantic
160	z	Z	Burst of evolution of new species of saurians, leading up to horned ceratopians, armored stegosaurs and tyrannosaurs (see 165, 150 Ma)
160	z	W	"Dino Death Trap" with 100's of skeletons of proto-triceratops, proto-crocodilians, 5 small guanlong CGI (proto-Tyrannosaurus.rex) dinosaurs stacked on top of each other, toothed and tooth-less theropods (changed from carnivore to herbivores), trapped in a mud pit, Junggar Basin, NW China
160	z	Z	Epidendrosaurus, sparrow-sized theropod, smallest dinosaur excl. birds, disproportionately large hands and 3rd fingers, China
160	z	AB	Anchionis.huxleyi, chicken-sized oldest bird ancestor, long feathers over feet as well, suggesting 4-winged dinosaur, NE Liaoning Province, China (see 150 Ma)
155	g	H	"Solnhofen limestone slates", Jura mountains, Southern Germany, Minette ores, Lorraine, France
155	g	H	Sierra Nevada orogeny, California, USA
155	g,e	Z	End of violent period of breaking up of continents and climate changes (see 165 Ma)
155	z	7	Short-tailed pterosaurs evolve, prosper until 65 Ma
≥150	z	AF	Anchiornis, chicken-sized proto-bird, covered in symmetrical feathers unsuitable for flight, China
150 ±70	c	X	1,6km diameter meteorite impact crater, Liverpool, Northern Territory, Australia
150 ±20	c	X	1,3km diameter meteorite impact crater, Tabun-Khara-Obo, Mongolia
150	g	H	Pangaea ends, Gondwana a separate super-continent (see 205,2 and 175 Ma)
150	g	H	Penninian Sea starts between Africa and Eurasia as the Iberian and Penninian cratons drift between Europe and Africa (see 45 Ma)
150	g	H	"Dinosaur grave-yard", Morrison Formation, North America (see 160 Ma)
150	g	I	Earliest known earthquakes in California, USA (60 Ma)
150	e	S	Ice age of relatively short duration, South Africa
150	e	H	Sundance Sea floods large part of North America
150	e,b	Q	Semi-arid savanna, Moab, Utah, USA (see 285 Ma)

	Subject Ref.	Source Ref.	
150 **Ma**	z	H	Braarrudisphaera.bigelowi, a calcareous nano-plankton species (see 64 Ma)
150	z	7	Fossilized horse-shoe crab, North America
150	z	Y	Turiasaurus.riodevensis sauropod, 36,5m long, 45t (= mass of 6 male elephants), Spain
150	z	I,3	Young dromaeosaur (theropod) shares 100 anatomical features [wishbone, swiveling wrists etc.] with bird, primitive feathers for warmth, not flight, China
150	z	3,W	Archaeopteryx: dinosaur/bird, earliest feathers, teeth and feet like dinosaurs, Sonthofen, Germany (see 160 and 140 Ma)
150	z	W	Europasaurus.holgeri, group of small-sized 6m long dinosaurs, Harz, Germany
150	z	W,Z	Maritime pliosaur, 16m long, size of a bus, Svalbard Island, Arctic Sea
150	z	AF	Grottenolm evolves, a cave dwelling lizard, blind, lungs and gills, Adriadic Mountains, Istria, Croatia
150	z	1	Stegosaurs die out (see 165 Ma)
150	z	Q	Limbic brain system develops from rhinen-cephalon ("swelling brain") in mammals (see 100 Ma)
148	z	P	Termites appear, start social organization, cementing their nests, first villages, then cities (see 165, 100 and 40 Ma)
145 ±0,8	c	W,X U	25km diameter stony meteorite rich in Fe silicates and NiFe sulfides caused 70km diameter impact crater, (suggestion: possibly caused Jurassic extinction ?), identified 1996, Morokweng, South Africa
145	g	AC	Gondwana begins to rift into continents (see 140 Ma)
144	z	7	Long-tailed pterosaurs die out (see 220 Ma)
144	b,z	H	Limited extinction of fauna and flora

144,0 Ma to 65,0 Ma Cretaceous Period

144	z	Z	Proliferation of crocodilians, Gondwana
142,5 ±0,8	c	X	22km diameter meteorite impact crater, Gosses Bluff, Northern Territory, Australia
142 ±2,6	c	X	40km diameter meteorite impact crater, Mjoelnir,Norway
140	c	X	6,8km diameter impact crater, Arkenu 1, Libya
140	c	X	10km diameter meteorite impact crater, Arkenu 2, Libya
140	g	U AC	Gondwana breaking up into Africa/South America and Antarctica/Australia/India/Madagascar, possibly due to mantle plume beneath Mozambique, creating the Southern Indian Ocean (see 182, 145, 120 and 50 Ma)
140	g	P	Elbsandstein mountain formed, Saxony, Germany
140	g	W	End of clay deposits under Paris, London, Oxford and most of France and England (see 195 Ma)
140	b	G	Neocalamitales (horse-tails) extinct (see 175 Ma)

	Subject Ref.	Source Ref.	
140 **Ma**	b	G	Chrysophyta, non-vascular plants
140	z	G	Sponge reefs, primitive skates, marine crocs, Central Europe
140	z	H	Last therapsidae disappear (see 200 Ma)
140	z	G	Pterodactylus (flying saurian), Central Europe
140	z	W	Pterodaustro (flying saurian), bird-like,1 000 tiny teeth, 2m wing span, 100s of fossils, Argentina
140	z	5	Proto-bird shenzhoiuraptor fossil: no teeth, very long tail, able to fly, China (see 160, 150 Ma)
135	g	S	Diabase (dolerite) eruptions, Namibia
135	g	I	Age of rocks from sea floor, found by "Glomar Challenger" expedition, Pacific Ocean
135	z	Y	Psittacosaurs appear (see 100 Ma)
135	z	P,Q	Dakosaurus.andiniensis, a jumbo carnivorous marine reptile "Godzilla", distant relative of crocodiles, paddles instead of feet, rudder-like tail, Pacific Ocean (then a deep tropical bay), off Chili
130	g	H	Western alpine orogeny starts (see 80 and 40 Ma)
130	g	5	Limestone rocks change to dolostone (dolomite), due to interaction of water and magnesium, Montpellier le Vieux, France (see 170 and 65 Ma)
130	e	Q	Global warming (see 330, 240 Ma)
130	b	G,7 I	Monocotyledons (1-seeded leaves) oldest angiosperms incl. buttercups, magnolia, followed by dicotyledons (2-seeded leaves), 3 basal lineages based on DNA: amborellaceae (probably woody), nymphaeaceae (water lilies), illiciaeceae (star anises) (125, 100 Ma)
130	z	Z	Amargasaurus, double row of bony spines, Argentina
130	z	P	Repenomanus.robustus mammal, 60cm long, 7kg, ate small psittacosaur, ripping like a crocodile, which changes our perception of saurian/mammal relation, also found Repenomanus.giganticus mammal, 90cm long, 13,6kg, Liaoning, China (see 125 Ma)
130	z	W	Proto mammal, 1st evidence of renewable teeth, Germany
128 ±5	c	X	55km diameter meteorite impact crater, Tookoonooka, Queensland, Australia
128	z	K	Flying incivosaurus, buck- toothed, cross between dinosaur and rabbit, herbivore, part of carnivorous theropod family, China
125	g	P	Fine-grained basalt, Southern Sweden
125	g	I	Northern Pacific floor was 3 000km south of the equator, drifted north, then south, then north again (see 65 and 55 Ma)
125	g	W	Seas repeatedly cover southwestern USA
125	b	C	Freshwater angiosperms, flower above water, cpl. stem, roots, leaves, reproductive organs, China (130 Ma)
125	b	G	Selaginellales, modern form of pleuromeiales (175 Ma)

	Subject Ref.	Source Ref.	
125 **Ma**	z	Q,Y AF	Volcanic gases killed, and thick rain of volcanic ash preserved Dilong.paradoxus, a proto-tyrannosaur (160) with hair-like proto-feathers, adult psittacosaur (130) and 34 juveniles (day care?), Hyphalosaurus. lingyuanensis, aquatic predator, protopteryx (150), a theropod primitive bird with 3 types of feathers, probably evolved from reptile scales, China
125	z	I	Jeholodens, placental mammals, mobile shoulder girdle allows increased range of motion (see 165 Ma)
125	z	P	100's of falcarius.utahensis, 1st transitional herbivore therizinosaur, bone structure of carnivore, body of herbivore, lost serrated teeth, Utah, USA
125	z	I	Eomaia.scansoria: furred proto- placental "dawn mother", tree-living, 50 My earlier than previously thought, ex Asia or Gondwana (see 190, 167 Ma)
121 ±2,3	c	X	9km diameter meteorite impact crater, Mien, Sweden
120	c	X	2km diameter impact crater, B.P. Structure, Libya
120	c	X	±18km diameter meteorite impact crater, Oasis, Libya
120 ±10	c	X	2,7km diameter impact crater, Rotmistrovka, Ukraine
120	g	U	India/Madagascar separate from Antarctica/Australia, Australia has reached its present place (see 140 Ma)
120	g	1	Plateau lava out-pour ends, Antarctica (see 160 Ma)
120	g	S,U	Start (mitochondrial DNA) of rifting between Africa and South America, eventually creating the South Atlantic, Falkland Plateau (as part of South America) separates from Africa (see 100 Ma)
120	g,e	AB	Antarctica already occupying the South Pole, but still ice-free (see 35 Ma)
120	e	AB AM	Tidal friction slows down Earth's revolutions by 3,82s per 100ky, length of day only 23 hours (see 400 Ma)
120	b	K	Rare sub-species of eudicots now dominant, China
120	z	I	Archaeoraptor.liaoningensis.sloan = a forgery, China
115 ±10	c	X	39km diameter impact crater, Carswell, Sask./Canada
115	b,z	3	Flowering plants and flying insects in "co-evolution" (pollination), both becoming highly specialized
110	c	X	4km diameter impact crater, Mt. Toondina, S.Australia
110	g	AM	Begin of kimberlite intrusions, producing most of the diamond deposits, South Africa (90 Ma)
110	g	H	Tethys floods parts of England, France, North Germany, depositing chalk, Dover, Champagne, Isle of Ruegen
110	g	AM	Atlantic, rifting from south to north (160 Ma)
110	e	Q	Australia starts to be flooded (see 98 Ma)
110	b,z	U	80 species of fauna and flora, including lemurs, are endemic to Madagascar
110	z	7	River crocodile, 10t, (= 10-15x Nile crocs), Sahara
110	z	Q	11t kronosaurs and woolungasaurs, marine predators

	Subject Ref.	Source Ref.	
110 **Ma**	z	z	Nigersaurus, a diplodocoid herbivore sauropod, 80% of skeleton with light-weight skull bones, paper-thin vertebrae, 600 teeth, muzzle like a lawn mower, Niger
105	b	G	Caytoniales (gymnosperms) extinct (see 175 Ma)
105	z	AG	Pakasuchus kapilimai, a cat-like Gondwana crocodile, short head with differentiated teeth, only the tail armored, Tanzania
100	c	X	13km diameter impact crater, Sierra Madera, Tex./USA
100	g	I,U	Volcanic Kimberlite diamond pipes reach surface due to erosion of surrounding rocks, South Africa (see 2,0 Ga and 90 Ma)
100	g	K	Uluru (= Ayers Rock) appears, remnant of vast sandstone plateau, Central Australia (see 800 Ma)
100	g	A	Ocean between North/South America and Eurasia/Africa has widened considerably (see 120 and 80 Ma)
100	g	AB	Breakup of Laurentia, western part of Svalbard now northern tip of North America, opening of Arctic Sea (see 17,5 Ma)
100	g	AG	Yellow Mountain formed, glaciers of Quaternary ice age shape granite pinnacles, Anhui, East China
100	g	AC	South America separates from Africa, starting the South Atlantic
100	e	H	Sea levels and global temperatures very high, probably highest average temperatures since then (see 440, 250, 70 Ma)
100	b	G	Palms, laurus, cinnamonum appear
100	b	H	Diatoms and foraminifera present in the oceans
100	b	K	Idiospermum, thought extinct angiosperm, found living in Queensland, Australia
100	b	I	Magnoliids 1st non-basal angiosperm, petals evolve for angiosperms, starting their "great radiation" (130)
100	z	Z	Leatherback turtles evolve (see 80 Ma)
100	z	Z	Modern crocodilians evolve, including Nile crocodile, Africa, saltwater crocodile, SE Australasia, alligator, North America
100	z	K,P	Nothomyrmecia proto-ant, evolved from solitary tiphiid wasps, forced to organize to compete with termites, thought extinct, found living in Australia (165, 148)
100	z	G	Octopods appear, ichthyosaurs decline, various plesiosaurs, salamanders
100	z	Y	Psittacosaurs disappear (see 135 Ma)
100	z	3	Marsupials spread globally (see 190 Ma)
100	z	Q	Cerebral cortex developed (see 150 Ma)
100	z	I	DNA data says most modern mammal groups appear (60 Ma)
99 ±4	c	X	13km diameter impact crater, Deep Bay, Sask./Canada
98	g	Q	Flooding of "Great Artesian Basin" ended, Australia (see 110 Ma)

		Subject Ref.	Source Ref.	
98	**Ma**	z	AB	2 new sauropod saurians (largest herbivores ever and up to 30t) and a 2m carnivore with 3 huge claws on each extremity, Queensland, Australia
97		c	X	13km diameter impact crater, Kentland, Ind./USA
97		z	Z	Spinosaurus, 15m long, with 2m long dorsal spines, largest terrestrial carnivore ever, North Africa
96		z	AB	Polypterus.senegalus, a present fish family long thought extinct, has skin built up by 4 nano-structured alternating soft and hard layers, Senegal
95		c	X	12km diameter impact crater, Avak, Alas./USA (3 Ma)
95		g	AC	India/Madagascar rift from each other, India moving north at 15cm/a (a plate tectonic record !), Madagascar got stuck on the African plate (110 Ma)
95		g	H	Mowry Sea flooding from Caribbean to Artic, developing into the cretaceous Interior Seaway, N.America (67)
95		b	G	Filicales (spore ferns) prosper (see 225 Ma)
95		b,z	H	Sea weeds, rudist reef builders symbiotic with algae (see 85 Ma)
95		z	W	Carcharodontosaurus.iguidensis (shark lizard), size of Tyrannosaurus.rex, teeth banana-sized, Morocco similar C.saharicus, a shallow sea covering the intervening land lead to 2 species, Niger
94		z	Q	Thalassomedon plessiosaurs, marine predators, 6m neck carried stones in stomach for ballast, North America
91	±7	c	X	25km diameter impact crater, Steen River, Alta./Canada
90		c	AB	Supernova SN 2007 exploded then, visible (X-rays) only now
90		g	S	Diamond-bearing kimberlite pipe in volcanic caldera, Orapa, Lesotho (see 120 Ma)
90		g	AM	End of kimberlite intrusions, South Africa (110 Ma)
90		g	AM	Plateau lava out-pour ends, Antarctica (see 160 Ma)
90		b,z	S	Oldest South African angiosperm and insect fossils
90		z	S	Frogs look like at present, South Africa (200, 180 Ma)
90		z	AF	End of ichthyosaur ("fish lizard") run (see 250 Ma)
90		z	I	Argentinosaurus, 39m long herbivore, South America
89	±2,7	c	X	19km diameter meteorite impact crater, Dellen, Sweden
88		b	W	Predominance of angiosperms, Patagonia, Argentine
88		z	W	70% of skeleton of 33m futalognkosaurus, of the titanosaur family, also pterosaurs, megaraptors, Patagonia, Argentine (see 80 Ma)
85		g	H	Sea levels high, continents covered by shallow seas
85		g	AB	Western China covered by up to 35°C tropical sea
85		b,z	H	Rudists up to 1m long build reefs together with algae, at the expense of corals (see 95 Ma)
85		z	H	Snakes appear, related to modern boa and python
85		z	H	Mammals (marsupials and placentals) exist

	Subject Ref.	Source Ref.	
85 **Ma**	z	AB	Gigantoraptor.erlianensis, bird-like dinosaur with a beak, small legs and probably feathers, 1,5t, 8m long, 5m high, 35x larger than closest relative caudipteryx, West China
82	g	I,K	New Zealand separates from Australia/Antarctica Tasman Sea starts to open (see 80 and 70 Ma)
82	z	W	Mzamba Fossil Formation, petrified forest, ammonites, inoceramus (giant clams), etc., Natal, South Africa
82	z	Z	Carnotaurus "meat-eating bull", battering ram head with horns, short arms, long legs, small teeth, Patagonia, Argentine
82	z	I,K	Bats the only mammals to survive the separation of New Zealand from Australia, (mitochondrial DNA) (60, 47)
81 ±1,5	c	X	6,5km diameter impact crater, Wetumpka, Ala./USA
80 ±20	c	X	3,5km diameter impact crater, Zeleny Gai, Ukraine
80	g	1	Europe, Russia, North America, North Africa, Australia, Arabia flooded
80	g	A	African axis from east-west to north-south (300 Ma)
80	g	AB	Driftwood on beaches of shallow sea petrified to fossil forest, since then land has risen over 400m, Natal South Coast, South Africa
80	g	H	Eastern alpine orogeny starts (see 130 and 40 Ma)
80	g	H,3 P	Chalk formations by protist fossils, coccoliths and algae, isle of Ruegen, Baltic Sea, Germany
80	g	1	Coal deposits in Siberia
80	g	7	New Caledonia separates from Australia (see 82 Ma)
80	g	A	North America consolidates, North/South America and Eurasia/Africa are closer again (see 160 and 100 Ma)
80	g	H	Appalachians now largely eroded (see 280 Ma)
80	b	G	Cycadeoidales extinct (see 185 Ma)
80	b	3	Oldest amber, Indian Ocean
80	b	G	Isoetales, modern form of pleuromeiales (see 125 Ma)
80	b	H	So-called sea grass develops, not a grass
80	b,z	W	Bee with oldest orchid pollen, Costa Rica
80	z	Q	Green turtles, Pacific Ocean (see 100 Ma)
80	z	Z	Modern crocodiles evolve (see 240 Ma)
80	z	I	1 000's of titanosaurus egg clusters swamped by flood, aucasaurs attacked young, Auca Mahueva, Patagonia (see 88 Ma)
80	z	I	Fossilized killing by velociraptor (carnivore) of proto-ceratops (herbivore), Gobi Desert, Mongolia
80	z	U	Indication that birds evolved from small light-boned theropod saurischians (reptile-hipped), not from ornithischians (bird-hipped) (see 200, 70 Ma)
76	z	Z	Parasaurolophus.walkeri, herbivore saurian, N.America
75	c	X	6km diameter impact crater, Maple Creek, Sask./Canada
75	g	H	Corsica, Sardinia, Sicily are minor cratons

	Subject Ref.	Source Ref.	
75 **Ma**	g	Q	Western Interior Seaway (Mowry Sea) splits N.America
75	z	Z	Styracosaurus, nose spike, profusion of head horns, rhino-sized herbivore, Alberta, Canada
75	z	P	8 albertosaurs found, hunted in icy conditions, Canada
75	z	I	Duck-billed dinosaur, Baja California
75	z	Q	Mosasaurs, marine raptors, North America
73,8 ±0,3	c	T,X	Manson crater, 4,5km deep, 35km across, by 10 bn ton 2,5km across rocky meteorite, Iowa, USA
73,3 ±5,3	c	X	23km diameter impact crater, Lappajaervi, Finland
70,3 ±2,2	c	X	65km diameter meteorite impact crater, Kara, Russia
70	c	X	3,5km diameter impact crater, Ouarkziz, Algeria
70	c	X	6km diameter meteorite impact crater, Chukcha, Russia
70	c	X	6km diameter impact crater, Tin Bider, Algeria
70	c	X	12km diameter impact crater, Vargeao Dome, Brazil
70	g	H	Africa, South America, India separated, Australia and Antarctic still connected (see 40 Ma)
70	g	1	Seychelles separate from drifting India (see 95 Ma)
70	g	K	Tasman Sea at present configuration (see 82 Ma)
70	g	Q	North Western Hawaiian Islands formed
70	g	I	Vast chert deposits created by skeletons of opalinida micro organisms, North Atlantic sea bed
70	g	V	Start of orogeny of Sierra Madre Oriental by subduction of Cocos plate, Mexico (see 40 Ma)
70	g,z	W	Giant frog "Devil Toad", 4,5kg, armored, not related to African, but to S.American ceratophrys, suggests that Madagascar still was, via much warmer than present Antarctica, part of Africa (see 110 Ma)
70	e	H	Global temperatures and sea levels recede again (100)
70	b	7	Welwitschia appears, lives more than 2 000 years, still existing, Namibia
70	b	H	Angiosperms now dominant over gymnosperms
70	z	U	Fossil beds, some of the fish fossils still show color spots on scales, Stompoor crater, South Africa
70	z	1	First butterflies
70	z	Q	Cluster of eggs and dinosaur pelvis with 2 un-laid eggs, closer to birds than reptiles, China (80 Ma)
70	z	Z	Deinocheirus, possibly ornithomimid saurus, with 2,45m extra long arms, 25cm claws, Mongolia (80 Ma)
70	z	Z	Masiakasaurus, Alsatian-sized carnivore, Madagascar
70	z	P	Bird and eggs fossils, Romania (see 80 and 60 Ma)
70	z	1	Archaic creodonta (carnivorous mammals) (see 45 Ma)
68	z	W	Molecular evidence of protein fragments of T.rex suggest relation to birds (see 160 Ma)
67	g	H	Closure of cretaceous Interior Seaway (see 95 Ma)
67	z	Z	Dracorex, herbivore pachycephalosaur with spiky head and snout, South Dakota, USA
67	z	7	"Sue", most cpl. skeleton of T.rex ever found, London

	Subject Ref.	Source Ref.	
66 **Ma**	z	I	Coprolite of Tyrannosaurus.rex, Saskatchewan, Canada
66	z	W	Tyrannosaurus.rex not found in Africa
65,17 ±640ky	c	X	24km diameter meteorite impact crater, Boltysh, Ukraine
65	c	X	9,5km diameter impact crater, Vista Allegre, Brazil
65	c	H	Quartz grains from iridium-rich zones with concussion-wave metamorphosis ex meteorite impact, global distribution, possibly a meteorite shower, Nitrogen of atmosphere burned, creating sulfur and acid rain
65	g,e	AJ L	Deccan Traps, 2km thick, 500 000km^2, include 500 000km^3 of basalt, sulfuric acid rain, contributing to K/T extinction ?, India
65	e	T	Global iridium levels 300-500 times higher than normal
65	e	H	Iridium in thin clay band (border clay), Gubbio, Italy
65	e,b	H	Fern spores 99% of micro-flora before extinction, afterwards only 15-30%, most extinct plants with un-serrated leaves used to warm climates, suggesting strong cooling as cause of extinction
65	z	G	Ammonoids extinct, nautiloids almost extinct
65	z	H	Marine reptiles and triceratops the last major dinosaur groups to die out
65	z	L	Carnivore marsupials: lions, dogs, herbivore marsupials: rhino-like, ground sloth, giant kangaroo, tapir-like, giant capybara, also giant lizards, all extinct, Australia (see 50 Ma)
65	z	6	Cretaceous/Tertiary (K-T) boundary extinction of 60 to 70% of fauna species globally, incl. saurians
64,98 ±50ky	c,e	3,Q	12km diameter meteorite hit (see 160 Ma), 180km diameter crater half under Caribbean water, 3 000 ring cenotes along crater perimeter, globally 10x normal iridium levels in thin clay layer Yucatan, Mexico, (see 205,7 Ma)

Part II Paleocene Epoch = KT Boundary to 5 000 BP

65,0 Ma to 5,0 ka **C e n o z o i c E r a**

65,0 to 1,8 Ma **Tertiary Sub - Era**

65,0 to 23,8 Ma **Paleogene Period** = early Tertiary Period

65,0 to 54,8 Ma **Paleocene Epoch**

	Subject Ref.	Source Ref.	
65 **Ma**	g	G,K	Africa collides with Europe, forming the Atlas mountains, North Africa, Pyrenean orogeny "rejuvenated Hercynian chain" (see 320 and 300 Ma)
65	g	5	Les Causses limestone plateaux, south of Massif Central, France (see 130 and 10 Ma)
65	g	Q	Greenland rifts from Scotland/Scandinavia (see 60 Ma)
65	g	I	Movement of Northern Pacific floor reversed direction, drifting south (see 125 and 55 Ma)
65	g	W	Rocky Mountain orogeny starts, USA (see 300, 35 Ma)
65	e	S	O_2 levels 30% of atmosphere (see 200 and 50 Ma)
65	b	S	Diatoma (but not 92% of foraminifera) survived
65	b	Q	Myxomycetes fungus (slime mould) with fused swarm cells = sexual intercourse
65	b	K	Microbialithes = co-habitation of cyano-bacteria/ bacteria thought extinct, alive in 25m depth, Pacific
65	z	U	Of the many reptilian species only 3 groups survived: lizards/snakes, crocodiles/alligators and birds
65	z	L	400 to 500 species of mega fauna survived globally, but only 4 marsupial species, Australia
65	z	S	Toads, corals, nautiloids (but not ammonites) survived
65	z	3,H	Turtles, crocodiles and lizards just survived, but now adaptive radiation of birds and mammals
64	c	X	10km diameter impact crater, Eagle Butte, Alta./Canada
64	z	H	Calcareous nano-plankton disappears (see 150 Ma)
63	e	AB	Huge river system connecting Okavango Delta and Makgadikgadi Lake = Kalahari Basin, Botswana (see 55 and 5,0 Ma)
63	z	7	Extinct hoofed archaic ungulates split into mesonychidae, early whales (55 Ma) and even-toed ungulates (see 30 Ma)
60	c	K	350m diameter asteroid hit, crater 3km diameter, 300m deep, concentric fractures for up to 19km, North Sea
60	c	X	9km diameter impact crater, Conolly Basin, W.Australia
60	g	A	Atlantic ocean narrower than now (see 20 Ma)
60	g	H	Beringia land bridge in existence, rifting between Greenland, North America and Europe starts (65, 50)

	Subject Ref.	Source Ref.	
60 **Ma**	g	7	"Giant's Causeway", lava flows into the sea, instant cooling, 1 000s of hexagonal blocks, Northern Ireland
60	g	1	Renewed flooding of Europe (see 26 Ma)
60	g	5	Rhein-Graben, triple junction rift between Black Forest and Vosges, Germany/France
60	g	W	Separation of Northern Europe and North America created layer-cake of related igneous rocks, Isle of Rhum, Scotland
60	g	W	Bryozoan chalk with flint bands, Moensted, Sealand, Denmark (see 250 Ma)
60	g	1	Laramide orogeny, mountains rise 2km, later Grand Canyon developed there, Colorado, USA (see 45 Ma)
60	g	I	Earliest known <u>strong</u> earthquakes, California (150 Ma)
60	e	U	CO_2 concentration then was 3 500 parts, now 360 parts per million
60	b	H	Appearance of the only still existing gingko species, China (see 210 Ma)
60	b	H	Grasses appear, need long recuperation after being grazed (see 50 Ma)
60	z	G	Nearly all modern bird species exist (see 70 Ma)
60	z	3	Diatryma, giant flightless carnivorous bird (40 Ma)
60	z	G	Multi-tuberculates extinct (see 175 Ma)
60	z	W	Indohyus, a badger-sized herbivore aquatic land mammal, thought to be common ancestor of whales and hippos, initiating return to the sea (see 55, 50 Ma)
60	z	P	Mammal with poison fangs, Canada
60	z	I	Fossils say most modern mammal groups appear (100 Ma)
60	z	V	Bats evolve, nocturnal, paper-thin wings, echolocation (see 82 and 47 Ma)
60	z	4	Plesiadapidae, proto-simian proto-anthropoid, Europe, North America
60	z	C,S I	Madagascar lemurs and tarsiers share common ancestor with lemurs, tarsiers survive in interior of SE Asian islands (see 57 Ma)
58 ±2	c	X	12,7km diameter impact crater, Marquez, Tex./USA
57	z	4,H S,L	Anthropoids, ancestor to Old World monkeys/primates/ hominoids, tree-living, hands and feet hominoid, split from proto-simians (tarsiers, bush babies, lemurs), Africa (see 60, 45, 35 Ma)
56	z	Z	Hyracotherium, a horse ancestor, (the 5-toed horses ?) North America (see 45 Ma)
55	g	AC	Laurasia rifts into Laurentia and Eurasia, opening the North Atlantic (see 160 Ma)
55	g	P	Volcano in Skagerrak Straits, youngest in Scandinavia, lighter than water Mo-clay deposits: ⅓ clay mineral smectite, ⅔ diatoma fossils, interspersed by 179 volcanic ash layers over few My, isle of Mors, Denmark

	Subject Ref.	Source Ref.	
55 **Ma**	g	I	Northern Pacific floor drifts north again (125, 65 Ma)
55	g	1	Italy rotated 43° clockwise (see 45 Ma)
55	e	U	Ancestral lake Makgadikgadi formed, Kalahari River captures Karoo River to form Orange River, S.Africa (see 63 and 5,0 Ma)
55	z	I	Mammals now larger, up to pig size
55	z	Y	Gomphos.elkema, common ancestor of rodents and lagomorphs (rabbits, pikas, hares), Mongolia
55	z	I	Phosphatherium.escuilliei, oldest proboscidean (elephant group), fox-sized, no trunk, straight "mouth", Morocco (see 54 and 50 Ma)
55	z	W	Whales and hippos split from common ancestor, they are now not considered related (see 63, 60, 55 Ma)
54,8	e	D,Y	Oceanic frozen methane "belch" causes global maximum temperature, destroying many maritime life forms, fresh-water ferns, crocodiles in Greenland, Arctic and Antarctica ice-free (see 40 and 14 Ma)

54,8 to 33,7 Ma Eocene Epoch

54,5	z	AB	Anthrasimias.gujaratensis, proto-anthropoid, very small teeth, 60 -80g, India (see 50, 47, 45, 30 Ma)
54	z	L	Proto-elephant, 1m high, swamp-living, (originally aquatic ?), Algiers (see 55 and 50 Ma)
53	z	H	Most of modern animal genera exist
51	g	AG	Insect fossils in amber show less divergence from specimen from Africa or Madagascar than expected after assumed long separation, Cambay, India (95 Ma)
50,5 ±760ky	c	X	45km diameter meteorite impact crater, Montagnais, N.S./Canada
50	c	X	5,1km diameter impact crater, Goat Paddock, Australia
50	g	I	Philippines emerge due to tectonic plate movements
50	g	U	Australia separates from Antarctica (see 140 Ma)
50	g	W	India collides with Asian plate, moving fastest ever at 20cm p/a because there is a hot spot underneath, causing start of Himalayan orogeny, having increased plate thickness to 100 km (see 5,0 Ma)
50	g	Q	Andes orogeny accelerates to 25mm/100a since then (see 200 and 16 Ma)
50	g	W	Volcano eruption creates St.Barthélemy Is., Caribbean
50	g	V	Uplifted Central Mexican Plateau (see 2,0 Ma)
50	g,e	Q	Beringia land bridge exposed due to dropped sea levels, Alaska (see 60 Ma)
50	e	Y	O_2 levels 18% (see 200, 65 and 40 Ma)
50	b	G	Cacti, leguminosae, ficus, eucalyptus prosper
50	b	H	Grasses prosper, "inventing" continuous growth (60 Ma)
50	z	AF	Eels develop (see 47 Ma)

	Subject Ref.	Source Ref.	
50 **Ma**	z	I	Mola fish develops, weighs up to 2 000kg
50	z	AG	Chiloe-like marsupial rat, South America, common ancestor of all marsupials, Australia ?? (100, 65 Ma)
50	z	7	Pakicetus = common ancestor of cetacea (whales/hippos and horses/pigs/cows/sheep): 4-pedal, hoofed, furry, co-living with marsupials, squirrel-sized anthropoids (54,5), Himalayas/ Pakistan (60, 55 Ma)
50	z	I	Indricotherium, elephant group, largest ever land mammal, mass of several elephants, no trunk, Asia (see 55 and 54 Ma)
50	z	I	Oldest whale with terrestrial habitat, Himalayas/ Pakistan (see 60, 55, 48 Ma)
50	z	I	Pezosiren.portelli, quadruped, maritime ancestor of manatees
49 ± 0,2	c	X	25km diameter meteorite impact crater, Kamensk, Russia
49 ± 0,2	c	X	3km diameter meteorite impact crater, Gusev, Russia
48	z	7	Walking/swimming fresh water whale, 4-toed feet, hooves, indicating they re-migrated from land to sea (see 50 and 45 Ma)
47,5	z	AB	Whale with fetus in head-first position, indicates proto-whales rested and gave birth on land, Pakistan
47	e	AG	El Niño effects stronger than at present, Messel, Germany
47	z	W,3	Kopidodon.macrograthus, 1m long European fruit eater, crocodiles, fish, eels (50), ungulates, turtles, reptiles, snakes (85), birds, lemurs, marsupials, insects, oldest fully developed bats (47), semi-tropical forest shale pit, Messel, Germany
47	z	AB	Darwinius.marsillae, 95% complete female skeleton "Ida", perfectly fossilized missing link between pro-simians and anthropoids, absence of pro-simian and presence of anthropoid features, 3m long 1m high, opposable thumbs, 5-digit hands, semi-tropical forest shale pit, Messel, Germany (see 54,5 and 45, 30 Ma)
46 ±7	c	X	5,5km diameter impact crater, Chiyli, Kazakhstan
46 ±3	c	X	9km diameter meteor. impact crater, Ragozinka, Russia
45 ±10	c	X	2,8km diameter impact crater, Shunak, Kazakhstan
45	g	H	Iberian and Penninian cratons wedged between African and Eurasian plates, Atlas and Pyrenees, Alps and Carpathians start to form, the Penninian Sea (part of Tethys) closed, some sea floor now on 4 477m Matter-horn mountain, Switzerland (see 150, 20 Ma)
45	g	1	Italy rotated 25° anti- clockwise (see 55 Ma)
45	g	H	Laramide orogeny ends, North America (see 60 Ma)
45	g	H	India collides with Indochina on the Eurasian plate (see 20 Ma)

	Subject Ref.	Source Ref.	
45 **Ma**	g	3	South America an island, Pacific/Atlantic connected (see 3,5 and 3,0 Ma, 12 ka)
45	z	7	Whales are now true marine mammals (see 48 and 40 Ma)
45	z	I	Creodonta, omni/carnivorous mammals extinct (70 Ma)
45	z	H,3	Proto-horse, 5-toed horse ancestor, size of small dog, 4 toes in front, 3 at back, North America (56, 20 Ma)
45	z	I	Eosimia, anthropoid, grasping hands/feet, color vision (see 57 Ma)
42,3 ±1,1	c	X	15km diameter meteorite impact crater, Logoisk,Belarus
42	b	H	Rose plant and upright tree fossils, Colorado, USA
42	z	Z	Icadyptes and another penguin species, during hot climate period, Ica, Peru (see 36 and 10 Ma)
40 ±20	c	X	8km diameter meteorite impact crater, Beyenchime Salaatin, Russia
40 ±20	c	X	20km diameter meteor. impact crater, Logancha, Russia
40	g	H	Atlantic ocean widens between Scandinavia and Greenland, rifting between N.America and Greenland stops
40	g	H	Alps reach nearly present form (see 130, 80, 8,0 Ma)
40	g	H	Start of Turgai Sea east of Ural, connecting Tethys and Arctic Sea (see 30 Ma)
40	g	H AC	Australia, moving north at 5cm/a, separates from Antarctic, finalizing the break-up of Gondwana (70)
40	g	1	Eastern Pacific floor develops
40	g	I	Limestone outcrops from ocean floor still rise, Cuba
40	g	V	Sierra Madre Oriental established, Mexico (see 70 Ma)
40	e	H	Begin of period of 5 abrupt temperature drops with global transgression over most continents (see 31 Ma)
40	e	A	Equator near present position (see 200 Ma)
40	e	Y	O_2 levels reach 23% (see 50 Ma)
40	e	I	Global temperature back to normal (see 54,8 Ma)
40	e	H	Antarctic glaciation starts, psychrosphere (cold sea bottom layer), cold seas (see 54,8 and 34 Ma)
40	b	H	Lignite (brown coal) deposits with extensive plant fossil beds, Geisel Valley, Halle/S, Germany
40	z	P	Wars between termites and ants (how does one know that ??), ants develop formic acid as a weapon (148)
40	z	H	Diatryma flightless birds extinct (see 60 Ma)
40	z	P	Mekosuchinae fossils of modern-like freshwater crocodiles, Queensland, Australia
40	z	7	1st modern whales spread from Tethys Sea (see 45 Ma)
40	z	Q	Nearly complete skeleton of whale-like dorudon, with detached pelvis and little legs
40	z	H	Mammal families reach 100, almost present number
39	c	X	23km diameter impact crater, Haughton, Nunavut, Canada
38,5	g	AM	Start of most recent volcanic eruptions, Southern Africa (see 35,7 Ma)
37,2 ±1,2	c	X	7,5km diameter impact crater, Wanapitei, Ont./Canada

	Subject Ref.	Source Ref.	
37 **Ma**	g	G	Aegean, Adriatic, Western Mediterranean seas formed
37	g	Q	Badlands clay stone deposits start, S.Dakota, USA (25)
37	g	G	Volcanoes: Vesuvius, Etna, Stromboli, Italy, and Massif Central, France (see 12 Ma)
37	b	H	50% of our extant plant genera in existence
37	z	H	Medium severe extinction of Mesozoic mammals, North America
37	z	AF	1 000's of Basilosaurus, a whale (!), 2 tiny webbed hind legs, Wadi Hitan, Egypt
37	z	7	Proto-canidae, North America (see 8,0 and 5,0 Ma)
36,4 ±4	c	X	38km diameter impact crater, Mistastin, Newf./Canada
36	g,z	I	Land bridge connects Cuba and South America, primates (new-world monkeys) migrate to Cuba
36	z	Z	1,5m tall Icadyptes.salasi penguin, 30cm long thin beak, during hot climate, Peru (see 42 and 10 Ma)
35,7	g	AM	End of most recent volcanic eruptions, Southern Africa (see 38,5 Ma)
35,5 ±0,3	c	Q,X	90km diameter asteroid crater, waves 100s of meters high race 100s of km inland, Chesapeake Bay, Va, USA (see 33,7 Ma)
35,5 ±0,2	c	U,X	Meteorite 100km diameter crater, Popigai, Siberia (see 33,7 Ma)
35	c	X	10km diameter impact crater, Flaxman, Australia
35	c	X	8,5km diameter impact crater, Crawford, Australia
35	g	AC	India starts to collide with Asia (see 20 Ma)
35	g	I	Fiji Islands appear
35	g	S,U	Drake Passage between Australia and Antarctica opened, starting circum-Antarctic oceanic circulation (7,5)
35	g	1	Central Rocky Mountains rising, North America (65 Ma)
35	g,e	AB	Land bridges between Antarctica and South America and Australia disappeared, glaciers increased, cooling of surrounding seas increased the plankton, leading to development of whales and dolphins (120, 14 and 7,5)
35	z	3	Marsupials only mammals in Australia, cover all niches (see 1,9 Ma and 70 ka)
35	z	I	Some hyrax rhino size, others with legs like gazelles
35	z	H	Tithanotheroids, rhino family North America, (31 Ma)
35	z	L,S	New World monkeys split from anthropoids (see 36 Ma)
35	z	S	Aegyptopithecus, ape-like anthropoid, Egypt
35	z	L	Modern mammals with 4-5x larger relative brains than older ones
34	g	D	Tasmania separate from Australia (see 43 ka)
34	e	7	Ice sheets start to form for 1st time, Antarctica (see 40 and 30 Ma)
34	z	I	Catopithecus, anthropoid with same dentals as humans: 2 incisors, 1 canine, 2 premolars, 3 molars each half (see 30 Ma)

	Subject Ref.	Source Ref.	
33,7 **Ma**	c,z	U	Major extinction of mammalians, possibly connected to 2 meteorite impacts, allowed development to modern mammals (see 35,5 and 31 Ma
33,7	e	AB	Eocene-Oligocene climate transition, severest since 65 Ma, CO_2 double current levels, rapidly falling, creating start of Antarctic ice sheet
33,7	e	D	Eocene/Oligocene boundary, glaciation maximum

33,7 to 23,8 Ma Oligocene Epoch

32	z	AB	Oldest proto-whales, proto-penguins, Waitaki Valley, New Zealand (see 25 Ma)
31	e	H	End of period of 5 abrupt temperature drops, climate turns arid, sea levels recede, Antarctic ice cap develops (see 40 Ma)
31	z	H	Tithanotheroids, rhino family, extinct, North America (see 35 Ma)
31	z	P	Oldest modern kolibri with feathers in Old World and 2 others slightly younger, Germany
31	z	V	Reported kolibri fossils may not be true humming birds
31	z	H	Further medium extinction of mammals, N.America (33,7)
30	c,e	W	Red giant Mira Ceti starts to have comet-like 13Ly long tail, 1st time seen now, speed 468k km/h, since then 40k tons of cosmic dust deposited annually on Earth, He^{-3} content 5 000 times higher than on Earth
30	g	U	Africa reaches its present geographic position (10 Ma)
30	g	W	East African "Graben" (rift) starts (see 27,5 Ma)
30	g	I	Ethiopian highlands created by volcanic eruptions (20)
30	g	H	European flooding reaches Russia and Himalayas, connecting via Turgai Straits with Arctic Ocean (40 Ma)
30	g	Q	Pacific plate with Kure Atoll travels over "hot spot" at 8cm p/a, Hawaii (see 5,6 Ma)
30	g	V	Start of Sierra Madre Occidental by extensive volcanic eruptions ,Mexico (see 20 Ma)
30	g	H	Orogeny of the Cascades (Mt.St.Helens), still in progress today, USA
30	e	U	Major expansion of ice sheet, Antarctica (34, 23 Ma)
30	b	K	Volvoxes (green algae) developing 2 different kinds of cells: ±16 germ cells, and ±2 000 somatic paddlers, developed from free-swimming chlamydomonas
30	b	R	Succulents thrive, Namibia
30	z	H	Even-toed now outnumber odd-toed ungulates (see 63 Ma)
30	z	H	Saber-toothed cats appear (see 2,6 Ma)
30	z	AF	Glyptodonts appear, 2t armored mammals, Americas (see 10 ka)
30	z	4,S	Anthropoid "Proconsul", $150cm^3$ brain, split into Old World monkeys and hominoids, Africa (34, 20 and 15)

	Subject Ref.	Source Ref.	
30 **Ma**	z	H	Multi-tuberculata extinct (see 175 Ma)
27,5	g	AF	Arabia starts separating from Africa, creating the Red Sea and Afar Basin and Nubian and Somalian plates, extending into the Rift Valley of East Africa (see 30 Ma, 250 ka)
27	z	I,3	Middle of Africa's "Dark Period", 2 272kg rhino-like largest arsinoitherium (31), 5 new proboscidea species (54), incl. 3 species of palaeo-mastodon (3,0), deinothere (1,0), gomphotherium (55) migrated to Eurasia, Chilca, Ethiopia
26	g	H	End of Turgai Sea east of Ural, connecting Tethys and Arctic Sea (see 30 and 24 Ma)
25	g	H	African plate stationary over mantle since then
25	g	AB	A rift creates start of Baikal Sea, largest liquid freshwater reservoir (20%) of 23 000km³,160 bar pressure, 1 637m deep, 673km long, 48km wide, Siberia
25	g	Q	Badlands deposits end, S.Dakota, USA (see 37 Ma)
25	g	AH	Cape Peninsula high mountains an island, South Africa
25	b	H	Compositae (herbs) and other low growing wood-free plants
25	z	AB	Proto-dolphin with shark-like teeth, proto-baleen whale similar to present blue whale, with teeth instead of baleens, huge eyes, only 3,5m long, Waitaki Valley, New Zealand (32, 15 and 5,0 Ma)
24	g	B	African plate collides with Eurasia, closing off E. Mediterranean Sea (see 10 Ma)
24	g	H	Global maritime regression: Europe, Turgai Straits dry again, Southern Russia (see 40 and 26 Ma)
24	z	B	Lions, saber-toothed cats, hippos, hyenas, antelopes migrate from Eurasia to Africa, large African mammals mainly disappear (see 5,5 Ma)
23,8	e	D	Oligocene/Miocene boundary, global glaciations

23,8 to 1,8 Ma Neogene Period

= late Tertiary Period

23,8 to 5,3 Ma Miocene Epoch

23	e	U	Antarctic ice sheet reaches coast line (30 and 6,0 Ma)
23	z	D	Caribbean corals extinct
20	c	C	Beta Pictoris creates local solar system, planets, cosmic bombardment, high CO_2 concentration, CO_2 ice
20	g	H	Start of Ethiopian and Kenyan "Domes", E.Africa (30)
20	g	7	Isle of Madeira, volcanic stock 6km above ocean floor, 4km above sea level, South Atlantic

Ma	Subject Ref.	Source Ref.	
20 **Ma**	g	W	Fuerteventura Is. appears, Canary Is., South Atlantic (see 15 Ma)
20	g	G	Apennines start folding, Italy (see 45 Ma)
20	g	A	Atlantic ocean in present form (see 60 Ma)
20	g	K	Lake George Range rises, Australia
20	g	H	Start of Himalaya orogeny by Indian plate pushing underneath Tibet (see 35 and 15 Ma)
20	g	V	Sierra Madre Occidental in present form by erosion of lava and ash, Mexico (see 30 Ma)
20	e	2	East Africa covered by forests (see 10 Ma)
20	z	AB	Vipers evolve with live births
20	z	3,H	Fanged venomous snakes, rats, mice, singing birds
20	z	Y	Pelicans appear in their present form
20	z	H	Para-hippus (leaf eater) changes to proto-hippus (grass eater), later to equus (horse) (45 and 4,0 Ma)
20	z	W	Pigs the only mammals to loose thermogenin gene due to warm climate, now piglets need warmth to survive
20	z	L	Apes migrate from Africa to Eurasia
20	z	S	Gibbons split off hominoid lineage (DNA), Asia (see 30, 15 Ma)
<20	g	H	Afar triangle lifted as oceanic crust, Indian Ocean
18	g	H	Start of collision of Eurasia/Africa (see 14 Ma)
18	g	Z	Oldest recorded eruption of Yellowstone super-volcano, a 560km string of calderas across Idaho, Oregon and Nevada due to SW move of tectonic plate, USA (2,1 Ma)
17,5	g	W	Previously isolated Arctic Ocean, during a temperature maximum, now opened to Atlantic by Fram Straights between Greenland and Svalbard, North Atlantic (100)
17	g	7	Old bed of Orange River, diamonds washed downstream from Kimberley fields, South Africa
17	z	AF	Orangutans split from hominoid lineage, Asia (20, 15)
16	g	1	Main Andean orogeny (see 200 and 50 Ma)
16	g	AJ	175 000km^3 basalt flow, Columbia River Plateau, USA
15,1 ±0,1	c	K,X	Ries crater, 24km diameter, caused by a chondrite stone meteorite, size 1,5 x 1km, 10^9t, high pressure mineral coesite found on site, Southern Germany
15 ±1	c	X	3,8km diameter impact crater, Steinheim, Germany
15	g	L	Ethiopian/Kenyan "domes" by ±3km plate movements (20)
15	g	1	Zagros mountains rise, Iraq/Iran
15	g	W	Gran Canaria, Lanzerote appear, Canary Islands, South Atlantic (see 20 Ma)
15	g	5	Island of Borneo appears, Indonesia
15	g	H	Australian plate collides with Asian plate (20 Ma)
15	g	AM	India collides with Asia (see 20 and 5,0 Ma)
15	g,e	AH	Antarctica separates from Gondwana, drifts to South Pole, ice cap starts to form (see 5 Ma)

	Subject Ref.	Source Ref.	
15 **Ma**	e	W	500m deep fresh water lake kept liquid by pressure of 4km of ice, largest of 150 similar bodies connected by underground rivers, signs of microbial life ?, coldest place globally -80°C, Lake Vostok, Antarctica
15	z	W	Megalodon, giant whale-eating shark, could swallow a rhino, 48t and 18m long, ancestor of Great White shark, only a tooth found, Zululand, S.Africa (1,0)
15	z	Q	Tiger sharks unchanged since then
15	z	V	200kg wingless Terror bird, Patagonia (see 2,0 Ma)
15	z	Z	Amazon dolphins, the largest of 4 river species, evolve from cetaceans before marine species appear, Amazon basin, South America (see 25 and 5,0 Ma)
15	z	I	Camels originate in North America (10, 6,0 Ma, 100 ka)
15	z	I,4 S	Ramapithecus "Man-Ape", split off hominoid line (DNA), 1st hominid (??), probably related to sivapithecus, ancestor of pongos (orangutans), Asia (20, 17, 10)
14	g	H	North Sea floods lower parts of Europe up to Cologne, creating extensive brown coal deposits, N.Germany
14	g	H	End of collision of Eurasia/Africa (see 18 Ma)
14	e	Y	North Pole ice cap similar to present (see 54,8 Ma)
14	e	U	Rapid global cooling, especially Antarctica, start of cold Benguela current, South Atlantic/Africa, causing arification of Namib desert, Namibia (see 7,5 Ma)
13	g	I,Q	Huge earthquakes, with intervals of ca. 2 000 years along Teton Valley create Teton Range, North America (see 12 ka)
13	z	K	Proto-fur seals evolve from proto-bears (brown bears?)
12	g	W	Huge volcanic eruption of Massif Central, France (see 37 Ma, 900 ka)
12	g	V	Start of Baja California rifting, moving north, California/Mexico (see 6 Ma)
12	g	V	Arc of volcanic islands fused, Caribbean plate starts to move them towards present Panama
12	z	7	Proto-duck/goose, 700kg, largest ever bird, not related to emu, ostrich, etc., Australia
11,8	e	AB	Amazon river source now in Andes mountains, earlier sources in central mountains, South America
10	g	U	African plate in present position versus mantle (30)
10	g	5	Les Cirques limestones collapse, France (65, 6,0 Ma)
10	g	1	Western Mediterranean Sea closed off from oceans, deposited rock salt (see 24 and 5,0 Ma)
10	e	2 AL	East Africa covered by fragmented forests, alternating seasons of wet and dry (see 20 Ma)
10	b,z	I,H	High salinity killed all life when Western Mediterranean Sea was closed off
10	z	Z	Dominant theory held, that penguins evolved in Antarctica and moved to moderate climes much later (42, 36)

	Subject Ref.	Source Ref.	
10 **Ma**	z	W	Recovered usable bone marrow of Rana.pueyoi, a frog species, Spain
10	z	I	Camels, horses, canidae migrate from North America to Eurasia (see 15 Ma)
10	z	G	Placental carnivores exterminate marsupials, S.America
10	z	Q	Hawaiian monk seals, oldest of the pinnipedia sub-order, the only tropical seal, all others cold water
10	z	2	[illegible]20 species of apes in East Africa (see 15 Ma)
10	z	2,4 S,W	Chororapithecus.abyssinicus or Dryopithecines, man-like primates, knuckle walkers, ancestors of gorillas, chimpanzees, hominids, Africa and Eurasia (see 15, 9,5 and 7,0 Ma, 500 ka)
9,5	z	AF	Gorillas split off hominoid line (DNA), Africa (10 Ma)
9,0	g	Q	Volcano at Atlantic mid-ocean rift forms Iceland
8,0	g	W	Mauritius and Reunion appear, Indian Ocean
8,0	g	H	Alpine orogeny ends (see 40 Ma)
8,0	b	W	Proto-bacteria with 270 (currently 300 million) base pairs defrosted, still alive, doubling every ½ hour, previous "record age" 300 ka, Antarctica
8,0	z	K	700kg herbivore guinea pig, enemies: crocs, Venezuela
8,0	z	7	Epicyon, wolf-sized precursor of canidae, North America (see 37 and 5,0 Ma)
7,5	c	W	Supernova explosion, "lace nebula" in constellation Cygna still visible, 1,5 Ly away, fragments fly with 600k km through nebula, heating gas and matter to 1M°C, producing metals heavier than Fe (Cu, Hg, Au, Pb), same process as in our solar system
7,5	g,e	S	"Terminal Miocene Event", caused by the separation of Australia and South America from Antarctica, creating cold Benguela current, 40-70m sea level drop results in land bridge at Gibraltar, Mediterranean (35, 14)
7,5	z	2	Ape species decline, monkeys prosper, East Africa
7,0	c	I	Supernova, 6 Ly across, a pulsar at the center spins 30 times/sec, remnants now Crab Nebula
7,0	z	S,I AF	Chimpanzees split off hominid lineage, (DNA analysis), 1st African bipedal primate species (see 10 Ma)
6,9	z	T	Sahelanthropus.tschadensis hominid fossils, possibly should be Sahelpithecus, an early ape, West Africa
6,7	z	W	African and Asian elephants separate (see 2,6 Ma)
6,5	e,z	C	Fossil ape "Toumai", $350cm^3$ brain, close to final common ancestor of chimpanzees and hominids, lived at 400 000km^2 Lake Chad, West Africa
6,5	z	AL	Common ancestor of alcelaphinae (arid browser specialists, ±40 species since then) and aepycerotinae (generalists, few species) (see 5,5 Ma)
6,5	z	AB	Assumed last common ancestor of chimpanzee and Homo, a species not yet discovered, East Africa (5,8, 4,4)

	Subject Ref.	Source Ref.	
6,0 **Ma**	g	Z	Collision of Pacific and North American plates causes rise of Alaska Range, highest point of North America with 6 194m Mt.McKinleay, Alaska
6,0	g	V	Baja California in present position, Mexico (12 Ma)
6,0	e	H	Warming and sea levels increase again (see 5,4 Ma)
6,0	e	S	Antarctica reaches present ice thickness (see 23 Ma)
6,0	g	N	Cirque de Navacelles formed, 285m deep and 500m wide limestone sinkhole, Massif Central, France (10 Ma)
6,0	z	W	Argentavis.magnificus, 75kg, 7m wing span, largest flying bird ever, size of a Cessna 152, Argentine
6,0	z	AB	191 footprints of hitherto unknown and largest species of camels, oldest in Europe, Jumilla, Spain (see 10 Ma and 100 ka)
6,0	z	K	Barbary macaques, Morocco
6,0	z	5	Orrorin.tugenensis "Millennium Man", bipedal, 1,5m tall, lived in trees and on ground, omnivore, Tugen Hills, Kenya
5,8	z	AF	Ardipithecus.kadabba, fragmentary hominid bones, Ethiopia (see 4,4 Ma)
5,6	g	H	Kauai, oldest (volcanic) island of Hawaii, appeared and moved over "hot spot" at 5cm/annum (30, <1,0 Ma)
5,5	g	7	Colorado River starts Grand Canyon (see 250 Ma)
5,5	z	2	Alcelaphinae with only 1 antelope species, now there are 10, including wildebeest and blesbok, East Africa (see 24, 6,5 and 5,0 Ma)
5,5	z	I	Lower jaw and molar of hominid, East Africa
5,4	g	W	Land bridge closing Mediterranean by submarine mountain rising 70mm per 100 years, dropping sea levels >2km, happened several times, Gibraltar and Messina, creating 2 separate basins (7,5 and 5,0 Ma)
5,4	e	H	Messinian Event = Mediterranean Sea isolated, dried out temporarily, accumulating ±6% of global sea salts, Antarctic glaciation extended, sea levels sink ±50m, at later glacial periods sea levels reduced by >100m against present levels (see 6,0 and 5,0 Ma)

5,3 to 1,8 Ma Pliocene Epoch

5,0 ±3	c	X	8km diameter impact crater, Bigach, Kazakhstan
5,0	c	X	52km diameter impact crater, Kara-Kul, Tajikistan
5,0 ±1	c	X	10km diameter meteorite impact crater, Karla, Russia
5,0	c	P	Speculation a 45m deep 720k km^2 sea gushed from the interior, instantly frozen, now covered with iron oxide, Mars
5,0	g	H AM	Main Himalayan orogeny starts, caused by Indian plate colliding with Asian plate, still active at 5cm/a (see 15 Ma)

	Subject Ref.	Source Ref.	
5,0 **Ma**	g	I,H	Mediterranean Sea again connected to oceans, salinity normalized, sea levels rise again (see 5,4 + 5,3 Ma)
5,0	g	AB	Tectonic movements cause several islands to converge, create mountain ranges, New Zealand
5,0	g	AG	Galapagos Archipelago rises from sea floor due to still very active volcanic eruptions, South Pacific
5,0	g,e	U	100m uplift of western, 900m of eastern South Africa, cutting off moist sea winds results in formation of Kalahari Desert, South Africa/Namibia (20 and 1,4 Ma)
5,0	e	3	Dense forest becomes sparse, East Africa (see 4,0 Ma)
5,0	e	AB	Makgadikgadi Lake covering 80 000 km_2 and 30m deep, Botswana (see 63, 2,0 Ma, 35 ka)
5,0	e	AH	Ice cap reducing, higher sea levels, Antarctica (see 15, 6,0 Ma)
5,0	b	G	Gnetales (gymnosperms) appear
5,0	z	S	Hemphillian extinction almost annihilated grazing animals, horses reduced to 1 species, S.Africa (5,5)
5,0	z	S	750kg carnivorous bear, relative of panda, South Africa (see 2,0 Ma)
5,0	z	7	Eucyron, fox-sized early canidae, later evolves into wolves, jackals, coyotes (see 8,0 and 1,5 Ma)
5,0	z	7	Walrus-like dolphins (see 25, 15 Ma)
5,0	z	AB	Dipoides, proto-beavers, ⅓ size of present species,
5,0	z	AL AC	Dinofelis (false saber-toothed cat) appears, dominant prey later seems to be australopithecus, Eurasia (see 1,2 Ma)
5,0	z	W	35% of chimpanzees carry the M and N types of the HIV retrovirus, the O type is carried by gorillas, PtERV1 retro-virus infects primates but not Homo, this may explain why primates despite infection are immune to the HIV1 retrovirus (see 10,0 ka)
5,0	z	2,4	Divergence of bipedal hominids and apes (chimpanzees), molecular evidence (see 1,5 Ma)
4,5	z	1,S	**Australopithecus**, bipedal ground dwelling hominid 2 genera, stone tools/implements, East Africa (4,1)
4,4	z	AF S	Ardipithecus ramidus female "Ardi", (related to **Au.** ?), 1,2m, 50kg, partially bipedal, not knuckle-walking but long arms, Aramis, Central Awash, Tim White 1994, Ethiopia 1997 (see 6,5 and 5,8 Ma)
4.1	z	P,C	**Au.**anamensis: small carnivore hunters, small brain, 1st confirmed bipedal, Mrs.Leakey 1995, Kenya (see 4,5 and 3,9 Ma)
4,0	c	P	Most recent eruption of a volcano, Mars (see 3,8 Ga)
4,0	e	3	Sparse forest turns into savannah, East Africa (see 5,0 and 2,8 Ma)
4,0	e	H	Climax of global warming, glaciers melt, Antarctica

Subject	Source	
	Ref. Ref.	
4,0 **Ma**	z Z	Horses develop, via mesohippus, archeohippus, parahippus, hippidion, dinohippus and other species to equus, North America (see 20, 3,0 and 1,6 Ma)
4,0	z 5	Mammoths develop in Africa, later migrate to Siberia and North America (see 7,0 and 5,0 ka)
3,9	z P	**Au.**afarensis almost cpl. skeleton incl. ankle bones, complete tibia, thighbone, Afar, Ethiopia (4,1 + 1,8)
3,7 ±0,3	c X	2,5km diameter impact crater, Roter Kamm, Namibia
3,7	z C,3 S	Fossilized footprints of 3 hominids, "1st Family", probably **Au.**afarensis, walked upright like **H.**habilis Mrs.Leakey 1976, Laetoli, Tanzania, East Africa
3,6	z AG	**Au.**afarensis fossil bones in excellent condition, Afar, Ethiopia 2005
3,6	z S	Oldest **Au.**afarensis fossil in South Africa, 1925
3,5 ±0,5	c X	18km diameter impact crater, El'gygtgyn, Russia
3,5	z S	Fossil beds, almost all species found there are now extinct, Swartkrans, South Africa
3,5	z S,C	"Little Foot", **Au.**afarensis, a complete skeleton may be found, excavations continue, R.Clarke 1994, Sterkfontein, South Africa
3,5	z C	**Au.**bahrelghazali "Abel", M.Brunet 1995, Chad
3,4	z AG	**Au.**afarensis used stones to scrape meat from animal bones, Dikika, Ethiopia (see 2,5 Ma)
3,3	e H	Cooling on northern hemisphere, start of oscillating present ice age cycles, alternating glacials every ±10ky and inter-glacials, at maximum glaciation 50% of oceans covered by shelf and drifting ice
3,3	z 7	**Kenyanthropus**.platyops (rudolfensis ?), Lake Turkana, Kenya, Mrs.Leakey 1999 (see 3,0 and 2,4 Ma)
3,3	z W	Very complete skeleton of 3 year old **Au.**afarensis "Selam", shoulders and arms like gorilla's, Ethiopia
3.18	z S,C	"Lucy", herbivore **Au.**afarensis, 1-1,2m tall, brain 400cm^3 (chimpanzee 320-480cm^3, modern human 1 400cm^3), D.Johanson, R.Leakey, Y.Coppens 1974, Hadar, Ethiopia
3,0	c X	12km diameter impact crater, Avak, Alas/USA (95 Ma)
3,0 ±0,3	c X	390m diameter impact crater, Aouelloul, Mauritania
3,0	c X	1,75km diameter impact crater, Talemzane, Algeria
3,0	g K	Mt.Kenya volcano starts to erupt, East Africa (750 ka)
3,0	g W	Under-sea lava flow of 5 000 000km^2, larger than the entire USA, Ontong Plateau, Java, Indonesia (<3,0 Ma)
3,0	g,e AB	North and South American plates collide, deviating warm equatorial current to become Gulf Stream, changing global climate, causes Arctic to be ice-free, creating glaciation elsewhere, Panama seaway closes, Isthmus of Panama (see 45 Ma and 12 ka)
3,0	e I	Siberian permafrost starts
3,0	z W	Start of Great Barrier Reef by corals, Australia

	Subject Ref.	Source Ref.	
3,0 **Ma**	z	AB	Terrestrial fauna migrate in both directions but maritime fauna are divided after North and South American plates collide
3,0	z	W	5m tooth, thigh bones of 25 year old 6t mastodon, 3,5m high, Greece (see 27 Ma, 50 ka)
3,0	z	Z	Equus (horse) emigrated from North America to Eurasia and Africa (see 4,0 and 2,0 Ma)
3,0	z	I	Gelada primates roam Africa and India, only 1 species survives, Ethiopia
3,0	z	1	Fossil skull differs from other **Au.**, possibly **K.**platyops ?, Lake Rudolph, East Africa (see 3,3 Ma)
3,0	z	S	**Au.**africanus 1,3m tall, walked upright, hands/feet human-like, mixed herbivore/carnivore, 480cm^3 brain
<3,0	g	AJ	Ontong Java Plateau, 5 Mkm^2 of sea-bed lava, near Borneo (see 3,0 Ma)
2,9	e	AL	Arctic Sea freezes
2,8	c	Q	Supernova explosion deposits Fe 60, near Hawaii, Northern Pacific
2,8	e	Q	Climate changes to more arid conditions, Africa (4,0)
2,7	z	2	**Au.**aethiopicus, East Africa (see 2,4 Ma)
2,6	e	P	Laurentide ice shield from Arctic Ocean to Mexico
2,6	z	D	Separation of African savannah elephant from Laxodonta.cyclotis, a forest dweller (see 6,7 Ma)
2,6	z	4	Saber-toothed cats in Americas (see 30 Ma and 12 ka)
2,6	z,d	4,C	**Au.**africanus thought to have evolved to **Homo.**habilis, East Africa (see 1,9 and 1,6)
2,6	z,a	I	**Au.**aethiopicus (or **H.**habilis ?) make oldest fabricated stone tools =Oldovan pebble culture, 1997, Lokalelei, Kenya and Gona, Ethiopia
2,5	z	S,2	"Taungs Child", now known to be young **Au.**africanus boy 3-4 years old, probably killed by a raptor, R.Dart 1924, Taungs, South Africa
2,5	z	AG	2nd oldest use of stone tools by **Au.**afarensis to scrape meat from animal bones, Bouri, Ethiopia (see 3,4 Ma)
2,5	z	AF C	**Au.**garhi, cranium 450cm^3, better bipedal than other **Au.**, but typical **Au.** dentition, T.White 1999, Hata, l'Awash, Ethiopia
2,5	z	C	"Black Skull", **Au.**aethiopicus, East Africa
2,5	z	2	Expansion of hominid brain, Africa (3,18 and 3,0 Ma)
2,5	z,f	L	Meat eating by hominids, East Africa
2,4	z	G	Dwarf hippos, dwarf elephants, probably shortage of grazing, Mediterranean islands, Malta (see 95 ka)
2,4	z	C	**Au.**aethiopicus extinct, East Africa (see 2,7 Ma)
2,4	z	C	**K.**rudolfensis (platyops ?), Kenya, East Africa (see 3,3 and 1,7 Ma)

	Subject Ref.	Source Ref.	
2,4 **Ma**	a	S,P	**H.**habilis used Oldovan tools, 1st to build shelters, Broca's area of skull suggests rudimentary/articulate speech, East Africa (see 1,6 Ma)
2,15	z	S	"Miss Ples" (originally classified as Plesianthropus. transvaalensis) ,adult female **Au.**africanus, Dr.R.Broom 1990, Sterkfontein, South Africa
2,1	g	Z	Explosion of Yellowstone super-volcano >2 000x the Mt.St.Helens explosion, leaving a hole 72km across, USA (see 18 and 2,0 Ma, 640 ka)
2,1	d	W	Speculated appearance of **H.**erectus, East Africa (1,9)
2,0	g	V	Death Valley, a tectonic rift valley between two mountain ranges, 86m below sea level, maximum temperature 57°C, California, USA
2,0	g	Q	Hotspot under Yellowstone Park 200km deep, magma chamber in 8 - 16km depth, caldera 65 km across, Mammoth Hot Springs with 300+ geysers globally greatest concentration (see 40 ka), "Old Faithful" blows every 74 min, USA (see 2,1 Ma, 640 ka)
2,0	g	V	Yucatan peninsula emerges from ocean, Mexico (50 Ma)
2,0	g	AB	River Main digs 100m deep valley in shelly limestone deposited by "Muschelkalk" Sea, Germany (230 Ma)
2,0	g b,z	5	Ngorongoro volcano explodes, 18km crater with 100m walls, creating unique closed habitat, East Africa
2,0	e	AB	Kalahari Basin starts to dry up due to rivers changing course and less rainfall, Botswana (5,0 Ma, 10,0 ka)
2,0	e	AB	Antarctica starts to freeze over (see 400 ka)
2,0	e	U	Dramatic global cooling, ocean temperature lowest ever since start of Cenozoic Era
2,0	e	AF	Glaciers start spreading over Greenland (see 1,0 Ma)
2,0	b	P	Wollemi pine was considered extinct, but now found again in Australia (see 200 Ma)
2,0	z	W	60cm tall mini Panda, now 1,2m, South China (5,0 Ma)
2,0	z	V	Terror Birds vanish, possibly due to land bridge between Americas, South America (see 15 Ma)
2,0	z	Z	Horses emigrate from North to South America (see 3,0 and 1,6 Ma, 10 ka)
2,0	z	C,S	**Paranthropus** ("almost human") hominid side line, probably evolved from **Au.**afarensis, genus with 2 species: **P.**robustus and **P.**bosei, East/South Africa (see 1,9 and 1,8 Ma)
2,0	m	I	**H.**habilis reaches Sterkfontein cave, South Africa
2,0	m	C	Possibly 1st "Out-of-Africa" migration by **H.**habilis or **H.**erectus (see 1,78 Ma)
1,9	z	G	Marsupials radiate like placentals, Australia (35 Ma)
1,9	z	C,2	**P.**robustus, 1,7m tall, brain 550cm^3, almost complete skull found, Drimolen, South Africa (2,0, 1,0 Ma)
1,9	d	Q	Oldest **H.**habilis fossils, Koobi Fora, Kenya (2,6 Ma)

	Subject Ref.	Source Ref.	
1,9 **Ma**	d	W	**H.**habilis, lived with **H.**erectus (largely carnivore) for 500ky, who would have evolved independently from him (Mrs. Leakey), Kenya (see 2,1 and 1,78 Ma)
1,9	m,a	T	**H.**erectus leaves Africa with primitive Oldovan tools (see 1,7 Ma)
1,865	z	AF AG	**Au.**sediba, almost cpl skeletons, boy and women, said to be new species, link between **Au.** and **H.**, small brain, long legs and arms **Au.**-like; pelvis, shape of teeth, long cranium **H.**-like, (R.Leakey not convinced) Berger 2008 Malapa, Maropeng, S.Africa
1,8	z	S	**Au.**afarensis disappear, Africa (see 3,9 Ma)

1,8 Ma to 5,0 ka **Quarternary Period**

1,8 Ma to 42,0 ka **Lower Paleolithic Age**

1,8	z	S	**P.**bosei, (originally called zinjanthropus), even more robust than **P.**robustus, large brain, omnivore, sagittal crest along the top of skull, East Africa (see 2,0, 1,8 and 1,5 Ma)
1,8	z	C	**K.**rudolfensis, large brain, 1,4m tall, 25-45kg, Kenya (see 3,3, 2,4, 1,7 Ma)
1,8	z d,m	1,2 S	**H.**ergaster (possibly **H.**erectus ?) coexists with **AU.**, Swartkrans, South Africa (see 1,9 Ma)
1,8	m	Q	**H.**erectus, Mojokerto, Java, Indonesia (see 1,7 Ma)
1,78	e	Q	Reversal of Earth magnetic field, dating Dmanisi excavations (see 780 ka)
1,78	z	I,S	Saber-tooth cat, rhino, horse, giant ostrich, short-necked giraffe, 10% are African species, found 1999, Dmanisi, Georgia, Caucasus
1,78	d,m	C,D	Group of **H.**erectus, 1st "Out-of-Africa pioneers", tiny brow ridge, short nose, huge canines, 1st smallest brain yet, 2nd much larger (2 species or male/female difference was larger than), primitive tools, 1999, Dmanisi, Georgia, Caucasus (2,1 and 2,0 and 1,9 Ma)
1,78	d,f	Q	**H.**erectus switches to being carnivore because of seasonal cold weather, Dmanisi, Georgia (1,9 + 1,44)
1,7	z	C	**K.**rudolfensis extinct, East Africa (3,3, 2,4, 1,8 Ma)
1,7	d,a f	S	**H.**erectus, 1 100cm^3 brain, used (but could not make) fire, hunted in teams, East Africa (1,6 Ma, 300 ka)
1,7	m	S	Re-dated **H.**erectus, Java, Indonesia (1,8 Ma, 800 ka)
1,7	m,a	Q	Oldest stone tools by **H.**erectus in East Asia, Nihewan, China (see 1,9 and 1,5 Ma)
1,7	a,f	T	**H.**erectus female with deformed bones and growths due to hyper-vitaminosis, caused by eating the livers of carnivores, had been cared for, Lake Turkana, Kenya

	Subject Ref.	Source Ref.	
1,6 **Ma**	z	Z	Equus (horse) develops, N.America (2,0 Ma, 10,0 ka)
1,6	d	H	**H.**erectus, originally classified as a Pithecanthropus (see 700 Ma)
1,6	a	AI	**H.**erectus, Proto-Acheulean tools, up to 30km between place of origin and of use, East Africa (see 1,1 Ma)
1,6	a	2,4	**H.**erectus with partial language, use of fire, East and South Africa (see 2,4 and 1,7 Ma)
1,55	d	W	**H.**erectus small skull, female ? (Mrs.Leakey), Kenya
1,54	d,a	C,I S	**H.**erectus "Turkana Boy", super-bipedal, 1,3-1,6m tall, 12 years, 850cm^3 brain, small teeth, Proto-Acheulean tools, first weapons, R.Leakey 1984, Kenya
1,5	z	7	Wolf-like canidae (see 5,0 Ma and 400 ka)
1,5	z	AF	Bonobo (pygmy chimpanzee) separates from chimpanzee (see 5,0 Ma)
1,5	z	C	**P.**bosei extinct, East Africa (see 2,0, 1,9, 1,8 Ma)
1,5	m	I	**H.**erectus reaches Swartkrans, South Africa
1,5	m,a	Q	Oldest stone tools of **H.**erectus in Europe, Orce Ravine, Spain (see 1,7 and 1,1 Ma)
1,5	a	AC	Proto-Acheulean culture of **H.**erectus and his Oldovan tools, Ubeidija, Israel
1,5	a	T	**H.**erectus makes 1st sophisticated Proto-Acheulean stone tools in huge numbers, mostly used for ceremonial purposes, Oldovan, East Africa (see 1,2 Ma)
1,44	d,f	W	Part of upper jaw with some teeth, skull of **H.**erectus, largely herbivore (Mrs.Leakey), Kenya (see 1,78 Ma)
1,4 ±0,1	c	X	3,44km diameter impact crater, New Quebec, Quebec, Canada
1,4	g	R	Coastline 100m higher than now South Africa (see 20 and 5,0 Ma, 25 ka)
1,2	z	AL AC	Dinofelis (false saber-toothed cat) disappears, dominant prey seemed to be **Au.**, Eurasia (5,0 Ma)
1,2	d,m	W,Z	**H.**antecessor, (**H.**erectus ?), 1st **H.** fossil in Europe, Atapuerca, Spain (see 780 and 700 ka)
1,2	a	T	Proto-Acheulean tool "factory", Olorgesailie, Kenya (see 1,5 Ma and 200 ka)
1,1	a	AI	Oldovan tools but no hand axes, Guadiz-Baza, Spain (see 1,5 Ma)
1,1	a	AI	Standardized basic forms of hand axes, up to 80km between place of origin and of use, East Africa (see 1,6 Ma and 29 ka)
1,07	c	X	10,5km diameter impact crater, Bosumtwi, Ghana
1,0	c	AB	A double star in Orion Nebula, each 0,41 sun mass, should be identical, but light emission shows 50%, diameter and temperature 10% differences
1,0	c	X	460m diameter impact crater, Monturaqui, Chile
1,0	e	AF	Glaciers merge into 1,7 Mkm^2 and 3km thick ice sheet, depressing central plateau by 1km, Greenland (2,0 Ma)

	Subject Ref.	Source Ref.	
1,0 **Ma**	z	Q	Megalodon extinct, cartilage skeletons like sharks, 5t, 15m long, teeth only fossils found (see 15 Ma)
1,0	z	B	Deinothere (proboscides) extinct, Eurasia (see 27 Ma)
1,0	z	2	3-toed horse, saber-toothed cat almost extinct, E.Afr
1,0	z	S	**P.**robustus disappears, Swartkrans, South Africa (1,9)
1,0	d	AG	Suggested divergence date for claimed "X-Woman" **H.** species, possible relation of **H.**antecessor ? (see 1,2 Ma and <48 ka)
<1,0	g	H	Hawaii Is., the youngest of the archipelago, appears (see 5,6 Ma, 700 ka)
900 **ka** ±100	c	X	14km diameter impact crater, Zhamanshin, Kazakhstan
900	g	W	Eruption of group of volcanoes south of Massif Central, France (see 12 Ma)
900	b	G	Psilotales, modern form of psilophytales (see 370 Ma)
840	m	Q	Tools of **H.**erectus, Soa Basin, Flores Is., Indonesia
800	m	I	**H.**erectus reaches Ceprano, Italy
800	m	C	**H.**heidelbergensis, (I suggest **H.**erectus), Europe
780	e	P,Q	Most recent Matuyame-Brunhes polarity reversal of Earth's magnetic poles, Tahiti, Chili, Hawaii, Las Palmas (see 1,78 Ma and 30 ka)
780	d	N	**H.**antecessor (**H.**erectus ?), cannibalism on 6 hominids, Atapuerca, Spain (see 1,2 Ma)
750	g	I	Eruption of Kilimanjaro (5 895m), East Africa (3,0 Ma)
750	g	AF	Globally largest sand island, Fraser Is., Australia
740	e	U	"Dome C" ice drilling core records global temperatures to present, Antarctica (see 420 ka)
700	g	P	Basalt "organ", exposed columns, St.Thibery, France
700	g	Q	Big Island created by volcanic action when drifting over a stationary "hot spot", Hawaii (5,6 + <1,0 Ma)
700	d	AB	Hominid fossil, attributed to Pithecanthropus.erectus (old name for **H.**erectus), claimed to be "a twin" of "Java Man", Germany
700	d	Z	Ancestral **H.**sapiens and **H.**sapiens.neanderthalensis start to split (see 500 and 370 ka)
700	m	I	**H.**erectus "Java Man" reaches Trinil, Java
700	a	AB	Proto-Acheulean artifacts of **H.**erectus living near pools of standing water, Saldanha Bay, S.Africa
680	e	AC	Begin of a series of glacials/interglacials, Guenz (1st) glacial starts, Western Europe (3,3 Ma, 620 ka)
670	m	Q	**H.**erectus "Peking Man", China (see 460 ka)
640	g	Z	Most recent explosions of Yellowstone super-volcano 1 000x the strength of the Mt.St.Helens explosion in 1980, USA (see 2,1 Ma, 70 ka)
620	e	AC	End of Guenz glacial and start of Guenz-Mindel interglacial, Western Europe (see 680 and 455 ka)
600	d	AF	**H.**erectus skull, Bodo, Central Awash, Ethiopia 1976

	Subject Ref.	Source Ref.	
600 **ka**	a	AC	Hand axes, **H.**erectus, Western Europe
540 ±1,5	c	X	170m diameter meteorite impact crater, Boxhole, Northern Territory, Australia
500	g	7	Natural limestone bridge over the Ardeche, Pont d'Arc, Massif Central, France
500	e,z	Q	Hippopotamus larger than at present, indicating warm climate, England (see 24, 2,4 Ma, 6,0 ka)
500	z	W	Mus.cypriacus, differs from house mouse, Cyprus
500	z	W	Primitive ancestors of Dessert Bighorn sheep migrate from Asia via Beringia land bridge to America
500	z	4	Gigantopithecus fossil ape extinct, China (see 10 Ma)
500	d	V	Last common ancestor of **H.**sapiens.neanderthalensis and **H.**sapiens (see 700 and 370 ka)
500	d	3,4	**H.**sapiens, East Africa (see 400, 200 ka)
500	m	4,S	"Boxgrove Man", oldest **H.**erectus in England
500	a	AC O	Proto (Lower)-Acheulean culture of **H.**erectus or **H.**sapiens starts, core and flake tools, Western Europe (see 350 ka)
460	m	V,I	**H.**erectus.pekinensis "Peking Man"in caves, Choukoutien, China (see 670 and 220 ka)
455	e	AC	Guenz-Mindel interglacial ends, Mindel (2nd) glacial starts, Western Europe (see 620 and 340 ka)
450	g	AB	Volcanic appearance of Marion Is., South Atlantic
450	z	I	Pithecanthropus fossil hominoid in France
420	e	U	Vostok ice drilling core reveals global temperatures to present, 4 periods of abrupt warming and gradual cooling, Antarctica (see 740 ka)
420	a	AC	Ashe wood spear tip, Clacton-on-Sea, UK
410	z	Z	Woolly mammoth appear, northern Eurasia, America (120)
410	d	Q	**H.**erectus extinct, China (see 300, 100 ka)
400	e	AB	Antarctica freeze-over is complete (see 2,0 Ma)
400	z	Q	Proto-elephant Paleoloxodon.antiquus found during excavation for Channel tunnel, France/UK (see 100 ka)
400	z	7	Wolves start living near humans, scavenging detritus (see 1,5 Ma, 14 ka)
400	m	P	**H.**sapiens in Middle East (see 500 ka)
400	a	O	Use (not making) of fire by **H.**erectus, China)
400	a	K,N	**H.**sapiens, 8 wooden throwing spears, Helmstedt, superb condition, Schoeningen, Germany
380	a	4,8	1st human structure, use of fire by **H.**sap., France
370	d	Z	Estimated lineage separation of **H.**sapiens and **H.**sapiens.neanderthalensis, based on genetic data (see 700 and 500 ka)
365	m	K	**H.**sapiens skull, had a brain tumor, Southern Germany
350	a	AC O	Old (Middle) Acheulean culture of **H.**sap. starts: flaking hand axes with wooden baton, Western Europe (see 500, 250 ka)

	Subject Ref.	Source Ref.	
350 **ka**	a	K	Sharpened rose quartz Acheulean axe head found with 27 **H.**sap. skeletons, Attapuerca, Spain and Mapungubwe National Park, Limpopo, South Africa
345	c	X	12,6km diameter impact crater, Aorounga, Chad
340	e	AC	Mindel (2nd) glaciation ends, Mindel-Riss interglacial starts, Western Europe (see 455 and 200 ka)
300	c	X	870m diameter impact crater, Wolfe Creek, W.Australia
300	g	7	Mt.Shasta explodes, lava tubes, California, USA
300	e	H	Illinoian glacials/interglacials start, North America (see 130 and 122 ka)
300	d	2	**H.**erectus disappears in Africa (see 1,7 Ma, 410 ka)
300	m	T	Only ancient human fossil (**H.**erectus or **H.**sapiens ?) ever found in India
300	m	S	**H.**sapiens "Saldanha Man", Saldanha Bay, South Africa
300	m,a	AB P	Sangoan Industry (culture) stone artifacts, antelope teeth ,considered 1st expansion into tropical climes by **H.**sap., Port Edward, Natal and Mapungubwe National Park, Limpopo, South Africa(see 120 ka)
300	a	AC	More than 30 bodies thrown down a pit, Sima de los Hueses, Sierra de Atapuerca, Spain
275	z	AF	Darwin's fox separates from South American grey fox (see 120 ka)
270	c	X	270m diameter impact crater, Dalgaranga, W.Australia
260	d,m	V	1,68m tall, 78,5kg female **H.**sapiens, largest known such fossil, also most northern and eastern human habitation, Jinniushan, Chinese/Korean border
259	d,m	S	Skull of **H.**sapiens, upright gait, pronounced brow ridges, "Florisbad Man", Florisbad, South Africa
250	g	Z	Ruapehu volcano starts, still active, New Zealand
250	g	H	Victoria Lake created as part of ongoing widening of the Rift Valley, East Africa (see 27,5 Ma)
250	g	AB	Eruption of Piton de la Fournaise, Reunion (see 350 Ma and 65 ka)
250	a	O	Old (Middle) Acheulean culture/tools of **H.**sapiens, Western Europe (see 500, 350, and 170 ka)
230	d,m	Z	**H.**sapiens.neanderthalensis only counted about 15 000, hunting and gathering in Eurasia from Atlantic to Siberia, central Eurasia to Mediterranean (45, 28 ka)
230	a	V	Start of Mousterian culture of **H.**sap.neanderthalensis, later probably used by **H.**sapiens, Southern France and Northern Spain (see 200 ka)
225	m	1	**H.**sapiens, Swanscombe, UK and Stuttgart, Germany
220 ±52	c	X	1,13km diameter crater, Tswane, formerly Pretoria Saltpan, South Africa
220	g	AB	Eruption of El Chichon, Mexico
220	m	V	Last of **H.**erectus.pekinensis in caves, China (460 ka)
220	m	3	"Petralona Skull" of **H.**sapiens, Greece

	Subject Ref.	Source Ref.	
200 **ka**	g	AB	Heavy volcanic activity, Eifel mountain, Germany (11)
200	e	Z	Lake Megafezzan, the size of England, perennial rivers, Fezzan, Libya
200	e	AC	Mindel-Riss interglacial ends, Riss (3rd) glacial starts, Western Europe (see 340 and 130 ka)
200	z	P	Polar bears evolve from grizzly bears, Arctic
200	d	S	3 calcified footprints by **H.**sapiens, Nahoon Point, East London, South Africa (see 500 Ma)
200	d	V	1st **H.**sap.sap. probable, **H.**sapiens likely disappears, East and South Africa (500, 195, 160, 150, 100 ka)
200	d,a	I	Fossils of **H.**sapiens.neanderthalensis: snout-like jaws, 100 000 worked stones, bones of rhinoceros, elephant, archaic cow, near Perpignan, France (230)
200	a	T	End of tool "factory", Olorgesailie, Kenya (1,2 Ma)
200	a	4	Oldest wooden tool, England
200	a	N	Double-sided **H.**sapiens Acheulean stone axe, start of flint production to create sparks for fires and use for weapons, Pataud, France (see 180, 35 ka)
195	e	W	Start of global ice age (see 165 and 135 ka)
195	d	V,Y	Oldest fossils of **H.**sap.sap., previously thought to be 135 ky old, Omo Kibish I + II, Ethiopia (200, 160 ka)
180	a	C	1st inhabitants (who?) worked pebbles, Soleihac, France
180	a	N	Double-sided stone axe re-cut, Pataud, France (200 ka)
170	a	AC O	Late (Upper) Acheulean culture, Western Europe (see 350 and 75 ka)
165	e	W	Sea levels up to 125m lower than at present (195, 135)
164	a	AB	Fire is occasionally used to manufacture weapons and tools from silcrete, which, when heated, allows easy splitting, Southern Africa (see 72 ka)
164	a,f	W	Oldest coastal habitation by **H.**sap.sap., shellfish, brilliant red hematite, Pinnacle Point, South Africa
160	d	V	**H.**sap.sap. fossils, Herto Ethiopia
160	m	Z	**H.**sap.sap. child, Jebel Irhoud, Morocco (see 200 ka)
157	d	AF	Skull of **H.**sapiens.sapiens, 1 450cm^3 crane (larger than present average), Herto, Ethiopia 1997
150	z	AB	Cichlidae (multi-colored bass) populate Victoria Lake, East Africa (see 15 ka)
150	d	V,7	1st **H.**sap.sap. women "Black Eve", identified by mtDNA and DNA in X chromosome already in its present form, today found in San people and 2 African tribes having similar languages, South and East Africa (200, 59 ka)
140	b	P	Tomato mosaic virus ToMV found alive, Greenland
140	m,f	AG	Start of **H.**sap.sap. 1st temporary occupation cycle, determined by Optically Stimulated Luminescence (OSL) and Thermo-Luminescence (TL), shell fishing, Blombos Cave, South Africa (see 70 ka)

	Subject Ref.	Source Ref.	
140 **ka**	a	U AG	Clay tablets with engraved red ochre bands, earliest evidence of cognitive abilities and 1st use of symbols by **H.**sap.sap., Blombos Cave, Cape Province, S.Africa
135	e	W,V	End of global ice age, sea levels 6m higher than now (see 195 and 165 ka)
130	e	AC	Riss glacial ends, Riss-Wuerm interglacial starts, Western Europe (see 200 and 110 ka)
130	e	H	Illinoian glacials/interglacials end (see 300 ka)
130	e	7	Coral reefs provide early El Niño records up to the present, New Guinea
130	z	W	Felis.silvestris.lybica (African wild cat) (9,0 ka)
130	m	Z	**H.**sap.sap. lived in Fezzan, Libya (see 70 ka)
130	m	T	**H.**sap.sap. fossils, Klasiesrivier, South Africa
125	g,z	K	Coral reef atop a volcano rim rises from the sea, home of rhea (flight-less bird), giant tortoise, Aldabra Is., Seychelles, Indian Ocean
125	e	H	Sea level maximum (see 105, 82 ka)
125	e	W	**H.**sap.neanderthalensis lived in near-tropical climate, hunted elephant, rhino, aurochs, Northwest France
122	e	H	Wisconsin glacials/interglacials start, North America (see 300 ka)
120	e	P	Tsunami, caused by landslide, deposits sand 500m up on Mt.Kohala, Mauna Loa, Hawaii
120	e,z	Z	Woolly mammoth decline dramatically due to global warming, but survive (see 410 ka)
120	z	Q	Arctic foxes established as a species, Arctic (275 ka)
120	d	?	**H.**sap.sap. split into Negroids (see 30,0 ka) and Non-Negroids (see 100, 70, 50 and 35 ka)
120	a	1	**H.**sap.neanderthalensis used stone and wood for tools, buried dead, used skins, Europe and Asia (see 100 ka)
120	a	W	Hut of **H.**sap.neanderthalensis, Ukraine
120	a	AC	Sangoan culture, South/East/Central Africa (300 ka)
110	e	AC	Riss-Wuerm interglacial ends, Early Wuerm glaciation starts, Western Europe (see 130 and 75 ka)
105	e	H	Sea level high, but lower than 125 ka levels (see 125 and 82 ka)
100	c	X	450m diameter meteorite impact crater, Amguid, Algeria
100	c	X	4,5km diameter impact crater, Rio Cuarto, Argentina
100	e	AB	Baltic Sea, North Sea and low lying coastal Arctic permafrost strips exposed, seas have receded by 100m due to global cooling
100	z	7	Proto-dogs (see 14 ka)
100	z	W	Elephant-sized dromedary camel, El Kowm, Syria
100	z	Q	Proto-elephant Paleoloxodon.antiquus extinct (400 ka)
100	z	I	Camels become extinct in California, migrated to Middle East and Africa (see 15 Ma)
100	d	S	**H.**erectus extinct in Eurasia (see 410 ka)

	Subject Ref.	Source Ref.	
100 **ka**	d	K	When leaving Africa on 1st major exodus, **H.**sap.sap. had to lighten his black skin color to produce the necessary vitamin D (see 120 ka)
100	d,m	4	**H.**sapiens last fossils in China (see 200 ka)
100	m	2	"True" **H.**sap.neanderthalensis in Southern Europe and Middle East
100	m	V	1st fossils (a skull) of **H.**sap.sap. outside Africa, Qafzeh cave, Palestine (see 90, 60 ka)
100	a	AG	End of 1st occupation cycle, ochre working tools, Blombos Cave, S.Africa (see 140, 80 ka)
100	a	V	Oldest rock paintings by Khoi-San, Apollo cave, Namibia (see 27 ka)
100	a	O	Mousterian culture of **H.**sap.neanderthalensis: flake tools improved, inserted in wood/bone handles, Western Europe (see 120, 30 ka)
95	z	Q	Cow-sized stegodonts (extinct elephant ancestors prone to dwarfing) and giant rats, Flores Is., Indonesia (see 2,4 Ma)
95	d,a	Q	Claimed new species **H.**floresiensis, hunters, used fire and stone tools, Flores Is., Indonesia (see 18 and 12 ka and *Notes*)
92,5	e	H	Fluctuation of Earth circulation around the Sun as now, according to 92,5ky cycle (see 22 ka)
90	z	I	Musk oxen migrate from Siberia to North America
90	z	Y	Only known complete skeleton of 18 months old extinct narrow-nosed rhino, 1st thought a donkey, then a prehistoric bear, La Peruyal, Spain
90	m	V	1st wave of African emigrants extinct, Near East (100)
82	c	5,P X	Hoba NIFE meteorite largest known: 9m^3, originally 15t, broke into 77 pieces in area 360 x 110km, largest piece 650kg, Gibeon, Namibia
82	a	AB	Nassarius shells, perforated, with color enhancements are the oldest known examples of human jewelry, Grotte des Pigeons, Taforalt, Morocco (see 75 ka)
80	z	7	Grey wolves migrate from Asia to N. America (100 ka)
80	a	AG	2nd occupation cycle, bone tools, ochre engravings, Blombos Cave, South Africa (see 100, 73 ka)
80	a	N	Stone scraper by **H.**sap.neanderthalensis, France
77	a	5	Engraved human designs, Western Europe
75	e	AC	Early Wuerm glaciation ends, Lower Paleolithic interglacial starts, Western Europe (see 110 and 30 ka)
75	a	P	Oldest jewelry found: beads made from shells, Blombos cave, South Africa (see 82 and 43 ka)
75	a	AC	Upper Acheulean culture, Western Europe (see 170, 28)
75	a	O	Levalloisian culture of **H.**sap.neanderthalensis, Western Europe (see 43 ka)

	Subject Ref.	Source Ref.	
74 **ka**	g,e	V,Q	Extreme eruption Mt.Toba, 100 x 30km crater, 48km high ash cloud, 96km long caldera, 3 000x stronger than Mt.St.Helens, "volcanic winter", Sumatra, Indonesia
73	a	AG	3rd occupation cycle, bone tools, engraved ochre, Blombos Cave, South Africa (see 80 ka)
73	a	AG	Pressure flaking technique found 55 ky earlier than in Europe (transferred by emigrants or invented twice ?), Blombos Cave, South Africa (see 20 ka)
72	a	AB	Fire is routinely used to manufacture weapons and tools from silcrete, which, when heated, allows easy splitting, Southern Africa (see 164 ka)
70	g	Z	Most recent volcanic eruption, Yellowstone, USA (see 640 ka)
70	e,z	W	Giant kangaroos, wombat-like marsupials, gigantic emus starved to death due to extreme climate changes, Australia (see 40 ka)
70	d	Q	Only about 2 000 (?) people survived worldwide in aftermath of Mt.Toba explosion (see 74 and 35 ka)
70	d	4	Non-Negroids split (based on mtDNA) into a northern group of Caucasoids/Mongoloids and a southern group of SE Asians/Pacific Islanders, and New Guineans/ Australians (see 120, 50, 35 ka)
70	m	Z	People left arid Fezzan, Libya (see 130, 5,0 ka)
70	f	7	**H.**sapiens.sapiens salt water fishing with spears, Blombos Cave, South Africa (see 140 ka)
65	g	AB	Eruption of Piton de la Fournaise, Reunion (250 ka)
62	d,m	T 7,D	Aboriginals settled, extinct **H.**sap.sap. genetic lineage Lake Mungo, South Australia (50 and 45 ka)
60	c	Q	Meteorite "Dar al Gani 670" ex Mars, Libya
60	g	V	Borneo and Sumatra joined as Sunda, separated by 100km of open sea from Australia, Tasmania and Indonesia joined as Sahul
60	d	V	Hyoid bone of **H.**sap.neanderthalensis suggests ability of speech, Kebara cave, Mt.Karmel, Israel (see 43 ka)
60	d,m	W	M130 Y chromosome, suggests arrival of 1st **H.**sap.sap., India
60	d,m	V	Major migration of **H.**sap.sap. from Africa to Near East, ancestors to all non-Negroids (see 100 ka)
60	d,a	V	"Great Leap Forward": tools are getting more refined, food is exploited more efficiently and art develops, indicating a change in conceptual thought by a more modern language, a distinct genetic change (see also *Notes* at end of this section)(see 50, 35 ka)
60	a	AC	Fauresmith culture, South Africa (see 38 ka)
60	a	V	**H.**sap.neanderthalensis cave community cared for severely injured member, Shanidar, Iran

	Subject Ref.	Source Ref.	
59 **ka**	c	K	Last time Mars close (56M km) to Earth prior to 2003
59	d	V	Khoi-San the oldest **H.**sap.sap. survivors but not the 1st, have more ancient evolutionary DNA than any other people, their language !Xu, probably the oldest, has 141 sounds, Southern Africa (see 200, 150 ka)
59	d	V,Q	Genetic analysis has traced the Y chromosome of all present **H.**sap.sap. males back to one "Adam" in Africa, M96 chromosomes of Negroids (see 150 ka)
55	e	P	Start of a global wet cycle (see 25 ka)
52 ±6	c	X	1,83km diameter meteorite impact crater, Lonar, India
52	d	K	**H.**sap.sap. "Cro-Magnon" brought "deletion at 508 gene of CF" (cystic fibrosis) to Western Europe (40 ka)
50	c	X,K	160m diameter meteorite impact crater, Odessa, Tex/USA
50	e	Y	Interruption of long term desertification, Sahara (30)
50	z	7	Genyornis, flightless 200kg birds extinct, Australia
50	z	W	Mastodont fossils, Alaska (see 3,0 Ma and 13 ka)
50	d	V	M168 Y chromosome found in all Non-Negroids (70, 40)
50	m	Q	**H.**sap.sap., Malakunanja, Australia (see 62 and 40 ka)
50	m	P	Negroids (I suggest: relatives of Australian aboriginals) settle Nicobar and Andaman Is., Indian Ocean (see 62 ka)

Note: *arrival dates of Amerindians in Americas prior to 17,5 ka have been marked by (?) pending clarification, see Notes at end of section*

	Subject Ref.	Source Ref.	
50	m,a	P	Stone tools and charcoal, Topper, S.Carolina, USA (?)
50	a	4	**H.**sap.sap. has fluent speech, art, symbolic thought, complex religious beliefs, body ornaments (60, 40 ka)
49 ±3	c	H,T X	Fragment of 42m diameter meteorite, broke up 14km above ground, 20m across, hit at 43 000km/h, 150x power of A-bomb, crater 1,18km diameter, 175m deep, ring wall 35m high, Barringer, Arizona, USA
48	m	P	Humans at Serra da Capivara National Park, Brazil (?)
<48	d	AG	"X-Woman", a child, claimed to be new **H.** species, (another Hobbit?) based on mitochondrial DNA, Denisova, Siberia (see 1,0 Ma)
46	z	AG	Major extinction of mega-fauna, probably by climate change and/or (controversially) humans, aborigines and settlers, Australia (see 70, 30 ka)
45	d	2	**H.**sap.neanderthalensis disappears in Middle East (28)
45	d,m	Q	M89 Y chromosome marks a major migration out of Africa, mostly found in Middle East (see 12 ka)
45	m	V	**H.**sap.sap. reached southeastern Australia (62, 40 ka)
45	a	4	Musical instrument (flute), North Africa (see 40 ka)
43	g	D	Tasmania is again part of Australia (34 Ma and 14 ka)

	Subject Ref.	Source Ref.	
43 **ka**	d	Z	Fossils of 9 **H.**sapiens.neanderthalensis had skulls and long bones smashed to gain brain and marrow tissue, faint traces of DNA genes MC1R and FOXP2 indicate red hair and pale skin, capacity for speech, El Sidron, Asturia, Northern Spain (see 60 ka)
43	a	P	2nd oldest jewelry: perforated teeth and egg shells, Balkans (see 75 and 40 ka)
43	a	2	Chatelperronian (= Old Perigordian) culture, use of **H.**sap.sap. culture by **H.**sap.neanderthalensis, ritual burials, no sexual mix between these groups, France (see 23 ka)

42,0 ka to 10,0 ka **Upper Paleolithic Age**

42	a	7,8 AC	Levalloisian (Chatelperronian) culture of **H.**sap. neanderthalensis, maybe later used by **H.**sap.sap., narrow blades, eyed needles, carving, engraving bones and antlers (see 75 and 42, 41,5 and 40,5 ka)
42	a	P	**H.**sap.neanderthalensis in lowest of 3 levels in a cave, Chatelperron, Massif Central, France
41,5	a	P	**H.**sap.sap. in 2nd lowest cave level
40,5	a	P	**H.**sap.neanderthalensis in top cave level
40	g	7	Uzar caldera, 2nd largest geyser field, Kamchatka, Siberia (see 2,0 Ma)
40	z	I	Oldest fossils of La Brea asphalt pit: saber-toothed cat, mammoth, camel, bison, wolf, giant ground sloth, pig, horse, Californian lion, antelope, rodents, tapir, 125 bird species Los Angeles, USA (see 5,0 ka)
40	z	I	Large carnivorous kangaroos, truck-sized wombat-likes, marsupial lions twice the size of leopards, Tasmania, Australia (see 46, 30 ka)
40	z	Z	Most complete mammoth ever found, a calf, NW Siberia, Russia (see 7,0 ka)
40	d	E	6 gene groups ex Cro-Magnon live in Europe (7,0 ka)
40	d	V	M9 Y chromosome in Eurasian people (see 50, ka)
40	d,a	K	Cro-Magnon people (**H.**sap.sap.) had the modern lowered larynx enabling distinct speech, Southern Europe (see 50 and 15 ka)
40	m	Z	**H.**sap.sap. arrives, northern Eurasia
40	m	4	Aboriginals (**H.**sap.sap.) reach Indonesia on foot, 130m sea level drop has created a land bridge: Sahul (New Guinea, Australia, Tasmania) (62, 50, 45, 38, 32 ka)
40	m	Q	**H.**sap.sap. at Niah Cave, Borneo
40	m	Z	Earliest fossil of **H.**sap.sap. "Cro-Magnon" in Europe (see 52 ka)
40	a	P	3rd oldest jewelry, ostrich egg shell beads, Kenya (43)
40	a	Y	Sturdy shoes said to have been developed (see 26 ka)

	Subject Ref.	Source Ref.	
40 **ka**	a	AB	Flutes found (**H.**sap.sap. or **H.**sap.neanderthalensis ?), Ulm, Germany (see 45 ka)
38	d	W	1st **H.**sap.neanderthalensis genome to be deciphered by 454 Life Sciences, USA/Max Planck Institute, Germany
38	m	D	**H.**sap.sap. settles Tasmania (see 40 ka)
38	a	AC	Stilbay culture, South Africa (see 60 ka)
37	d	P	Penultimate genetic mutation of human brain, effecting 70% of global population (see 6,0 ka)
37	m	AC	**H.**sap.sap. settles Pesteracu oasis, Romania
36	m	W	Skull of **H.**sap.sap. claimed to be contemporaneous with similar Cro-Magnon people of France, 1st such fossil since 70 ka, Hofmeyr, South Africa
35	g,e	W	Super-lake Makgadikgadi, 100m deep, now dry salt pan due to tectonic movements, Botswana (see 5,0 Ma)
35	d	?	Northern group of Non-Negroids splits into Caucasoids and Mongoloids (see 70, 15 and 12 ka)
35	d	?	Southern group of Non-Negroids splits into SE Asians/ Pacific Islanders (see 70 and 8,0 ka) and New Guineans/Australians (see 70 and 12 ka)
35	d	Q	Major population expansion started, Altai Mountains, Central Asia (see 60 ka)
35	d,m	K	Ainos with Caucasian racial characteristics (related to Cro-Magnon ? = my speculation), Japan (32, 9,5)
35	m	4	**H.**sap.sap. in China and Siberia (see 17,5 ka)
35	a	AB	6cm female ivory statue "Venus", earliest example of 3-dimensual figurative art, exaggerated sexual attributes, parts of 25 items found, Tuebingen, Germany (see 25 ka)
35	a	AC	Mammoth figurine, 2007, Vogelherd, Germany
35	a	N	Flint production by Cro-Magnon people to create sparks for fire and use for weapons, France (see 200 ka)
33	m	P	Human skull bones, Chimalhuacan, Mexico (?)
33	m,a	P	Stone and bone tools, San Luis Potosi, Mexico (?)
33	a	7 AC	Amongst oldest rock paintings/engravings of cave lion, horse, cave bear, rhino, leopard, bison, mammoth, monkey, correct perspective (my comment: compare lack of this in Middle Ages !), Chauvet Cave, France (11)
32	m	4	Colonization of Micronesia starts from New Guinea (40)
32	m	4	**H.**sap.sap. reaches Japan (see 35 ka)
32	a	7	"Lion Man", artifacts of Aurignacian culture made from mammoth ivory, Southern Germany
32	a	5	Start of gigantic rock engravings, Aurignacian art, cave of Cussac, Dordogne, France
>30	f	H	Amerindians arrive in America, unlikely that they succeeded with their un-sophisticated weapons in eradicating many species of large animals (14, 11)

	Subject Ref.	Source Ref.	
30 **ka**	g	K	Start of erosion of a mountain of clay at Mt.Colombis, France (see 18 ka)
30	e	AC	Lower Paleolithic interglacial ends, Main Wuerm (4th) glacial starts, Western Europe (see 75 and 12 ka)
30	e	I	Probable reversal of Earth's geomagnetic field about every 2 500 years (see 780 ka)
30	e	Y	Maximum of long term desertification, Sahara (50 ka)
30	z	W	2m high, 3m long, 3t giant wombat, Australia (40 ka)
30	d	Q	M173 Y chromosome found in most Western Europeans, M20 Y chromosome originated in Iran/India
30	m	4	Most southerly point in Asia reached prior to the end of the last Ice Age by **H.**sap.sap., Tasmania (as part of Australia)
30	m	P	The "Pie del Diablo" (Devil's Foot) is a human foot impression size 34 in volcanic ash, Mexico (?)
30	m	7,8	Preliminary mitochondrial DNA research suggests possible human presence in Americas (?) (see >30 ka)
30	a	V	End of Mousterian culture of **H.**sap.neanderthalensis, Southern France, Northern Spain (see 100 ka)
29	a	AI	Standardized basic forms of hand axes, up to 200km between place of origin and of use ,Western Europe (see 1,1 Ma)
28	e	W	Cro-Magnon people living at a cave now 40m below the sea, Cap Morgiou, Provence, France
28	d	4	Last **H.**sap.neanderthalensis extinct, Gibraltar, Spain (see 230 and 45 ka)
28	a	V,8 AC	Aurignacian culture by **H.**sap.sap. spreads from Middle East to Western Europe (see 75, 23 ka)
27	m	4	San people and Khoikhoi in arid Namibia (see 20 ka)
27	a	5,S	Paintings on portable stones, oldest Khoi-San rock paintings, Hundsberg, Namibia and South Africa (see 100, and 15 ka)
26,5	e	AB	Start of maximum extension of last Ice Age, northern and southern hemisphere simultaneously (see 19,5 ka)
26	c	1	Penultimate time Pole Star stood true North
26	a	Y	Sturdy shoes almost certain to be in use (40 + 10,5)
25	g	R	Coastline similar to now, South Africa (20 and 1,4 Ma)
25	g	V	Plinian pyroclastic eruption of Vesuvius, Italy (see 22,5 ka)
25	e	P	End of a global wet cycle (see 55 ka)
25	d	4	Mongoloid fossils, China (see 35 ka)
25	d	K	Khoi-San people in South Africa, 85 000 still survive now (see 10,0 ka)
25	a	4	Evidence of self-awareness in **H.**sap.sap., Europe
25	a	I	Artifacts similar to Mousterian near Beirut, Lebanon
25	a	4	"Venus of Willendorf", Austria (see 35 ka)
25	p	7	1st social stratification, Russia

	Subject Ref.	Source Ref.	
24,5 **ka**	d	T	Skeleton of **H.**sap.sap. 4 year old child with some ancient features (**H.**sap.neanderthalensis ?), Portugal
24	m	I	Male human skull, Los Angeles (?)
24	a	4	Burial with hooded jacket and beads, near Moscow
23	e	AB	Intensity of solar radiation at minimum
23	e	AB	Start of cold polar air flows into Mediterranean basin more often, but not more strongly than now (19 ka)
23	a	N,O AC	Gravettian (=Late Perigordian) culture starts, pressure flaking produces thin blades, 1st straight-backed knife, awl to perforate skins for clothing, more modern tools, nets, spear slingshots, textiles, La Gravotte, Cussac cave, Dordogne, France (see 28, 20 and 11,5 ka)
22,5	g	V	Plinian pyroclastic eruption of Vesuvius, Italy (see 25 and 17 ka)
22	e	AB	Ice cover looks like at present-day Greenland and Antarctica, Northern and Central Europe
22	e	H	Fluctuation of Earth axle position as now, according to 22ky cycle (see 92,5 ka)
22	a	I	Ground stone tools, Hoabinhian culture, Australia (14)
21,4 ±9,7	c	X	1,9km diameter impact crater, Tenoumer, Mauritania
21	g,e	AF	Bahamas limestone plateau mostly exposed, sea level 120m lower than at present (see 18 ka)
20	g	AB	Present sand dunes start to form, Natal, S.Africa
20	g,e	R	Coastline of Southern Africa 60m lower than now, rivers dig deep off-shore channels (see 25 ka)
20	e	AB	Minimum age of extreme dryness, indicated by unchanged levels of sand since then, Atacama dessert, Chile (see 11 ka)
20	e	H	European climatic zones moved south by 20°C, but Beringia between Siberia and Alaska ice-free (11 ka)
20	e	7	Glaciation in N.America reaches maximum extend to southern tip of Great Lakes, Arctic Ocean frozen from northern Britain to southern tip of Greenland (10)
20	e	W	Glaciers gouging out Yosemite Valley etc., leaving behind cold, wet, vegetation-less land and lakes, California (see 18 ka)
20	z	K	Cave paintings of Przewalski's Takhi (Mongolian wild) horse, only remaining wild horse species
20	d	?	Split of New Guineans and Australians (see 35 ka)
20	m	5	1st human habitation by San people in the Drakensberge mountains, South Africa (see 27 ka)
20	a	AG	Oldest boomerang found, Poland (see 16 ka)
20	a	Z	Red hand-prints, Gibraltar, Spain (see 12 and 10,0 ka)
20	a	AC	Start of Solutrean culture, Western Europe (23, 15 ka)
20	a	N	Bronze laurel-leaf shaped spearhead, bones of 100 000 horses, Solutré, France

	Subject Ref.	Source Ref.	
20 **ka**	a	7	Spiritual use of Lascaux cave, Massif Central, France (see 16 ka)
20	a	P,Y	457 fossilized footprints, from toddler-size to 2m tall adult, in calcareous clay, Willandra Lake, NSW, Australia
20	p	7	Oldest settlement of Genezareth (Nazareth), Palestine (see 12,8 and 10,0 ka)
20	p	7	1st man found killed by others, Nile valley, Egypt (14)
19,9	m	Z	**H.**sap.sap. at Gibraltar, Spain
19,5	e	AB	End of maximum extension of last Ice Age, northern and southern hemisphere simultaneously (see 26,5 ka)
19	e	AB	End of cold polar air flows into Mediterranean basin more often, but not more strongly than now (23 ka)
18	g	K	Oldest of the "hatted ladies": = clay columns topped by a glacial rock, Mt.Colombis, France (see 30 ka)
18	g,e	AF	End of Bahamas limestone plateau exposure (see 21 ka)
18	g,e	Z	Due to low ice age oceans Japan's main island is connected by a land bridge to Asia, not to Japan (10 ka)
18	e	W	Ice sheets move south, carving out Great Lakes, USA (see 14,8 ka)
18	e	U	Sea level drops by 130m, Southern African coasts
18	e	AB	Sea temperatures and CO_2 started to rise after ice had started to melt (see 23 ka)
18	e	W	Climate now arctic tundra, California (20 and 14 ka)
.18	e	1,7 Y	Last major global glaciation: temperatures 2,3°C, sea level 80m lower than now, North Pole ice maximum Eastern Siberia, Alaska, Yukon ice-free (see 14 ka)
18	d	Q,P	7 tiny bodies of **H.**floresiensis, (a tribe of "pygmies" **H.**sap.sap ?), including a 91cm tall 22,7kg female, brain <30% of modern humans, skull similar to Dmanisi people (?), nicknamed "Hobbits", speculation that children were born normal size but stopped growing, Flores Is., Indonesia (1,78 Ma, 95, 12 and 6,5 ka)
18	m	7	Stone tools similar to Solutrean culture of France, Cactus Hill, Virginia (?)
18	a	AB	Oldest pottery made, Yuchanyan cave, South China
17,5	m	V	1st migration of Paleo-Amerindians from Siberia to Alaska via Beringia, Arctic (timing hotly debated) (see 35, 17, 14,3 and 14 ka)
17	g	V	Plinian pyroclastic eruption of Vesuvius, Italy (see 22,5 and 15 ka)
17	m	7	Paleo-Amerindians reach Alaska (see 17,5 ka)
16	e	AB	Masula ice dam breaks and re-freezes repeatedly, causing devastating flooding, North America
16	m	4,V	Paleo-Amerindian rock shelter, date now accepted, Meadowcroft, Pennsylvania, USA
16	a	5	Huts of grass or skins by San people, Namibia

	Subject Ref.	Source Ref.	
16 **ka**	a	O AC	Early (Proto)-Magdalenian culture starts: needles with eyes, barbed spearheads, boomerangs, France (see 20 and 11,5 ka)
16	a	7	Magdalenian high art, cave paintings of Lascaux, France and Altamira, Spain (see 20, 10 ka)
15	g	V	Plinian pyroclastic eruption of Vesuvius, Italy (see 17 and 11,4 ka)
15	g	I	Southern crater of Ol Doinyo Lengai volcano erupts, 18km across, natro-carbonatite lava is 50% cooler than magmatic lavas, disintegrates in days, Tanzania
15	e,z	AB	Victoria Lake dries up almost completely, the multi-colored bass survive in small but deep Kivu Lake, preserving the genes of the original 500 species, East Africa (see 150 ka)
15	z	Q	Extinct horse, cameloid, giant armadillo found in cenotes, Yucatan peninsula, Mexico
15	d	?	Mongoloids split into NE Asians and Amerindians (see 35, 10,0 ka)
15	m	5	Paleo-Amerindians migrate to Alaska, related to Jomon, an ancient people in Japan (see 18 ka)
15	m	I	Paleo-Amerindians possibly in California
15	a	7	Solutrean culture fades, France (see 20 ka)
15	a	4	San Bushmen rock paintings, Kalahari, Namibia (27 ka)
15	a	3	Hut made of mammoth bones and hides, Ukraine
15	a	N	Clay sculptures of bison, Tuc-d'Audoubert Cave, France
15	a	P	Start of Basque language, (my speculation: since not related to any known one, maybe ex unknown Cro-Magnon language ?), SW France and NW Spain (see 40 ka)
15	a,p	AB	Earliest maps (cartography) (really ?) (see 8,2 ka)
15	f	I	Grinding of gathered grain, Nile valley, Egypt
<15	a	W	Brahmin's chants in unknown language, sound similar to bird song, claimed to have been used before human speech evolved, India
14,8	e	H	Glaciers reach south of the Great Lakes, North America (see 18 ka)
14,7	a	AG	3 human skulls used as drinking vessels, SW England
14,6	m,a	Q	Anvil stone, Big Eddy, Missouri, USA
14,3	m	AG	700 Amerindian coprolites dated by DNA, confirming agreement with Siberian population, Oregon, USA (see 17,5 ka)
14	c	P	Explosion of Supernova, now green beetle-shaped nebula
14	g	D	Tasmania finally separate from Australia (see 43 ka)
14	g	AB	Explosion of huge volcano, Laombok Is., Indonesia
14	e	4	Slow amelioration of global Ice Age (see 18 ka)
14	b	W	Pine, spruce, hemlock and alder grow then, California, (see 18 and 7,542 ka)

	Subject Ref.	Source Ref.	
14 **ka**	z,f	7 AG	Wolves domesticated to dogs, oldest dog bones in human remains, proving dogs were bred before humans settled (see 400 ka)
14	m	7	Main migration by Paleo-Amerindians from NE Asia to Alaska via Beringia land bridge (see 17,5 ka)
14	m	7	Paleo-Amerindian habitation, date now accepted, Monte Verde, southern Chile
14	m,a	I	Unifacial tools, chopper, burin from pre-projection point stage, with extinct sloths, cameloids, Ayacucho, Peru
14	m,a	7	Ivory tools/weapons made from Pleistocene horse, Aucilla, Florida
14	a	N	Magdalenian spear slingshot, wood or bone, Mas-d'Azil, copies found at Bedeilhac and Arndy, Pyrenees, France
14	a	7	Bone needle, Broken Mammoth, Alaska
14	a	I	Hoabinhian culture lasted 6 - 8 000 years, Spirit Cave, Thailand (see 22, 12 ka)
14	f	I	Start of large scale extinction of mammals, probably due to human activities, California (11 and 9,0 ka)
14	f	7	Big-game hunts, spear heads, "time barrier", Clovis, New Mexico, USA (see >30, 11 ka)
14	p	7	1st systematic killing of men, women, children, Sudan (see 20 ka)
13,5	a	Q	Oldest artifacts of Clovis people, Texas, USA
13	c	P	Mars meteorite "Alan Hills 84 001", Greenland ice
13	e	AB	Danube delta starts to form, Black Sea
13	z	7	Mastodons extinct, Florida (see 50 ka)
13	m	P	1st habitation, Richtersveld, Namibia
13	m	Q	Paleo-Amerindian female, Santa Rosa Is., California
13	m	7	"Luzia" skull, near Rio de Janeiro, Brazil
13	a	Q	Unfinished spear head, Big Eddy, Missouri, USA
13	a	7	Woven sandals found, Canada (see 10,5 and 7,5 ka)
12,8	p	V	Founding of Jericho, Palestine (see 20 and 10,0 ka)
12	g	W	North/South America are apart, oceans are connected, again, Panama (see 3,5 and 3,0 Ma)
12	g,e	Q	Glaciers carve canyons, Teton Range, Wyoming (13 Ma)
12	e	AC	Main Wuerm glaciation ends, Upper Paleolithic inter-glacial starts, Western Europe (see 30 and 8,0 ka)
12	e	W	Formation of Larsen B ice shelf, which has now collapsed, Antarctica (see 5,0 ka)
12	e	W	Start of Niagara Gorge and Falls, USA/Canada
12	z	7	Extinction of saber tooth cats in Americas (2,6 Ma)
12	z	I	Fossils of extinct goat, sheep, Grand Canyon, USA
12	z	AF	Goats and sheep domesticated
12	d	?	Hamitic/Semitic peoples split from Caucasoids (35 ka)
12	d	Q	Massive eruption ends "**H.**floresiensis" (see 95, 18 ka)
12	d	Q	M172 Y chromosome found mainly in Middle East (45 ka)

	Subject Ref.	Source Ref.	
12 **ka**	a	I	Jomon pottery, (stone and fired-clay pots), Japan, linked to Hoabinhian culture ?, or Wei Shui River and lower Yellow River culture ?, China (14 and 7,2 ka)
12	a	Q	Stencils of hands, shamanistic symbols, probably related to Australian aboriginals, jungle caves, Borneo (see 20 and 10,0 ka)
12	a	O	Rock paintings of horses, grotto of Pech-Merle, France
12	a,p	4	Permanent villages of several 1 000s, permanent stone and wood huts, mortars, grindstones, Levant uplands
12	f	I	Plant cultivation, Hoabinhian culture (see 14 ka)
12	f	4	Temporary field camps, reaping knives to harvest wild wheat and barley, Levant uplands
12	f	7	Dog buried together with human (see 14 and 5,5 ka)
12	f,p	4	Natufian society, "complex" hunter-gatherers settled down, some become slaves, class structure, wars, Levant uplands
11,65	c,e	P	Sirius B imploded, became a "white dwarf", surface 300x harder, interior density 3 000x higher than diamond, claimed to be "manna from Heaven", the red star
11,5	e	W	Strong rains green tropical Sahara, 150 archeological sites, Africa (see 10,0 and 7,3 ka)
11,5	a	V AC	End of Neo-Magdalenian, start of Late Gravettian culture, Western Europe (see 16 ka) of the Egyptians and to have caused end of ice age
11,4	g	V	Plinian pyroclastic eruption of Vesuvius, Italy (see 15 and 8,0 ka)
11.3	f	V	9 carbonized figs found with grains, acorns, tree species could not reproduce by pollination, only by planting branches, pushing back fruit cultivation by 5 000 years (? figs grow wild !), Palestine
11	c	AB	Cassiopeia A supernova explosion
11	g	P	Last volcanic eruption, Eifel, Germany (see 200 ka)
11	g,e	8	South coast of Arctic Sea near Iceland, Thames, Weser, Elbe tributaries of the Rhine in the area of the later North Sea (see 7,0 ka)
11	g,e	7	Beringia land bridge disintegrates, sea-levels 100m lower than now (see 20 ka)
11	e	P	Start of a global wet cycle (see 5,0 ka)
11	e	Q	Atacama desert habitable, more moderate climate than now, since then permanent drought, now globally driest place, Andes, Chile (see 20 and 6,0 ka)
11	z	AF	Pigs domesticated
11	z,f	L	"Pleistocene Overkill" by invading Clovis people, extermination of 57 species of large mammals incl. mammoth, glyptodont, elephant, mastodon, N.America (see >30, 14 and 9,0 ka)
11	m	7	Charlotte Is., Canada, is inhabited

	Subject Ref.	Source Ref.	
11 **ka**	m	4	Paleo-Amerindians reach Mexico
11	m	7	Skeleton of woman, Arch Lake, New Mexico, USA
11	m	4	Andes densely populated by hunters/gatherers
11	m,f	H	Amerindians arrive in North America via Beringia, advancing 16km/a, with their sophisticated weapons they could have eliminated many species of the larger animals (see >30 ka)
11	a	K	Dug-out boats appear, Middle East (see 8,0 ka)
11	a	4	Cave art ends in Europe (see 33 ka)
11	a	Q	Iberian immigrants create Nuragic culture, Sardinia
11	f	4	Beans cultivated, Andes
11	f	W	30 beehives in a row, 80cm long, 40cm diameter loam and straw cylinders, Palestine
10,8	p	AC	Founding of town of Asikh Hoeyuek, Turkey
10,75	f	V	Start of local culture with diversified diet of seeds, fruits, small game, Guila Naquitz, Mexico (8,67 ka)
10,5	g	AG	Start of Yoldia Sea ice reservoir (present Baltic Sea) (see 10,2 ka)
10,5	a	AB	Start of all-male 10 x 20m cemetery with earliest of 65 graves, hills of Nazareth, Palestine (see 8,75 ka)
10,5	a	Y	Oldest (?) sandal, Rock Cave, Oregon, USA (26, 13 ka)
10,5	a	AG	England's oldest house (suggest a shelter, locals were hunters/gatherers !), Scarborough, England
10,4	e	W	Monsoon winds proceed 800km north to Sahara, creating marshes and swamps in Nile valley, Egypt (7,3 + 5,5)
10,2	g	AG	End of Yoldia Sea ice reservoir due to amelioration of last ice age (see 10,5 and 8,9 ka)
10,2	f	AC	Goats domesticated, Zagros, Iran
>10	a	AG	Concrete (suggest mortar) used in buildings, Anatolia
10	c	X	100m diameter meteorite impact crater, Morasko, Poland
10	g	8	Japan finally an archipelago (see 18 ka)
10	e	AB	Climatic changes caused Makgadikgadi Lake to dry out, leaving behind huge salt pans, Botswana (2,0 Ma, 35 ka)
10	e	AC	Upper Paleolithic interglacial ends, Late Wuerm glaciation starts, Western Europe (see 12 and 8,0 ka)
10	e	L,7	End of global glaciation, Amazon basin with only fragmented forests, glaciation only north of Great Lakes, North America (see 20 ka)
10	e	W	Climate changes to warm and arid, all glaciers melted, California (see 14 and 6,0 ka)
10	z	G	Many mammal groups disappear, due to global warming or human activities ?
10	z	AF	Glyptodonts disappear, 2t armored mammals, Americas (see 30 Ma)
10	z	3	Giant sloth, glyptodont extinct in South America
10	z	Z	Horses extinct in Americas (see 1,6 Ma)

	Subject Ref.	Source Ref.	
10 **ka**	z	O	500kg cave bear (Ursus.spelaeus) extinct, bones of 50 000 found in a cave in the Austrian Alps, W.Europe
10	f	4	Hunter-gatherers disappear in Southern Europe

10,0 to 7,0 ka Mesolithic/Archaic Age

10,0	g	K	Puy de Dôme, part of a chain of volcanoes, Massif Central, France
10,0	g,e	H	Scandinavia starts rising after glaciers receded, so far by 100m (±1cm/a) in the center
10,0	g,e	J	Britain is now an island, North Sea and Channel are flooded (see 11 ka)
10,0	e	Q	African paleo-monsoon shifts northwards, inundating North Africa, hippos live there (see 6,0 and 5,0 ka)
10,0	e	4	Sahara from tropical vegetation to savannah (see 11,5 and 7,3 ka)
10,0	e	4	Forests spread, sea levels rise
10,0	e	7	Antarctic glaciation up to 5km thick
10,0	e,a	Z	Start of Kiffian culture due to intervening moist period, creating a large freshwater lake, "Green Sahara" (see 8,0 ka)
10,0	b	W	Present stromatolites start, Sharks Bay, Australia (see 1,5 Ga)
10,0	z	7	Asian lions live in Balkans, Anatolia, Persia, Northern India (see 100 ka)
10,0	z	AF	Cats domesticated (see 9,0 ka)
10,0	z,f	K	Aids virus theory: sick monkey eaten by chimpanzee (immune, but carry the virus), this eaten by Africans (see 5,0 Ma)
10,0	d	V	M3 Y chromosome in Amerindians (see 15 ka)
10,0	d,f	S	Khoi-San (Bushmen) split from Negroids, San people maintain hunter-gatherer style, Khoikhoi adopting pastoral ways, Southern Africa (see 25 ka)
10,0	m	AG	Human skeleton 60% complete, Mexico
10,0	m,a	7	Spray-painted hands, Cuevas de las Manes, Patagonia (see 20 and 8,3 ka)
10,0	a	4	Microliths (small stone tools), Western Europe
10,0	a	4	Copper working, Middle East (see 7,6 ka)
10,0	a	K	Murujuga, largest Aboriginal art site, 250 000 petroglyphs, Australia
10,0	a	N,W	Weaving, "pottery" made of stone, stone tablets with engraved primitive pictures and symbols (no writing), Jerf, Syria
10,0	f	N,W	Farming, goats, dogs, cake baked with mixture of various grains (oldest baked product), Jerf, Syria
10,0	f	7	Man's bones prove a marine diet, Alaskan coast
10,0	f	K	Sheep domesticated, Middle East

	Subject Ref.	Source Ref.	
10,0 **ka**	f	4	Incipient agriculture (cultivation of wild plants), 1st in Fertile Crescent: Iraq, Syria, Israel, then in SE Asia, Peru/Mexico, then neighboring areas (9,5 ka)
10,0	f	K	1st fishermen and farmers on isle of Ruegen, N.Germany
10,0	f	4	Bow and arrow, nets, snares, traps widely used
10,0	f	W	Capers found, Iran and Iraq
10,0	p	4	Fortified towns: Jericho, Damascus (12,8 and 9,2 ka)
10,0	p	7	Bands/clans become tribes/nations, battles intensify since leaders are not anymore personally endangered, Fertile Crescent
10,0	p	7	Division of labor leads to hierarchies and armies, also to progress and higher living standards, Fertile Crescent
9,9	a	K	Sun-dried (not fired) pottery, China/Middle East (9,5)
9,8	f	AC	Wheat, barley harvested, Turkey
9,6	a	AC	Pre-Ceramic A, Middle East (see 9,4 ka)
9,5	d,m	7,P	Skull form of "Kennewick Man" indicates Caucasian origin (?),possible Aino link (?), Washington State, USA (see 35, 32 ka)
9,5	m	5	Cyclades, Aegean Sea, are inhabited
9,5	a	I	Oldest level of settlement, Fritz Hugh Sound, British Columbia, Canada (see 9,0 ka)
9,5	a	O	Pre-pottery village, clay bins, houses with windows, double doors and 1m thick walls, Hacilar, Anatolia
9,5	a	K	Pottery is now fired in kilns, China/Middle East (9,9)
9,5	a,p	7	9km long coastal town: remains of 200m long building, 45m wide, near Surat, Gulf of Cambay, India (9,0 ka)
9,5	f	K	Pigs domesticated, rice cultivated, China (7,0 ka)
9,5	p	4	Class structures, wealth from surplus food, trade, chiefdoms, wars between cities start, Middle East
9,4	a	AC	Start of Pre-Ceramic B, Middle East (9,6 and 8,5 ka)
9,2	a,p	8	Jericho oldest fortified town, no pottery, mesolithic stone/bone tools, round huts, Palestine (10,0 + 8,0)
9,2	f	4	Potato farming, Peru
9,0	z,f	W	Domestic cat established, Fertile Crescent (130 ka)
9,0	m	I	Female skull "La Brea Woman", Los Angeles
9,0	a	I	Oldest level of settlement, Onion Portage, Alaska (see 9,5 ka)
9,0	a	V	Warriors and villagers threw about 15 000 weapons and articles like a deer antler axe into sacred Ljubljanica River, Slovenia
9,0	a	AB	3 human skulls with shell eyes and reconstructed noses and faces, Israel
9,0	a,f p	4	Multi-roomed/storied houses as status symbols in mixed agricultural/trading villages, Middle East
9,0	f	I	Peak of large scale extinction of mammals in California (by Amerindians ?) (see 14 and 11 ka)

	Subject Ref.	Source Ref.	
9,0 **ka**	f	O	Mattocks (primitive tools to break up soil without turning it), sledges, skis, rafts found at 190m^2 "factory", Star Carr, England
9,0	f	W	Fenugreek (a herb) found, Tell Aswad, Syria
9,0	f	4	Paleo-Amerindian bison hunters, North America (11 ka)
9,0	f	K	Barley, beans, olives cultivated, Middle East
9,0	f	AG	Pistacia vera cultivated, Turkey
9,0	f	K,4	Bananas, sweet potatoes, sugar cane, New Guinea
9,0	f	4	Rice farming, India
9,0	f	4	Farming, herding, Eastern Sahara
9,0	f	4	Farming in the Balkans
9,0	p	W	Large villages, Indus valley (see 9,5 and 5,3 ka)
8,9	g	AG	Fresh water Ancylus Sea (present Baltic Sea) has replaced the Yoldia ice reservoir (see 10,2 ka)
8,75	a	AB	End of all-male 10 x 20m cemetery with latest of 65 graves, hills of Nazareth, Palestine (see 10,5 ka)
8,67	f	V	End of local culture with diversified diet of seeds, fruits, small game, Guila Naquitz, Mexico (10,75 ka)
8,5	e	8	Baltic Sea a fresh water basin (see 11 and 7,0 ka)
8,5	e	8	Average temperature 2,5°C lower than now, Centr. Europe
8,5	a	K	Textiles, cords, cloths commercially made, Middle East
8,5	a	W	Early engraved seals of soft material, Iraq (5,0 ka)
8,5	a	Y	Possible age of rock paintings, Colorado, USA (8,0 ka)
8,5	a,f	AC	End of Pre-Ceramic B, raising sheep and goats, Cyprus (see 9,4 ka)
8,5	f	W	Coriander found, Palestine
8,5	f	AC	Gathering of legumes, Western Europe
8,5	p	Q	Oldest traces of human presence, Athens, Greece (5,2)
8,3	m	7	The final destination of Amerindians reached, modern man has conquered the whole world, Tierra del Fuego, southern tip of Argentine (see 10,0 ka)
8,3	a	V	Start of culture based on obsidian trade with Iran, Syria and Levant, Catal Hueyuek, Turkey (see 7,5 ka)
8,2	e	7	Ice dam collapses, causing massive floods, Canada
8,2	e	7	Shift in Gulf Stream, cooling of Greenland and Europe
8,2	e	AG	Start of continental warming, the fresh water of the Ancylus Sea rises and connects to the oceans and becomes salty (see 6,9 ka)
8,2	p	W	Oldest village plan, with 3 270m volcano, Hassan Dao, Anatolia, Turkey (see 15 ka)
8,0	g	V	Plinian pyroclastic eruption of Vesuvius, Italy (see 11,4 ka)
8,0	e	AC	Late Wuerm glaciation ends, present interglacial starts, Western Europe (see 10 and 5,0 ka)
8,0	e,m	AB	Large parts of present Baltic Sea inhabited by Germanic (??) peoples (see 6,0 and 5,0 ka)

	Subject Ref.	Source Ref.	
8,0 **ka**	e,a	Z	End of Kiffian culture and "Green Sahara" due to return of prolonged arid period (see 10,0 and 6,5 ka)
8,0	z	AF	Chicken domesticated
8,0	d	?	Split of SE Asians and Pacific Islanders (see 35 ka)
8,0	d	AB	Mutation creates 1st blue eyes for **H.**sap.sap.
8,0	m	4	Amazon basin populated, Brazil
8,0	m,a	8	Northern immigrants, rectangular houses, neolithic tools, no ceramics, Jericho, Palestine (see 9,2 ka)
8,0	m,p	8	Hamites from Southern Arabia migrate to Egypt and Ethiopia, create 1st Egyptian empire (see 6,0 ka)
8,0	a	Q	Jade earrings, Mongolia
8,0	a	Q	Nomadic hunters/gatherers made tools, created rock art, Moab, Utah, USA (see 8,5 ka)
8,0	a,f	5	Oldest boat found, Black Sea (see 11 and 7,5 ka)
8,0	f	4	Farming of yams, taro, Thailand
8,0	f	4	Farming established incl. cebus and cotton, India
8,0	f	4	Farming in Italy and Spain
8,0	f	K	Cattle domesticated, Middle East
8,0	f	4	Plow starts to oust stone hoe only in Eurasia, because there are no draft beasts elsewhere (see 7,0 ka)
8,0	f	AB	Milk production additionally to meat as reason for husbandry of cows, sheep, goats, Marmara Sea, Turkey
8,0	f,p	4	Irrigation scheme by the ancestors of Sumerians, Iraq (see 6,3 and 5,1 ka)
7,9	f	4	Millet farming, Yellow River, China
7,8	a	8	Cyprus population is isolated, farming, burial (see 7,2 and 8,5 ka)
7,8	f	4	Farming in Nile flood plain, Egypt
7,7	g	Z	600m deep crater lake, result of volcanic eruption, Mt.Mazama, High Cascades, Oregon, USA
7,6	a	K	Copper mines, metal is cold-hammered, Iraq (see 10,0 and 7,5 ka)
7,542	b	AB	Still living spruce tree takes root, Sweden (14 ka)
7,5	e	7	(Ice ?) wall breaks, Mediterranean is flooding Black Sea fresh water basin (Noah's Flood ?), Bosporus (see 7,1 and 6,5 ka)
7,5	m	4	Mesolithic hunter-gatherers in Scandinavia, Britain
7,5	m	P	Spessart mountain populated, Germany
7,5	a	K	Distillation of alcohol, Middle East
7,5	a	I	Smelting, melting, alloying, casting of metals, Middle East (see 7,6 ka)
7,5	a	V	End of culture based on obsidian trade with Iran, Syria and Levant, Catal Hueyuek, Turkey
7,5	a	AG	Oldest (?) sandal, made of plant fibers, Missouri, USA (see 13 ka)
7,5	a,f	K	Boats are now built with planks, Middle East (8,0 ka)
7,5	f	I	Dogs the only domesticated animals, Iron Gate, Balkans

	Subject Ref.	Source Ref.	
7,5 **ka**	f	4	Horses domesticated, Russia (see 6,0 ka)
7,3	e	4	Global warming to "Climatic Optimum" (see 6,0 ka)
7,3	e	W	Sahara turns to dessert, villages abandoned, monsoon winds reduced, Nile valley, Egypt (11,5, 10,4, 5,5)
7,3	a	4	"Bandkeramik", Balkans, spreading to Central Europe (see 6,5 ka)
7,3	p	4	Iraq densely populated (see 6,5 and 6,0 ka)
7,2	e	8	Taiga (steppe) starts, Siberia
7,2	a	8	"Bandkeramik" (?) of proto-Japanese Jomon culture (see 12 and 7,5 and 7,1 ka)
7,2	a,f	AC	Irrigated agriculture, ceramics, Cyprus (see 7,8 ka)
7,2	f	8	Proto-Chinese, Black Earth civilization, rice and probably silk farming (see 12 and 5,0 ka)
7,1	e	P	Tsunami caused by underwater landslide off Norway leaves sand layers on coasts around NE Atlantic
7,1	a	W	King Gilgamesh praise song in verses (which language and type of writing ?), Babylonian report: "Great Flood", 1 man and his family and animals are saved, Uruk, Iraq (see 7,5 and 6,5 ka)
7,1	f	W	Wild chili peppers possibly 1st cultivated, Amazon Basin and Central America (see 6,1 ka)
7,0	c	X	300m diameter meteorite impact crater, Macha, Russia
7,0	g	W	Last active volcano, France
7,0	e	8	End of last Ice Age, Northern Sweden
7,0	z	3	Last mammoths, Wrangell Island, Alaska (see 4,0 Ma)

7,0 to 5,0 ka Neolithic Age

7,0	e	8	Sea level rises 40m, North Sea and Baltic Sea are now salt water seas (see 11 and 8,5 ka)
7,0	e	H	Global temperatures higher than ever since then
7,0	d	E	One gene group ex Cro-Magnon in Near East (40, 9,5 ka)
7,0	m	K	Migrations/exchanges by boats between China and Hokkaido, Japan (see 18 ka)
7,0	a	Q	20 graves with alabaster items, Cairo, Egypt
7,0	a	W	Agate, carnelian, chalcedony, chrysoprase, jasper and rock crystal, all varieties of quartz, employed as ornaments, Egypt (see 6,4 and 6,0 and 5,0 ka)
7,0	a	M	Mud bricks in use, Iraq
7,0	a	K	Copper mine workings, Catal, Turkey (7,6 and 6,8 ka)
7,0	a	AB	Oldest "Pfahlbauten" (huts on stilts) on the shores of Alpine lakes and moors, Western Europe
7,0	a		Longhouse, burnt clay bottle, Goseck, Germany
7,0	a	AC	Cardial and Linear pottery, Western Europe
7,0	f	AC	Stock rearing, Western Europe
7,0	f	K	Stone hoe, Hessia, Germany (see 8,0 ka)
7,0	f	4	Maize farming, Central America (see 5,5 ka)

	Subject Ref.	Source Ref.	
7,0 **ka**	f	4	Rice farming, Yangtze, China (see 9,5 and 6,0 ka)
7,0	f	K	Sorghum cultivated, Sahel, North Africa
7,0	f,p	K,P	Farming community erects globally oldest 75m diameter circular calendar structure to determine winter solstice, Goseck, Germany (see 6,25 ka)
7,0	p	K	1 000s of trees felled with stone axes to build "road" connecting several moor villages, Vechta, Germany
7,0	p	I	Important village at Tigris source, Cayonu, Turkey
7,0	p	I	Yangshao dynasty (mythical/historic ?), China (5,3 ka)
6,9	g,e	AG	Scandinavia keeps rising, blocking the connection between the Ancylus Sea and the oceans, turning it into a fresh water sea (see 8,2 and 5,0 ka)
6,8	a	AC	Chalcolithic culture, copper metallurgy, Near East (see 7,0 and 5,8 ka)
6,8	f	5	Agriculture starts in the Cyclades, Aegean (9,5 ka)
6,7	a	N	Start of megalithic culture in Europe (menhirs, tombs, cairns), tumulus (megalithic tomb), Bongon, Bretagne Denmark, Portugal (see 6,5 and 5,2 ka)
6,5	e,a	8	Babylonian report: "Great Flood", 1 man and his family and animals are saved (see 7,5 and 7,1 ka)
6,5	e,a	Z	Start of Tenerian culture due to end of arid period, again "Green Sahara" (see 8,0 and 5,0 ka)
6,5	d	4	Pygmies separate from Negroids, West African rain forests (see 30, 18 ka)
6,5	a	K	Megalithic graves, Isle of Ruegen, Northern Germany (see 6,7 and 5,7 ka)
6,5	a	P	Sicilians mine obsidian on Lipari Is., Italy
6,5	a	4	End of "Bandkeramik", Central Europe (see 7,3 ka)
6,5	a	K	Furniture fabrication, building of bridges starts, Middle East
6,5	a	W	Bronze (copper/tin alloy) usage starts, Egypt
6,5	a	G	Trade contacts between Middle East and Egypt (5,2 ka)
6,5	f	4	Cultivation of yam, millet, sorghum at northern edge of West African rain forest
6,5	p	4	Eridu, Sumerian town of 5 000, Iraq (see 7,3 ka)
6,4	a	W	Turquoise mined, Sinai peninsula, Egypt (7,0 and 6,0)
6,3	f,p	4	Civilization has to emerge to organize irrigation, Iraq, (see 8,0, 5,1 ka)
6,3	p	M	Uruk, Sumerian city of 50 000, large public buildings of mud bricks on high kiln brick platforms, Uruk, Iraq
6,25	p	Q	365 day calendar in use, Egypt (see 7,0 and 5,5 ka)
6,1	f	W	Cultivated chili peppers farmed, Amazon Basin and Central America (see 7,1 ka)
6,0	e	4	End of "Climatic Optimum", slight global cooling (7,3)
6,0	e	W	Climate gets wet again, 1st closed canopy forests, California (see 10 ka)

	Subject Ref.	Source Ref.	
6,0 **ka**	e,z	Y	Hippos, needing water all year round, Sahara, Africa (see 10,0 ka)
6,0	e,m	AB	Burial sites, posts and ceramic shards, fossils of earlier habitation of present Baltic Sea (see 8,0 ka)
6,0	z	AF	Llamas and alpacas domesticated
6,0	d	P	Last genetic mutation of human brain, effecting 30% of global population (see 37 ka)
6,0	a	W,V	Gold seen as something valuable, oldest worked gold objects, golden artifacts in Thracian royal tombs, Thracian civilization, Varna, Bulgaria (see 5,1 ka)
6,0	a	AG	A basalt figurine of a culture of herders, oldest statue ever found in Jordan
6,0	a	4	Potter's wheel, weaving loom invented, Middle East
6,0	a	M	Pottery figurines: cult objects or children's toys ?, Iraq
6,0	a	O	Rock painting of cattle drive, Tassili-n-Ajjer, Sahara
6,0	a	W	Turquoise, olivine, chrysocolla, amazonite, jade, green fluorite and malachite, these green minerals used ritually, Egypt (see 7,0, 6,4 and 5,0 ka)
6,0	a	AB	Counting based on fingers and toes leads to systems using 5, 10 and 20 to count farmed animals (5,1 ka)
6,0	a	Z	"Cup Mark" art (hollows within hollows), Preseli Hills, Wales, UK
6,0	a	Z	200 graves of Kiffian and Tenerian cultures, Gobero, "Green" Sahara, Niger (see 6,5 and 8,0 ka)
6,0	a	W	Best preserved mummy of young woman "Miss Chile", Atacama, Chile (see 11 ka)
6,0	a	M	Pre-dynastic period, Hierakonpolis statues by hamitic
6,0	a,f	K	20 000 flint stone axes, adzes, saws found, hunters/ gatherers become farmers, Ruegen, North Germany people, Egypt (see 5,6 and 5,2 ka)
6,0	f	P	Neolithic farmers in Jutland, Denmark
6,0	f	4	Terraced rice paddies, villages abandoned when soils exhausted, re-occupied when recovered, China (7,0 ka)
6,0	f	K	Horses domesticated, Ukraine (see 7,5 ka)
6,0	p	4	Nile valley densely populated, Egypt (see 7,3 ka)
5,8	a	AC	Chalcolithic culture, copper metallurgy, Western Europe (see 7,0 and 6,8 ka)
5,7	a	J	Long barrows (chieftain's tombs) near Stonehenge and West Kennet near Avebury, England (see 6,5 ka)
5,6	a	P,M	Gerzean period, all elements of dynastic art, large rectangular tomb of an early ruler of Hierakonpolis, earliest known superstructure, wooden table, head of cow carved in flint, Edfu, Egypt (see 6,0 and 5,2 ka)
5,5	e	W	African Monsoon winds cease, creating fertile Nile valley, Sahara again dessert, Egypt (see 7,3 ka)
5,5	z	AF	Horses domesticated by Botais, Kazakhstan

	Subject Ref.	Source Ref.	
5,5 **ka**	a	4	Sumerian civilization 1st to use cart wheels, Iraq
5,5	a	G	Woven skirt with beads, Eridu, Iraq
5,5	a	K	1st mention of gold in the Vedas (Indian holy script)
5,5	a	K	Caravans are operating, Middle East
5,5	a	I	Gonorrhea first observed, Middle East
5,5	a	W	Cemetery with 33 middle and lower class graves, largest brewery, Tall-al-Farkla, Egypt
5,5	a	I	Clay tablets with Oroto-Elamite writing, Iran
5,5	a	W	King Enmerkar said to have invented cuneiform writing in message to Iran to buy lapis lazuli, Uruk, Iraq (see 5,4 and 5,3 ka)
5,5	a	W	Local writing, not deciphered, Harrappa, Indus valley
5,5	a	AG	Pig or cow leather shoe, including laces, Armenia
5,5	a	AK	Mosaic Standard, "picture book" of this civilization, also 1 000s of human sacrifices in a royal tomb, oldest structural stone arches, below a 2,5m clay layer indicating a huge deluge, Ur, Sumeria, Irak
5,5	f	K	Llamas, potatoes farmed, Andes, South America (5,1 ka)
5,5	f	K	Maize, turkeys in Central America (see 7,0 ka)
5,5	f	4	Farmers domesticate aurochs, pig, cultivate new strains of wheat, oat, barley, Britain, Scandinavia
5,5	f	7	Humans hunt with the help of dogs, Egypt (see 12 ka)
5,5	p	7	Major harbor city by pre-Canaanites, Ashkelon, Canaan
5,5	p	Q	Year of 12 months at 30 days each, plus 5 extra days, Egypt (see 6,25 ka)
5,4	a	W	Lapis lazuli from Afghanistan in use, Egypt (5,5 ka)
5,3	a	M,4 W	Proto-literate period, "Start of History", writing, originally 800+ pictographs, 5 000 cuneiform clay tablets, Great Temple, Uruk, Iraq (5,5 and 5,2 ka)
5,3	a	W	Spoken Sumerian with known pronunciation survived until 4 ka, written cuneiform language until 75 AD (see 5,5 ka)
5.3	a,f	P,7	"Oetzi", hunter/gatherer buried in glacier, arrow head in his back, 1,6m tall, 46 years, charcoal tattoos, oldest copper axe found in Europe, flint dagger, unfinished longbow, tinder fungus and iron pyrites/ flints for sparks, tool to sharpen flint, bran of einkorn wheat, Eisack Valley, South Tyrol, Italy
5,3	p	7	Indus Valley civilization starts (see 9,0 ka)
5,3	p	I	Liangzhou dynasty (mythical/historic ?), China (7,0)
5,2	a	4	Megalithic tomb of 200 000t of stones, world's oldest roofed structure, 85m long, 13m high, 10m wide with small opening to let in the sun to the floor during the winter solstice only, Newgrange, Ireland (see 6,7 and 6,5 ka)
5,2	a	5	Underground village of 50 inhabitants, Skara Brae, Orkney Islands, Scotland

	Subject Ref.	Source Ref.	
5,2 **ka**	a	5	1st European culture starts in Crete, metallurgy, ceramics, marble extraction in the Cyclades
5,2	a	Q,Y	Phoenicians sell cedar timber from Lebanon to Egypt (see 6,5 ka)
5,2	a	Q	Bone tags, bearing some of the oldest writing known, Abydos, Egypt (see 5,5 and 5,3 ka)
5,2	f,p	AC	Enclosed villages, Western Europe
5,2	p	I	Late Pre-dynasty starts, Egypt (see 6,0 and 5,6 ka)
5,2	p	Q	Oldest human settlement, Zagani Hill, Athens, Greece (see 8,5 ka)
5,1	m	G	Sumerians ex Iran, neither Indo-Europeans nor Semites (possibly Hamites ?)
5,1	a	4,G	Hieroglyphic pictographs, stone buildings, Memphis, Egypt
5,1	a	K	Gold medal of sun god Aton, used before silver, Egypt (see 6,0 ka)
5,1	a,p	K	Gold mines, golden treasures in royal graves, temple accountants used decimal and hexadecimal arithmetic, invented modern capitalism, credit, Ur, Sumer/Iraq (see 6,0 ka)
5,1	f	I	Evidence of agriculture, Peruvian highlands (5,5 ka)
5,1	f,p	4,G	Ancient dynastic civilization starts due to need of organizing irrigation, Egypt (see 8,0 and 6,3 ka)
5,1	p	4,G	1st dynasty, 8 or 9 kings including Menes, 1st unification of Upper and Lower Egypt, capital Memphis (5,0)
5,04	a	Z	Aubrey Holes burial pits, contemporaneous with ditch-and-bank monument, Stonehenge, England
5,0	c	1	Dragon constellation true North
5,0	e	P	End of a global wet cycle (see 11 ka)
5,0	e	4	Global climates similar to now
5,0	e	W	Formation of Larsen ice shelf A, Antarctic (see 12 ka)
5,0	e	Q	African monsoon shifts back to south, creating present desert conditions in the Sahara (see 10,0 ka)
5,0	e	AC	Present interglacial still in operation, Western Europe (see 8,0 ka)
5,0	e	AG	Rising oceans flood land bridge between Sweden and Denmark, creating brackish water Baltic Sea (6,9 ka)
5,0	e,a	Z	End of Tenerian culture due to renewed arid period, the freshwater lake dried up (see 6,5 ka)
5,0	z	I	Youngest fossils of La Brea asphalt pit: saber-toothed cat, mammoth, camel, bison, wolf, giant ground sloth, pig, horse, Californian lion, antelope, rodents, tapir, 125 bird species, Los Angeles, USA (see 40 ka)
5,0	z	AF	Water buffalo and dromedary domesticated
5,0	m	Q	Bantu speaking Negroes start displacing Pygmies and Khoi-San people, spreading south from their homeland, Nigeria/Cameroon

	Subject Ref.	Source Ref.	
5,0 **ka**	m	Y	Inuit migration from Siberia to Greenland, Arctic
5,0	m	5	Indo-European proto-Greeks reach Greek islands
5,0	m,a	7,8	Indo-European language group: the Proto-Europeans in S.Germany, Danube valley, E.Europe, S.Russia, the proto-Indians/Iranians in the Ukraine (see 8,0 ka)
5,0	a	K	Proto-Indo-European language splits into about a dozen groups: Germanic, Celtic, Slavonic, Greek, Italic, Thraco-Illyrian, etc. and the Indo-Iranian group
5,0	a	I	Oldest mummy in wooden coffin, only 2nd ever found untouched by thieves, Saqqara, Egypt
5,0	a	W	Galena, rock crystal, garnet, hematite, lapis lazuli beads, seals and pigments, Egypt (7,0 and 6,0 ka)
5,0	a	W	Gypsum is heated to form Plaster of Paris, Egypt
5,0	a	W	Meteoric nickel-iron worked, Egypt
5,0	a	W	Cylinder seals now made of harder materials, engraved by rotating bow drills, Iraq (see 8,5 ka)
5,0	a	W	Healers wrote clay tablet prescriptions, using caraway and thyme, Iraq
5,0	a	1	Chinese culture well advanced
5,0	a	C	"Tantaval Man" burial sites, France
5,0	a	Z	20x larger henge than Stonehenge, Durrington Walls, UK
5,0	a	AG	Double circle of megaliths, 10 000t shingles tumulus, 50m long, 8m high, inside 29 stones engraved with spirals, concentric circles, great broken 300t menhir, 25m high, Bretagne, France
5,0	a,f	Z	When Sahara rains stopped the people stayed, starting livestock farming, later oasis agriculture, (Garamantian civilization), rock engravings, Fezzan, Libya (see 70 ka)
5,0	a,f	Q	14 planked boats in mud-brick graves, oldest ever found, Abydos, Egypt
5,0	f	4	Farmers use Middle East cereals, Orkney Is., Scotland
5,0	f	C	Chinese princess Xi Ling Shi discovers silk thread (see 7,2 ka)
5,0	p	4	Slavery, militarists, Iraq
5,0	p	4	Unification of Egypt by Narmer (see 5,1 ka)
5,0	p	O	Mycenae founded by Proto-Greeks, Greece
5,0	p	P	1st inhabitants, Hisarlik (later called Troy), Turkey
5,0	p	P	300m ring wall fortification, near Dresden, Germany

D Source References, Queries, Addenda, Notes

Source References:

1 Dr.P.Cattermole/Patrick Moore, The Story of the Earth, 1985
2 R.Leakey, Origins Reconsidered, 1992
3 R.Fortey, Life - an unauthorized Biography, 1997
4 J.Haywood, The illustrated History of Early Man, 1995
5 News articles of various newspapers, popular magazines, 2000/1
6 TV series Earth Story, BBC, 1997
7 National Geographic Magazine, 2000/1
8 Alimen/Steve, Fischer Weltgeschichte (transl. from French), 1966
9 A.C.Bishop et al., Philips Minerals, Rocks and Fossils, 1999
A MS Encarta Encyclopedia (multimedia), 1997
B Nature, various issues, 2003/4
C L'Express, 2000/2, Le Point, 2001/2
D Science magazine, 4 and 8/2001, 7/2002
E B.Sykes, Seven Daughters of Eve, 2001
F Fokus magazine 17/2001
G Encyclopaedia Britannica, 1970/73
H S.M.Stanley, Earth and Life through Time, 1989
German translation: Historische Geologie, 1994
I National Geographic Magazine, 2002/3
J Prehistoric Temples of Stonehenge and Avebury, 1994
K News articles of various newspapers, popular magazines, 2002/3
L R.Leakey, Sixth Extinction, 1995
M S.Lloyd, Art of Ancient Near East, 1961
N L'Express, 2003/4, Le Point, 2003/4
O Life, The Epic of Man, 1963
P News articles of various newspapers, popular magazines, 2004/5
Q National Geographic Magazine, 2004/5
R Hamilton et al., Geology for South African Students, 1960
S Colin MacRay, Life etched in Stone, 1999
T Bill Bryson, A Short History of nearly Everything, 2003
U T.McCarthy/Rubidge, Story of Earth and Life, Southern Africa, 2005
V www.5nationalgeographic.com/genographic/html
W News articles of various newspapers, popular magazines, 2006/7
X www.unb.ca/passc/ImpactDatabase
Y National Geographic Magazine, 2006/7
Z National Geographic Magazine, 2008/9
AA A.Feldman, Space, 1988
AB News articles of various newspapers, popular magazines, 2008/9
AC www.en.wikipedia.org
AD Lesch/Mueller, Kosmologie, dunkle Seiten des Universums, 2008
AE Stephen Hawking, Brief History of Time, 1988
Stephen Hawking/Mlodinow, Briefer History of Time, 2005
AF National Geographic Magazine, 2010/11
AG News articles of various newspapers, popular magazines, 2010/11
AH Geological Journeys (South Africa), 2006

AI Ploetz, Weltgeschichte, 2008
AJ J.Farndon, Rocks of the World, 2007
AK C.W.Ceram, Goetter, Graeber und Gelehrte, 1995, quoted from:
S.N.Kramer, History begins at Sumer, 1956
AL B.Chatwin, The Songlines, 1987
AM T.McCarthy, How on Earth ? 2009

? No specific reference found = dates are my speculation

Notes and Addenda

Spelling of names and places, particularly of the Antique and scientific names and terms:
I have tried to follow the Encyclopedia Britannica, otherwise I have used the US spelling

Ecological/Cultural Timelines for Western Europe

For comparison purposes some additional information is given, regarding geological periods and the relevant contemporary cultures, ref.8 and AC adjusted by entries from Wikipedia, ref.AC

Mesolithic Age

ka	Geological period	Culture
8- 5 **ka**	Present Interglacial still in operation	
10- 8	Wuerm Post-Glaciation	Late Magdalenian

Upper Paleolithic Age

ka	Geological period	Culture
12-10	Upper Paleolithic Interglacial	
18-10		Main Magdalenian carinated cores, denticulated microliths
19-15		Solutrean: pressure flaking, producing thin blades, projectile points, bow and arrow, bifacial point
22-18		Early Magdalenian: needles with eyes, barbed spearheads
29-20		Gravettian =Late Perigordian: blunt straight-backed knifes, struck pointed blades
		2nd Cro-Magnon culture by **H.**sapiens.sapiens
30-12	Main Wuerm (4th) Glacial	
35-29		Chatelperronian = Old Perigordian: flint blades, denticulated tools
		1st Cro-Magnon culture in W.Europe by **H.**sapiens.sapiens, originally probably by **H.**sap.neanderthalensis
		Aurignacian: flint blades to burins from prepared cores, cave art by **H.**sapiens.sapiens
40-30		Levalloisian: flake tools from cores, domed shape by **H.**sap.neanderthalensis

Lower Paleolithic Age

ka	Geological period	Culture
60-40		Mousterian: flake tools improved, inserted in wood or bone handles, **H.**sap.neanderthalensis culture, later by **H.**sap.sapiens
75-30	Lower Paleolithic Interglacial	
110- 75	Early Wuerm Glacial	
130-110	Riss-Wuerm Interglacial	Final Acheulean culture of **H.**sapiens
200-130	Riss (3rd) Glacial	Main Acheulean culture of **H.**sapiens
380-200	Mindel-Riss Interglac.	Old Acheulean: flaking hand axes with a wooden baton, culture of **H.**sapiens
455-380	Mindel (2nd) Glacial	Middle Acheulean: bi-facial tools, by **H.**erectus or **H.**sapiens ?
620-455	Guenz-Mindel Interglac.	Lower Acheulean: core tools and uni-face flake tools by **H.**erectus brought from Oldowan, East Africa
680-620	Guenz (1st) Glacial	

Mediterranean Sea Levels:

Another interesting timeline for the Mediterranean world is provided by the increase in the sea-levels, according to ref. 8

52,0 **ka**	Levalloisian/Mousterian	Tyrrhenian III	by	± 6 m
100,0	Levalloisian/Mousterian	II		±15 m
380,0	Old Acheulean	I		±45 m

The Big 5 Extinctions: according to reference L

440 **Ma** end of Ordovician
365 late Devonian
225 end of Permian/Paleozoic,
210 end of Triassic
65 end of Cretaceous/Mesozoic

Major or moderate extinctions: every 26 My
Average life span of any species: 4 My

Note: the dates given by this reference are those of the Harland timeline of 1982 and do not agree with those used by me, which are based on the Bishop timeline of 1999, reference 9, which is more up-to-date,
and they keep changing

Basic Terms of Biological Hierarchy

extracted from Colin MacRay, Life etched in Stone, 1999, ref. S

Kingdom, Phylum, Class, Order, Family, Genus, Species
many subdivisions and other groupings abound

Woese's Tree of Live (1976)

extracted from B.Bryson, A short History……, 2003, ref.T

Bacteria: cyano b., purple b., gram-positive b., green non-sulfur b., flavo b., thermotogales
Archaea: halophilic a., methanosarcina, methanobacterium, methanoncoccus, thermoceler, thermoproteus, pyrodictium
Eukarya: diplomads, microsporidia, trichomonads, flagellates, entameba, slime moulds, ciliates, plants, fungi, animals

E Subject Lists Cosmic/Earth Sciences:

When checking these lists for mistakes, please watch out for (maybe) correct times at or near - but on the wrong side of - a boundary.

c cosmic: **Big Bang, universe, celestial, meteorites**

13,7 Ga to 4,6 Ga COSMIC EON

	Subject Ref.	Source Ref.	
13,7 **Ga**	c	K	Big Bang creating universe, eventually consisting of >100G galaxies each with 200G stars, 4% "normal" atoms, 23% "dark matter" and 73% "dark (anti-gravity) energy" (see Notes at end of this section)
13,7±100My	c	P	Big Bang (NASA microwave project 2003)
13,7-10^{-44}s	c	AD	Natural Laws start to operate (see 13,7 Ga -1s)
13,7-10^{-32}s	c	W	Temperature of universe dropped to only 11G°C (see 13,7 Ga -1min)
13,7-10,5s	c	AD	Universe cooled enough that quarks cannot exist any longer independently, 3 each cluster to form protons and neutrons, but not atoms yet (see 13,7 Ga -380ky)
13,7-0,01s	c	W	Universe in quark-gluon-plasma condition (13,7-380ky)
13,7-1s	c	AD	Neutrinos stop reacting with matter (13,7-10^{-44}s Ga)
13,7-1s	c	T	Gravity, strong and weak nuclear forces and the other physical forces appear (see 13,7Ga -10^{-44}s)
13,7-1s	c	AE	10G°C = temperature in H-bomb, mostly photons, electrons and neutrinos and their anti-particles with some protons and neutrons (13,7-100s Ga)
13,7-1min	c	T	Universe now 1,6 trillion km across, appearance of H and He, 98% of all universal matter now in existence (see 13,7 Ga-10^{-32}s)
13,7-100s	c	AE	1G°C = temperature inside hottest stars, protons and neutrons combine to atomic nuclei, 1 proton and neutron each = nucleus of deuterium (heavy hydrogen), then 2 protons and neutrons each = helium nucleus (see 13,7 Ga -380ky)
13,7-10ky	c	AD	Rate of expansion of universe dominated by energy up to now, from then on by matter
13,7-380ky	c	AD	Energy of photons insufficient to separate electrons from protons = recombination, end of plasma oscillation, echo horizon 220k Ly = extent of universe then, size increase since then 1 100x, temperature 3 000°K (see 13,7 Ga -0,01s and 13,7-380ky)
13,7-380ky	c	Q	Separation of energy and matter

	Subject Ref.	Source Ref.	
13,7 **Ga** -380ky	c	AB	H appears as 1st element by adding an electron to the nucleus, universe is now "transparent" for electro-magnetic radiation, there are no gravitational waves (see 13,7 Ga -10^{-5}s)
13,7 -1My	c	Q	Universe <0,1% of present size
13,6	c	AG	1st short-lived stars appear (see 13,45 Ga)
13,5	c	I	Universe plunged in darkness (see 13,2 and 12,8 Ga)
13,45	c	AG	Last of short-lived stars appear (see 13,6 Ga)
13,3	c	K	Primordial structure of universe now established
13,2	c	I	1st short-lived (< 1My) star produces hydrogen and helium, nuclear fusion of hydrogen atoms creates light, becomes supernova, creating heavier atoms (oxygen, carbon) (see 13,6 and 13,5 Ga)
13,1	c	AF	Age of small proto-galaxies seen by Hubble, blue light
13,07	c	AG	Supernova of short-lived star 13,1G Ly away
>13,0	c	AG	UDFy-38 135 539, the most distant galaxy found
12,8	c	P	1st stars, end of "Dark Age" (Sir Martin Rees) (13,5)
12,7	c	Q	Oldest planet found in Globular Cluster M4
12,7	c	Q	Universe <0,1% of present size
12,0	c	W	Milky Way started (see details at end of subject)
12,0 ±1Gy	c	AD	Average age of star clusters in the Milky Way halo (Hertzsprung/Russell diagrams)
11,7	c	K	2 000 galaxies already in existence
11,0	c	W	Supernova explosion is source of almost mass-less neutrinos, which can transverse planets, forming electrons, myons, tauons (see 5,0 Ga)
10,7	c	W	Very old spiral galaxy seen when very young, 30 gas accumulations 200M Ly across, no stars
7,0	c	AD	Expansion of universe until now braked by gravitation (see 6,0 and 5,0 Ga)
6,0	c	AD	Expansion of universe linear (see 7,0 and 5,0 Ga)
6,0	c	K	Number of red (dying) stars begins to exceed the number of blue (new) stars
5,5	c	W	Start of accelerating expansion of universe (5,0 Ga)
5,0	c	I	Supernova explosion creates natural atoms heavier than uranium (92 protons), e.g. a plutonium isotope of 94 protons, a component of rare earth bastnasite
5,0	c	AD	Expansion of universe starts to accelerate (see 7,0, 6,0 and 5,0 Ga)
*5,0	c	AE	Solar system is formed from supernova debris (4,7 Ga)
*4,7	c	Q	99,9% of a gas/dust cloud 24G km across became our Sun, 0,1% formed the planets, comets, meteorites (see 4,587 Ga)
*4,7	c	H	Formation of the solar system: planets and oldest meteoroids from debris of imploding star and subsequent exploding supernova (see 5,0 and 4,55 Ga)

	Subject Ref.	Source Ref.	
*4,7 **Ga**	c	Q	Sun temperatures: photosphere 5,7k°C, chromosphere 10k°C, corona 2M°C
*4,7 -20My	c	AB	Water exists in solar system, but source unclear (volcanic eruptions, proto-planet, asteroids ?), but inner planets Mercury to Mars lost all water (see 4,25 Ga)

4,6 Ga to 3,8 Ga Priscoan Era

4,6	c	P	Small baby (new) galaxies formed 100Ly away
*4,6	c	3,H	Bombardment of Earth and Moon starts, meteorites/ comets bring carbon and its compounds as carbonaceous chondrites (see 3,9 Ga)
*4,6	c	I	Moon forms from primeval solar nebula (4,53 Ga,700 Ma)
*4,6	c	I	Probable Moon temperatures: 90km outer crust at 440°K, intermediate zone 800km at 800°K, central core 900km radius at 1 100°K, assuming mostly olivine interior
*4,6	c	I	Probable configuration of the Moon: outer 6km "loose material", next 16km basalt, next 38km eclogite or anorthosite rocks
*4,6	c	I	"Genesis Bean", glass fragment ex drilling core, Moon
*4,6	c	K	Mt.Olympus crater, 24km high walls, 600km diameter, Valles Marineris canyon 7km deep, 4 000km long, Mars
*4,587	c	W	Interstellar 5 000°C molecular cloud 100's of Ly across, debris of dead stars, for 10My gravity draws particles together (see 4,7 Ga)
*4,57±30My	c	AD	Oldest solar system rocks and meteorites

***Note:** *in the light of the newest information, all entries regarding the solar system prior to 4,567 Ga have to be re-dated, but I have left the original dates given by the references unchanged, pending confirmation*

4,567	c	AM	A supernova causes collapse of a gas/dust cloud, rotation flattens the cloud into a disk shape, with the proto sun in the center, radiometric dating from meteorites (see 4,55 Ga)
4,55±70My	c	T	Age of solar system rocks (C.Patterson) (see 4,57 Ga)
4,55	c	T	Sun has 75% of present brightness
4,55	c	W	Mass of solar system contracts, spin increases and superheats, forming ±20 planets, during following 30My these start to collide (see 4,7 and 4,53 Ga)
4,55	c,g	AM	Start of planet formation(see 4,567 and 4,4 Ga)
4,54	c,g	AM	Best estimate of Earth's age
4,53	c	W	Moon was 15x closer than now (see 4,6 Ga and 700 Ma)

	Subject Ref.	Source Ref.	
4,53 **Ga**	c,g e	U F,Q	Earth struck a glancing blow by a Mars-sized object, which is mostly thrown into Earth's orbit, part falls back, vaporizing part of the mantle, rest forming Moon surface, tilted Earth's axis, now spins in a conical path for 26My, creating seasons and tides, increased revolutions, rotating NiFe nucleus creates magnetosphere, protecting atmosphere from solar wind (see 4,55 Ga)
4,5	c	W	Huge floods and glaciers formed 2 500km long, 3km deep and up to 500km wide Kasei Valles, Mars
4,5	c	7	Mars surface "active" but solid, no plate tectonics, plenty of water 200m below the poles, kept liquid due to overlay pressure (see 3,8 Ga)
4,5	c	W	CO_2 ice sublimes to gas from the bottom, carrying dust fountains to surface which causes dark areas, Mars
4,5	c	AG	New theory: ice covering a huge moon crashing into Saturn was stripped off, forming the rings, which are 95% ice("Nature")
4,5	c,b	P,W	Carbonaceous chondrite meteor contains 74 types of amino acids (8 used by Earthly proteins), strings of polyols sugar unknown on Earth, components of Earth life (left-handed amino, di-amino acids) came from space, maybe forming proteins, molecules, Murchison, Australia (see 4,0 Ga)
4,4	c	AM	Sun nuclear fusion starts, solar wind removes remainders of the gas/dust cloud (see 4,55 Ga)
4,4	c	Q	Planets have about ⅓ of present size
4,25	c,e	W	Impactor space craft (2005) proves much ice in meteorites, but water differs from ours, oceans are green (iron content), denser atmosphere reddish, now believed water reached Earth from outer asteroid belt meteorites, deflected into Earth orbit by Jupiter (see 4,7 Ga -20My)
4,0	c	I	Mare Imbrium result of meteorite impact, Moon (3,3 Ga)
3,9	c	7,H	Great Bombardment of Earth and Moon ends (4,6 and 3,8)

3,8 Ga to 2,5 Ga Archean Era

3,8	c	AF	2 asteroid storms hit Earth and Moon (see 3,9 Ga)
3,8	c	I	Age of Moon surface soil (see 3,7 Ga)
3,8	c	P	1st volcanic eruptions, Mars (see 4,0 Ma)
3,8	c	P	Phyllosilicate clays, result of basalt immersed in water for very long times, Mars (see 4,5 Ga)
3,7	c	I	Minimum age of Moon rocks (see 3,8 Ga)
3,7	c	I	Lava eruptions on Moon start (see 3,3 Ga)

	Subject Ref.	Source Ref.	
3,465 **Ga**	c	U,D	1st recorded 20km diameter super-meteorite impact, melting rocks to glass spherules, crater across Gondwana, Barberton, S.Africa, Pilbara, W.Australia
3,4	c	I	10 layers of asphalt at Hadley Rille (= gorge), Moon
3,3	c	I	Lava filling Mare Imbrium at Hadley Rille, Moon (4,0)
3,3	c	I	Lava eruptions on Moon end (see 3,7 Ga)
3,1	c	U	Indication of 18 day lunar month

2,5 Ga to 1,6 Ga Early Proterozoic Period

2,4	c	X	16km diameter impact crater, Suavjaervi, Russia
2,023	c	U,X	Vredefort Dome, result of 10 - 15km diameter asteroid impact with 300km diameter crater, 5km deep, world's largest, now eroded, South Africa
2,023	c,g	U	New theory of combination of Vredefort Dome meteorite impact with hot spot mantle plume, South Africa
2,0	c	X	30km diameter meteorite impact crater, Yarrabubba, Western Australia
2,0	c	P,W	Copernicus crater 93km diameter, 3,76km deep, 1,2km high cone, Moon
1,85 ±3My	c	X	200km x 100km oval meteorite impact crater, 10-19km diameter exploding meteorite, equivalent to 10bn Hiroshima bombs, Sudbury, Ont./Canada
1,8	c	X	30km diameter impact crater, Keurusselkae, Finland
1,8	c	X	10km diameter impact crater, Paasselka, Finland
1,64	c	X	20km diameter impact crater, Amelia Creek, Australia
1,63 ±5My	c	X	30km diameter meteorite impact crater, Shoemaker (formerly Teague), Western Australia

1,6 Ga to 650 Ma Riphean Period

1,4	c	X	3km diameter meteorite impact crater, Goyder, Northern Territory, Australia
1,0	c	X	3km diameter impact crater, Iso-Naakkima, Finland
1,0	c	X	4km diameter impact crater, Suvasvesi N, Finland
1,0	c	X	9km diameter meteorite impact crater, Lumparn, Finland
700 **Ma**	c	I	Moon captured by Earth gravitational forces (4,53 Ga)
700 ±5	c	X	14km diameter impact crater, Jaenisjaervi, Russia

650 Ma to 600 Ma Vendian Period

646 ±42	c	X	25km diameter meteorite impact crater, Strangways, Northern Territory, Australia
600	c	X	1,5km diameter impact crater, Saarijaervi, Finland
600	c	X	6,6km diameter impact crater, Soederfjaerden, Finland
600	c	X	60km diameter impact crater, Beaverhead, Mont./USA

600 Ma to 543 Ma Ediacaran Period

	Subject Ref.	Source Ref.	
590 **Ma**	c	X	90km diameter impact crater, Acraman, South Australia
570	c	X	13km diameter impact crater, Spider, W.Australia
560	c	X	6km diameter impact crater, Saeaeksjaervi, Finland
550 ±100	c	X	2,35km diameter impact crater, Holleford, Ont./Canada
550	c	X	10km diameter meteorite impact crater, Kelly West, Northern Territory, Australia
545	c	X	6km diameter meteorite impact crater, Foelsche, Northern Territory, Australia

543 Ma to 490 Ma Cambrian Period

515	c	X	18km diameter meteorite impact crater, Lawn Hill, Queensland, Australia
508	c	X	19km diameter impact crater, Glikson, Australia
505	c	X	6km diameter impact crater, Rock Elm, Wis./USA
500	c	AA	Greater Magellanic Cloud, a distant galaxy, came close (70k Ly) to our Milky Way galaxy
500 ±10	c	X	5km diameter meteorite impact crater, Gardnos, Norway
500 ±20	c	X	5km diameter impact crater, Mizarai, Lithuania
500	c	X	8km diameter impact crater, Clover Bluff, Wis./USA
500	c	X	3,2km diameter impact crater, Newporte, N.D./USA
500	c	X	24km diameter impact crater, Presqu'ile, Que./Canada

490 Ma to 443 Ma Ordovician Period

474	c	Q	Age of Mars meteorite rocks
470	c	X	3km diameter meteorite impact crater, Granby, Sweden
470	c	X	8km diameter meteorite impact crater, Neugrund,Estonia
470 ±30	c	X	16km diameter meteorite impact crater, Ames, Okla./USA
455	c	X	7km diameter meteorite impact crater, Kardia, Estonia
455	c	X	7,5km diameter meteorite impact crater, Lockne, Sweden
455	c	X	2km diameter meteorite impact crater, Tvaeren, Sweden
450 ±10	c	X	8,5km diameter impact crater, Calvin, Mich./USA
450	c	X	30km diameter impact crater, State Islands, Ont/Canada
445 ±2	c	X	6km diameter impact crater, Pilot, N.W.T./Canada

443 Ma to 417 Ma Silurian Period

430 ±25	c	X	8km diameter impact crater, Couture, Que./Canada
430	c	X	4km diameter impact crater, Glasford, Ill./USA

417 Ma to 354 Ma Devonian Period

	Subject Ref.	Source Ref.	
400 **Ma**	c	X	12,5km diameter impact crater, Nicholson, N.W.T.Canada
400 ±50	c	X	8km diameter impact crater, La Moinerie, Que./Canada
396 ±20	c	X	3,8km diameter impact crater, Brent, Ont,/Canada
395 ±25	c	X	8km diameter impact crater, Elbow, Sask./Canada
380 ±5	c	X	15km diameter meteorite impact crater, Kaluga, Russia
378 ±5	c	X	8,5km diameter impact crater, Ilyinets, Ukraine
364 ±8	c	X	40km diameter impact crater, Woodleigh, W.Australia
361 ±1,1	c	X	52km diameter meteorite impact crater, Siljan, Sweden
360	c	X	7km diameter impact crater, Piccaninny, W.Australia
360 ±20	c	X	3,8km diameter impact crater, Flynn Creek, Tenn./USA

354 Ma to 290 Ma Carboniferous Period

351 ±20	c	X	2,44km diameter impact crater, West Hawk, Man./Canada
345	c	X	14km diameter meteor. impact crater, Gweni-Fada, Chad
342 ±15	c	X	54km diameter impact crater, Charlevoix, Que./Canada
320	c	X	8km diameter impact crater, Serpent Mound, Ohio/USA
320 ±80	c	X	7km diameter impact crater, Crooked Creek, Mo./USA
300 ±50	c	X	2,5km diameter impact crater, Mishina Gora, Russia
300	c	X	6km diameter impact crater, Decaturville, Mo./USA
300	c	X	6km diameter impact crater, Middlesboro, Ky./USA
300	c	X	4km diameter impact crater, Ile Rouleau, Que./Canada
300	c	X	12km diameter impact crater, Serra da Cangalha, Brazil
290 ±20	c	X	26km/36km diameter meteorite impact crater, Clearwater East/West, Que./Canada
290 ±35	c	X	4,5km diameter meteorite impact crater, Dobele, Latvia

290 Ma to 248 Ma Permian Period

280	c	X	8km diameter impact crater, Des Plaines, Ill./USA
280 ±10	c	X	11km diameter impact crater, Ternovka, Ukraine
250 ±80	c	X	6km diameter meteorite impact crater, Kursk, Russia
250	c	X	4km diameter meteorite impact crater, Gow Sask./Canada

248,2 Ma to 205,7 Ma Triassic Period

244,4	c	X	40km diameter impact crater, Araguainha, Brazil
230	c	X	1,5km diameter impact crater, Karikkoselkae, Finland
220 ±32	c	X	40km diameter impact crater, Saint Martin, Man./USA
220	c	AH	1,1km diameter impact crater, Tswaing, South Africa
214 ±8	c	X	23km diameter impact crater, Rochechouart, France
214 ±1	c	D,X	Manicougan crater, 100km diameter, largest of 3 - 5 craters formed within a few hours by parts of a comet, Quebec, Canada

	Subject Ref.	Source Ref.	
210 **Ma**	c	W	M32 galaxy crashes through the center of the Andromeda spiral galaxy, 65k Ly diameter
205,7	c b,z	7,H	Triassic extinction (by comet impact, indicated by iridium abundance and a "fern spike" ?), mass extinction of marine species, mammal-like reptiles extinct, seed ferns disappear (see 215, 210, 140 Ma)

205,7 Ma to 144,0 Ma Jurassic Period

200 ±25	c	X	9km diameter impact crater, Red Wing, N.D./USA
200 ±100	c	X	12km diameter impact crater, Wells Creek, Tenn./USA
200	c	X	4,5km diameter impact crater, Riachao Ring, Brazil
190 ±30	c	X	7km diameter impact crater, Cloud Creek, Wyo./USA
190 ±20	c	X	2,5km diameter impact crater, Viewfield, Sask./Canada
180	c	X	3,5km diameter impact crater, Kgagodi, Botswana
170	c	X	10km diameter impact crater, Upheaval Dome, Utah/USA
169 ±7	c	X	20km diameter meteorite impact crater, Obolon, Ukraine
167 ±3	c	X	80km diameter meteorite impact crater, Puchezh, Russia
165 ±5	c	X	3,2km diameter impact crater, Zapadnaya, Ukraine
160	c	W	2 huge asteroids collided at edge of solar system, breaking into 140k pieces of >1km, 3oo pieces of >10km diameter, one later hitting Yucatan, Mexico (see 64,98 Ma)
160 ±10	c	X	8km diameter impact crater, Vepriai, Lithuania
150 ±70	c	X	1,6km diameter meteorite impact crater, Liverpool, Northern Territory, Australia
150 ±20	c	X	1,3km diameter meteorite impact crater, Tabun-Khara-Obo, Mongolia
145 ±0,8	c	W,X U	25km diameter stony meteorite rich in Fe silicates and NiFe sulfides caused 70km diameter impact crater, (suggestion: possibly caused Jurassic extinction ?), identified 1996, Morokweng, South Africa

144,0 Ma to 65,0 Ma Cretaceous Period

142,5 ±0,8	c	X	22km diameter meteorite impact crater, Gosses Bluff, Northern Territory, Australia
142 ±2,6	c	X	40km diameter meteorite impact crater, Mjoelnir,Norway
140	c	X	6,8km diameter impact crater, Arkenu 1, Libya
140	c	X	10km diameter meteorite impact crater, Arkenu 2, Libya
128 ±5	c	X	55km diameter meteorite impact crater, Tookoonooka, Queensland, Australia
121 ±2,3	c	X	9km diameter meteorite impact crater, Mien, Sweden
120	c	X	2km diameter impact crater, B.P.Structure, Libya
120	c	X	±18km diameter meteorite impact crater, Oasis, Libya
120 ±10	c	X	2,7km diameter impact crater, Rotmistrovka, Ukraine

	Subject Ref.	Source Ref.	
115 ±10 **Ma**	c	X	39km diameter impact crater, Carswell, Sask./Canada
110	c	X	4km diameter impact crater, Mt. Toondina, S.Australia
100	c	X	13km diameter impact crater, Sierra Madera, Tex./USA
99 ±4	c	X	13km diameter impact crater, Deep Bay, Sask./Canada
97	c	X	13km diameter impact crater, Kentland, Ind./USA
95	c	X	12km diameter impact crater, Avak, Alas./USA (3 Ma)
91 ±7	c	X	25km diameter impact crater, Steen River, Alta./Canada
90	c	AB	Supernova SN 2007 exploded then, visible (X-rays) only now
89 ±2,7	c	X	19km diameter meteorite impact crater, Dellen, Sweden
81 ±1,5	c	X	6,5km diameter impact crater, Wetumpka, Ala./USA
80 ±20	c	X	3,5km diameter impact crater, Zeleny Gai, Ukraine
75	c	X	6km diameter impact crater, Maple Creek, Sask./Canada
73,8 ±0,3	c	T,X	Manson crater, 4,5km deep, 35km across, by 10 bn ton 2,5km across rocky meteorite, Iowa, USA
73,3 ±5,3	c	X	23km diameter impact crater, Lappajaervi, Finland
70,3 ±2,2	c	X	65km diameter meteorite impact crater, Kara, Russia
70	c	X	3,5km diameter impact crater, Ouarkziz, Algeria
70	c	X	6km diameter meteorite impact crater, Chukcha, Russia
70	c	X	6km diameter impact crater, Tin Bider, Algeria
70	c	X	12km diameter impact crater, Vargeao Dome, Brazil
65,17 ±640ky	c	X	24km diameter meteorite impact crater, Boltysh, Ukraine
65	c	X	9,5km diameter impact crater, Vista Allegre, Brazil
65	c	H	Quartz grains from iridium-rich zones with concussion-wave metamorphosis ex meteorite impact, global distribution, possibly a meteorite shower, Nitrogen of atmosphere burned, creating sulfur and acid rain
64,98 ±50ky	c,e	3,Q	12km diameter meteorite hit (see 160 Ma), 180km diameter crater half under Caribbean water, 3 000 ring cenotes along crater perimeter, globally 10x normal iridium levels in thin clay layer (205,7 Ma), Yucatan, Mexico

65,0 Ma to 54,8 Ma Paleocene Epoch

64	c	X	10km diameter impact crater, Eagle Butte, Alta./Canada
60	c	K	350m diameter asteroid hit, crater 3km diameter, 300m deep, concentric fractures for up to 19km, North Sea
60	c	X	9km diameter impact crater, Conolly Basin, W.Australia
58 ±2	c	X	12,7km diameter impact crater, Marquez, Tex./USA

54,8 Ma to 33,7 Ma Eocene Epoch

	Subject Ref.	Source Ref.	
50,5 **Ma** ±760ky	c	X	45km diameter meteorite impact crater, Montagnais, N.S./Canada
50	c	X	5,1km diameter impact crater, Goat Paddock, Australia
49 ± 0,2	c	X	25km diameter meteorite impact crater, Kamensk, Russia
49 ± 0,2	c	X	3km diameter meteorite impact crater, Gusev, Russia
46 ±7	c	X	5,5km diameter impact crater, Chiyli, Kazakhstan
46 ±3	c	X	9km diameter meteor. impact crater, Ragozinka, Russia
45 ±10	c	X	2,8km diameter impact crater, Shunak, Kazakhstan
42,3 ±1,1	c	X	15km diameter meteorite impact crater, Logoisk,Belarus
40 ±20	c	X	8km diameter meteorite impact crater, Beyenchime Salaatin, Russia
40 ±20	c	X	20km diameter meteor. impact crater, Logancha, Russia
39	c	X	23km diameter impact crater, Haughton, Nunavut, Canada
37,2 ±1,2	c	X	7,5km diameter impact crater, Wanapitei, Ont./Canada
36,4 ±4	c	X	38km diameter impact crater, Mistastin, Newf./Canada
35,5 ±0,3	c	Q,X	90km diameter asteroid crater, waves 100s of meters high race 100s of km inland, Chesapeake Bay, Va, USA (see 33,7 Ma)
35,5 ±0,2	c	U,X	Meteorite 100km diameter crater, Popigai, Siberia (see 33,7 Ma)
35	c	X	10km diameter impact crater, Flaxman, Australia
35	c	X	8,5km diameter impact crater, Crawford, Australia
33,7	c,z	U	Major extinction of mammalians, possibly connected to 2 meteorite impacts, allowed development to modern mammals (see 35,5 and 31 Ma)

33,7 Ma to 23,8 Ma Oligocene Epoch

30	c,e	W	Red giant Mira Ceti starts to have comet-like 13Ly long tail, 1st time seen now, speed 468k km/h, since then 40k tons of cosmic dust deposited annually on Earth, He^{-3} content 5 000 times higher than on Earth

23,8 Ma to 5,3 Ma Miocene Epoch

20	c	C	Beta Pictoris creates local solar system, planets, cosmic bombardment, high CO_2 concentration, CO_2 ice
15,1 ±0,1	c	K,X	Ries crater, 24km diameter, caused by a chondrite stone meteorite, size 1,5 x 1km, 10^9t, high pressure mineral coesite found on site, Southern Germany
15 ±1	c	X	3,8km diameter impact crater, Steinheim, Germany

Subject Ref.	Source Ref.	
7,5 **Ma** c	W	Supernova explosion, "lace nebula" in constellation Cygna still visible, 1,5 Ly away, fragments fly with 600k km through nebula, heating gas and matter to 1M°C, producing metals heavier than Fe (Cu, Hg, Au, Pb), same process as in our solar system
7,0 c	I	Supernova, 6 Ly across, a pulsar at the center spins 30 times/sec, remnants now Crab Nebula

5,3 Ma to 1,8 Ma Pliocene Epoch

5,0 ±3 c	X	8km diameter impact crater, Bigach, Kazakhstan
5,0 c	X	52km diameter impact crater, Kara-Kul, Tajikistan
5,0 ±1 c	X	10km diameter meteorite impact crater, Karla, Russia
5,0 c	P	Speculation a 45m deep 720k km^2 sea gushed from the interior, instantly frozen, now covered with iron oxide, Mars
4,0 c	P	Most recent eruption of a volcano, Mars (see 3,8 Ga)
3,7 ±0,3 c	X	2,5km diameter impact crater, Roter Kamm, Namibia
3,5 ±0,5 c	X	18km diameter impact crater, El'gygtgyn, Russia
3,0 c	X	12km diameter impact crater, Avak, Alas/USA (95 Ma)
3,0 ±0,3 c	X	390m diameter impact crater, Aouelloul, Mauritania
3,0 c	X	1,75km diameter impact crater, Talemzane, Algeria
2,8 c	Q	Supernova explosion deposits Fe 60, near Hawaii, Northern Pacific

1,8 Ma to 42,0 ka Lower Paleolithic Age

1,4 ±0,1 c	X	3,44km diameter impact crater, New Quebec, Quebec, Canada
1,07 c	X	10,5km diameter impact crater, Bosumtwi, Ghana
1,0 c	AB	A double star in Orion Nebula, each 0,41 sun mass, should be identical, but light emission shows 50%, diameter and temperature 10% differences
1,0 c	X	460m diameter impact crater, Monturaqui, Chile
900 **ka** ±100 c	X	14km diameter impact crater, Zhamanshin, Kazakhstan
540 ±1,5 c	X	170m diameter meteorite impact crater, Boxhole, Northern Territory, Australia
345 c	X	12,6km diameter impact crater, Aorounga, Chad
300 c	X	870m diameter impact crater, Wolfe Creek, W.Australia
270 c	X	270m diameter impact crater, Dalgaranga, W.Australia
220 ±52 c	X	1,13km diameter crater, Tswane, formerly Pretoria Saltpan, South Africa
100 c	X	450m diameter meteorite impact crater, Amguid, Algeria
100 c	X	4,5km diameter impact crater, Rio Cuarto, Argentina

	Subject Ref.	Source Ref.	
82 **ka**	c	5,P X	Hoba NIFE meteorite largest known: 9m^3, originally 15t, broke into 77 pieces in area 360 x 110km, largest piece 650kg, Gibeon, Namibia
60	c	Q	Meteorite "Dar al Gani 670" ex Mars, Libya
59	c	K	Last time Mars close (56M km) to Earth prior to 2003
52 ±6	c	X	1,83km diameter meteorite impact crater, Lonar, India
50	c	X,K	160m diameter meteorite impact crater, Odessa, Tex/USA
49 ±3	c	H,T X	Fragment of 42m diameter meteorite, broke up 14km above ground, 20m across, hit at 43 000km/h, 150x power of A-bomb, crater 1,18km diameter, 175m deep, ring wall 35m high, Barringer, Arizona, USA

42,0 ka to 10 ka Upper Paleolithic Age

26	c	1	Penultimate time Pole Star stood true North
21,4 ±9,7	c	X	1,9km diameter impact crater, Tenoumer, Mauritania
14	c	P	Explosion of Supernova, now green beetle-shaped nebula
13	c	P	Mars meteorite "Alan Hills 84 001", Greenland ice
11,65	c,e	P	Sirius B imploded, became a "white dwarf", surface 300x harder, interior density 3 000x higher than diamond, claimed to be "manna from Heaven", the red star of the Egyptians and to have caused end of ice age
11	c	AB	Cassiopeia A supernova explosion
10	c	X	100m diameter meteorite impact crater, Morasko, Poland

10,0 ka to 7,0 ka Mesolithic/Archaic Age

7,0	c	X	300m diameter meteorite impact crater, Macha, Russia

7,0 ka to 5,0 ka Neolithic Age

5,0	c	1	Dragon constellation true North

Glossary of some terms used in this section, according to ref. AA

Sequence of layers of a dying star, starting at the surface:
hydrogen, helium, carbon, neon, oxygen, silicon, iron core
Sequence of observations after explosion of a supernova:
neutrons, X-rays, visible light, nebula of debris forming new star

Red Giant	remains of stars <1,4 solar masses, expanding exterior of dying star, largest stars in universe,
Blue Giant	because luminosity of red giant increases, deuterium is converted to iron, which is converted back to helium
White Dwarf	extremely hot imploding red/blue giant, neutron core, all fuel is being burned
Black Dwarf	the white dwarf after all fuel is burned
Supernova	neutron core (10 - 60km diameter) of a white dwarf explodes (see above), producing all the elements of the Mendeleyev Table of Elements beyond iron
Pulsar = Neutron Star	remains of stars of 1,4 to 2,5 solar masses, core of exploded supernova, spinning neutron star consists of tightly packed neutrons
Black Hole	remains of stars of >2,5 solar masses, as above, but so dense that light cannot emerge
White Hole	opposite of black hole, according to theory the connection between them is Einstein-Rossen Bridge or wormhole
Singularity	"cosmic egg", time 0, space 0 (my thought !), temperature infinite
Super-galaxy	group of 100's or 1000's of galaxies, revolving around each other
Quark	basic matter particles
Gluon	messenger particles
Plasma condition	the 4th state of matter: solid - fluid - gas - plasma)

Isotope: variants of elements, differing by number of neutrons and atomic mass, all have identical number of protons, which determine the specific element
Radio-active isotopes emit alpha particles (2 protons, 2 neutrons) or emit or absorb beta particles (1 electron)
Emission of a beta particle leads to conversion of a neutron to a proton, changing the nucleus loading and another higher element appears
Absorption of a beta particle leads to conversion of a proton to a neutron, changing the nucleus loading and another lower element appears

Thoughts on the Big Bang theory of Stephen Hawking

Amongst other things, the standard theory states, that at the time of the Big Bang (the singularity) all matter of the universe was concen-trated in a tiny ball so small that it had no dimension at all. This makes me suspicious, because this seems to violate common sense. Even the tiniest conglomeration of compressed matter has a dimension, but is definitely not a non-dimensional pin head. This line of speculation looks to me like mental acrobatics.
My layman's idea is, that at the Big Bang there was nothing but ENERGY, maybe in the form of (mass-less) photons (no Space, no Time, no Matter), because only Energy does not require any of the other components.
We know that there are things which behave like particles one moment, and as energy (radiation) the next. Energy could have exploded (similarly to ball lightning), creating Space and Time, which would have enabled Matter to be formed, requiring Space and Time to exist for the revolution of atomic particles around the nuclei.
We now have the theory of an inflationary universe, where matter is created piece-meal, so to speak, first the lighter and later the heavier elements. But here are also problems: the postulated initial expansion of the universe conflicts with the law that the Speed of Light is absolute (nothing can move faster than 300 000km/s). Was this law not existing yet ? If all matter was only created after the Big Bang, what then did the non-dimensional singularity consist of ? If the Big Bang is supposed to have created matter, why was then matter formed afterwards ?

The following statements were found in:
Hawkins, A Brief History of Time: 2 photons (without mass) can produce electrons and positrons, mass = matter
National Geographic Magazine 2008, Large Hadron Collider at CERN:
Violent collision of energy will create matter, which in turn will create sub-atomic particles
Search for the unstable Higgs bosun (possibly 100 -200x the mass of a proton), giving mass to fundamental particles
ALICE at CERN will re-create conditions immediately after the Big Bang

Any suggestions/criticisms ?

Quote: "This is one of those views which are so absolutely absurd that only very learned men could possibly adopt them" Bertrand Russel

Quote: "The scientists of today think deeply instead of clearly. One must be sane to think clearly, but one can think deeply and be quite insane" Nicola Tesla

Big Bang Notes 1 (ref. AD)

A singularity = infinity (impossible condition) means that a theory needs to be changed, because in nature there are no singularities.
A photon is a quantum of light (energy) without mass
Neutrinos are matter
Stars vary in size from 0,1 to 100 Sun masses
Hubble constant: 72 ±5km/s/Mpc
Mpc (megaparsec) = ±3,26 MLy = ±3 x 10^{19}km
Big Bang microwaves of 160 GHz, 2mm length and 2,735K temperature = proof of hot plasma of free electrons and protons and photons
Based on present knowledge: the universe is flat
We have no clue as to the character of dark matter nor dark energy, but the latter could possibly be repulsive vacuum energy

4 fundamental forces of the universe:
gravity, weak but universal and long distances, strong with large masses, causes celestial orbits, works by exchange of gravitons
weak nuclear force, 2nd weakest, causes radio-activity, effects all matter particles but not force-carrying particles, operates through W and Z bosons
electromagnetism, 2nd strongest, short distances, acts between charged particles, between 2 electrons 10^{24} times stronger than gravitation, causing electrons to orbit the nuclei, photons emit and exchange energy
strong nuclear force, shortest range, holds together the quarks forming the protons and neutrons and these to form the nuclei, using quarks = matter particles, but possibly carried by gluon particle

Present distribution of matter and energy in the universe:

baryonic shining matter (*)	0,4%
dark matter	3,6%
non-baryonic dark matter (**)	26,0%
dark energy	70,0%
	100,0%

(*) protons and neutrons bound in atoms = matter as we know it
(**) protons and neutrons as free particles, not bound in atoms
only baryonic matter closely tied to photons until 13,7 Ga less 380ky

Planck scale: 3 natural constants c = speed of light, G = gravitation
H = Planck's efficiency quantum (*)
resulting in: smallest possible length of 10^{-33}cm
shortest possible time of 10^{-44}s
weakest possible energy of 10^{-28}eV
1 eV = energy gained by an electron passing through a potential difference of 1 Volt
(*) representing the divide between classical physics (relativity theories) and quantum physics

Big Bang Notes 2 (ref. AE)

Neutrons and protons consist of 3 quarks each
H atom = 1 proton plus 1 electron
Macro-molecules formed very early on Earth, probably in oceans, self-reproducing, errors formed new macro-molecules, then prokaryotes

General Notes

The very earliest of the data of this "Cosmic Eon" has now taken on a more definite appearance, with the published results from the WMAP exercise being available, which claims a mere 1% margin of error. Later data are still very vague and contradictory, and have for this reason been left in the listing until further results from WMAP are published

The abbreviation "Ly" stands for "light year", a distance of
$9,4605 \times 10^{12}$km = 9 460 500 000 000km
GLy, MLy, kLy = multiples

Current universe theory: accelerating expansion, with 130G galaxies, each with up to 100G stars
Standard Model: 4% atomic, 21% "black" matter, (a gas, does not emit nor absorb light, exerts gravity, electrically neutral), 75% "black" energy

Milky Way: age 13,2Gy, a spiral galaxy with 6 arms, 300G stars, 600M sun masses of interstellar matter, surrounded by 165kLy diameter "halo" with 150 star clusters, rotating in 186My, 120kLy diameter, periphery 3kLy, center 16kLy thick in form of "beam" 27kLy* long (7kLy more than previously thought), old red stars, center of Milky Way is a Black Hole "Sagittarius A*" of 4M sun masses, source of quasars as bright as 100G stars, 100k stars ≤1 Ly away, sun 27kLy* away, revolves every 230 My
* query: 2 times 27kLy in one compilation ??

Peony Nebula star found by Spitzer infra-red telescope is 100 million times bigger, 3,2 million times brighter and 150x heavier than our Sun

Meteorite Impact Website:

Further details of meteorites are available on the internet at:
www.unb.ca/passc/ImpactDatabase
there appear to be many simultaneous impacts, like the recent Shoemaker meteorite(s)

g geological: **tectonics, volcanics, orogenies, sediments, oceans, ocean floods**

4,6 Ga to 3,8 Ga Priscoan Era

	Subject Ref.	Source Ref.	
4,6 **Ga**	g	F	Earth a ball of igneous molten rocks (see 4,4 Ga)
4,59	g	U	Earth has 65% of present size, largely segregated into core and mantle
4,55	c,g	AM	Start of planet formation(see 4,567 and 4,4 Ga)
4,54	c,g	AM	Best estimate of Earth's age
4,53	c,g e	U F,Q	Earth struck a glancing blow by a Mars-sized object, which is mostly thrown into Earth's orbit, part falls back, vaporizing part of the mantle, rest forming Moon surface, tilted Earth's axis, now spins in a conical path for 26My, creating seasons and tides, increased revolutions, rotating NiFe nucleus creates magnetosphere, protecting atmosphere from solar wind (see 4,55 Ga)
4,404	g,e	W AM	Oldest zircon crystal in globally oldest sandstone deposits, proof of presence of water, Pilbara, Western Australia (see 4,252 and 3,0 Ga)
4,4	g,e	7,F	Rocky islands in magma ocean, crust probably has present average thickness of 35km, first water (see 4,6 and 3,9 Ga)
4,3	g	7	Melting of the interior of the Earth, NIFE core
4,28	g	AB	Nuvvuagittuq volcanic greenstone belt, Quebec, Canada
4,252	g	W	Oldest diamond inclusions in zircon crystals, Pilbara, Western Australia (see 4,406 Ga)
4,1	g	F	Grano-diorite rocks of Acasta, Canada (see 4,03 Ga)
4,03	g	AB	Acasta gneiss, Northern Territory, Canada (4,1 + 3,9)
3,9	g	T	Earth crust completely solidified (see 4,4 Ga)
3,9	g	G,3	Greenland gneisses, metamorphic greenstone, possibly part of vanished north-western continent, Huronian orogeny, Arctic Canada (see 4,03 Ga)
3,9	g,e	U	Oldest sedimentary banded iron rocks, indication of surface water, Amitsoq terrane, Isua Group, Greenland
3,85	g	P AM	Quartz/clinopyroxene oldest water-lain sedimentary rocks, Isua Group, Greenland

3,8 Ga to 2,5 Ga Archean Era

3,8	g	5	Swaziland shield, oldest rocks of Africa, South Africa
3,644	g	AH U	Intrusion of 1st granites, , grano-diorite, high Na content, Komatiite basalt part of ancient continental and oceanic crusts, Kaapvaal craton, Barberton, South Africa (see 3,3 Ga)

	Subject Ref.	Source Ref.	
3,6 **Ga**	g	1	Siberian shield formed (see 2,5 and 1,5 Ga)
3,553	g	AH	Basement granites, Pongola, South Africa
3,45	g	AH	Start of formation of Barberton etc. greenstone belts, South Africa (see 3,0 Ga)
3,4	g	U	Oldest island arc by subduction of oceanic crust with associated batholiths, eroded sediments fill ocean trench, Barberton, South Africa (3,3 and 3,2 Ga)
3,3	g	U	Oldest island arc eroded, Barberton, S.Africa (3,4 Ga)
3,3	g	AH	End of formation of Barberton etc. greenstone belts, start of post-greenstone granite intrusions, South Africa (see 3,644 and 3,0 Ga)
3,2	g	U	Ripple marks in oceanic sandstones, Barberton, S.Afr.
3,2	g	U	Island arcs amalgamate, form oldest micro-continent, Kaapvaal craton, South Africa (see 3,3 and 3,4 Ga)
3,1	g	U	Granites, high K content, Kaapvaal craton stabilized, South Africa (see 3,074 Ga)
3,1	g	1	Baltic/Ukrainian shields exist
3,074	g	U	Rifting and thinning of Kaapvaal craton, eruption of rhyolites, South Africa (see 3,1 and 2,97 Ga)
3,0	g	U	UR super-continent starts to assemble: parts of southern Africa, Madagascar, India, western Australia, eastern Antarctica (see 1,5 Ga)
3,0	g	AH	End of post-greenstone granite intrusions, South Africa (see 3,3 Ga)
3,0	g	U AF	Oldest diamonds formed 100-200km below at 900-1 300 C, ejected by explosive volcanic eruptions at 10-30km/h (Eggler, 1989), last few km probably at several 100km/h, otherwise they would have turned into carbon, Southern Africa (see 2,0 Ga)
3,0	g	H	Pongola super group astride greenstone belt, South Africa (see 3,45 Ga)
3,0	g	AB	Globally oldest sand deposits, Jack Hills, Western Australia (see 4,406 Ga)
3,0	g	P	Northern Scandinavian orogeny, Kola peninsula, Russia (see 1,9 Ga)
2,97	g	U	Rifts subside, Kaapvaal craton submerged, start of Witwatersrand Supergroup (see 3,074 and 2,714 Ga)
2,914	g	AH U	Granitic crust sags, formation of large Witwatersrand Basin (inland sea), alluvial gold deposits laid down, Witwatersrand and Zululand, South Africa
2,9	g	AM	Formation of Great Dyke mineral deposits, Zimbabwe
2,9	g,b	S	Carbonaceous kerogen (bitumen) of biological origin (Hallbauer), Witwatersrand, South Africa
2,8	g	H	Start of Witwatersrand deposits of up to 8km thick and 400 000km^2 of mixed lava and sediment (conglomerates), South Africa (see 2,5 Ga)
2,8	g	R	Basement granite/gneiss laid down, Zimbabwe

	Subject Ref.	Source Ref.	
2,8 **Ga**	g	S	Extensive volcanic activity, Southern Africa
2,714	g	AH	Zimbabwe craton collides with and fractures Kaapvaal craton, Ventersdorp flood lavas cover the Witwatersrand Basin, 100 000km^2 magma outpours, 2km thick, creates 6km high mountain ridge (Limpopo Belt), now completely eroded, South Africa (see 2,97 Ga)
2,65	g	U	Kaapvaal craton again flooded, South Africa (2,714 Ga)
2,6	g	B	Black Reef, overlaying Schagen paleosols on Archean basement = oldest terrestrial ecosystem, Swaziland
2,6	g,e b	AH	Start of Transvaal stromatolitic dolostones, free oxygen generation, South Africa (see 2,4 Ga)
2,5	g	H	End of Witwatersrand deposits of up to 8km thick and 400 000km^2 of mixed lava and sediment (conglomerates), South Africa (see 2,8 Ga)

2,5 Ga to 1,6 Ga Early Proterozoic Period

2,5	g	H	Start of massive banded ironstone formation (1,8 Ga)
2,5	g	W	Granulite facies start to metamorph Archean granites into Charnockite group of gneissose rocks, but only in former Gondwana continents, Madras, India (550 Ma)
2,5	g	AH	Billions of tons of dolomitic limestone deposits, Transvaal/Griqualand West basin, South Africa
2,5	g	U	Start of Arctica super-continent: parts of northern Canada, eastern Siberia, Greenland (3,6 and 1,5 Ga)
2,4	g,e	AH	End of Transvaal stromatolitic dolostones, free oxygen generation, South Africa (see 2,6 Ga)
2,3	g	H	Start of extensive marine sedimentation (see 1,8 Ga)
2,2	g	AH	Transvaal iron formations deposited, South Africa
2,1	g	H	Australia has only half of present area, eastern Australia (Adelaide and Tasman orogenies) added later in conjunction with Samfrau orogeny (see 400 Ma)
2,061	g	U,5	Bushveld complex developed, globally largest Cr, Pt and V deposits, Merensky and UG2 reefs, largest igneous lopolith, 65 000km^2, 8km thick, South Africa (see 2,054 Ga)
2,054	g	AH	End of Bushveld complex intrusion, S.Africa (2,061)
2,049	g	U	Volcanic pipe carrying copper and apatite (phosphor mineral), Phalaborwa complex, South Africa
2,023	c,g	U	New theory of combination of Vredefort Dome meteorite impact with hot spot mantle plume, South Africa
2,0	g	U	Atlantica super-continent starts: parts of South America and West Africa (see 1,5 Ga)
2,0	g	K	Formation of diamonds, Kimberley, South Africa (see 3,0 and 1,6 Ga)
2,0	g	H W,T	Wopmay orogeny, gunflint cherts, metamorphosed quartzite rocks form mountains, Lake Superior, Canada

Age	Subject Ref.	Source Ref.	
2,0 **Ga**	g	W AJ	Great Unconformity, sedimentary base formed then, later overlaid by younger sandstones, from Arizona, USA to Alberta, Canada, sediments start to form Grand Canyon area, USA (see 1,7 Ga)
2,0	g	H	Tectonic rift formations look like at present, Canada
2,0	g,e	3,6 W	Banded Fe formation ends = free oxygen ±2% of present values (see 3,9 and 1,9 Ga, 580 Ma)
2,0	g,e	W	Continents and oceans similar to present appearance but in different shapes and positions
1,9	g	Q	Ocean crust subducted under African plate, creating rift along Richtersveld coast, Namibia (see 1,6 Ga)
1,9	g	P	Svekofennian orogeny, Southern Scandinavia (3,0 + 1,8)
1,9	g	H	Begin of consolidation of several cratons to North American continent (see 850 Ma)
1,9	g	AC	Formation of Columbia or Nuna (Nena ?) super-continent (see 1,8 and 1,6 Ga)
1,9	g	H	Canadian craton grows by accretion of Baltica
1,9	g,e	U	Sedimentary rocks stained red by iron oxide, proof of significant free O_2, Kaapvaal craton, South Africa (see 2,0 Ga)
1,85	g	H	North America/Greenland nucleus of Laurentia, added Northern Ireland/Scotland, Scandinavia, Siberia
1,8	g	U	Start of Columbia, a speculative super-continent of unspecified components (see 1,9 and 1,5 Ga)
1,8	g	H	End of extensive marine sedimentation (see 2,3 Ga)
1,8	g	H	End of massive banded ironstone formation (2,5 Ga)
1,8	g	W	Ocean is covering Southern Natal to Cape, South Africa
1,8	g	U	Collision of Congo craton with Kaapvaal/Zimbabwe craton, Ubendian Belt, Southern Africa
1,8	g	P	Gothic orogeny, Southern Scandinavia (see 1,9 Ga)
1,7	g	P	Filipstad granite strip and Dalarna volcanoes, Sweden
1,7	g	AJ W	Sandstones of the Great Unconformity are metamorphosed by magma intrusions to schist, Grand Canyon area, USA (see 2,0 Ga and 500 Ma)

1,6 Ga to 650 Ma Riphean Period

Age	Subject Ref.	Source Ref.	
1,6	g	Q	Richtersveld rift closed again, causing orogeny parallel to coast, Namibia (see 1,9 Ga)
1,6	g	U	Kimberlite pipes, Postmasburg, S.Afr. (2,0 + 1,2 Ga)
1,6	g	U	Nena super-continent of Arctica, Baltica, Ukraine, western N.America, eastern Antarctica (see 2,5 + 1,9 + 1,3 Ga)
1,6	g	H	Probable rifting of Angara (= Siberia) from North American plate, later drifting towards Baltica (= Europe), forming Ural
1,5	g	U	End of Columbia speculative super-continent (1,8 Ga)

	Subject Ref.	Source Ref.	
1,5 **Ga**	g	U	Formation of Ur, Arctica and Atlantica super-continents complete (see 3,0 + 2,5 + 2,0 Ga)
1,3	g	U	End of Nena super-continent (see 1,6 Ga)
1,3	g	Q	Basement granites/gneisses, Namibia
1,3	g	W	Antarctica drifts over and eliminates ocean, joins Africa, forming Namaqua-Natal Mobile Belt (see 1,1 Ga and 450 Ma)
1,2	g	AH	Cullinan, globally oldest kimberlite pipe, yielding largest diamond ever found, South Africa (see 1,6 Ga)
1,2	g	U AG	Nepheline syenite =alkaline (K and Na) volcanoes, Pilanesberg, South Africa, Kola peninsula, Siberia and in Greenland
1,1	g	U	Rodinia super-continent formed by collision of Nena, Ur and Atlantica super-continents (see 700 Ma)
1,1	g	H,U	Grenville orogeny, due to collision of Canadian shield with super-continent Rodinia, surrounded by the Panthalassan Ocean (see 1,0 Ga, 700 Ma)
1,1	g	AH	Start of Namaqua-Natal mountains S.Africa (1,1 + 1,0)
1,1	g	H	"Geo Catastrophe", an aborted continental rift, 100m wide, 1 500km long, USA
1,1	g	K	Porongurups Range appears, Australia
1,067	g	AB	Margate suite of metamorphic rocks laid down, S.Afr.
1,025	g	AB	Granite intrusions, Marble Delta, Natal, South Africa
1,0	g	AH	End of Namaqua-Natal mountain building, South Africa (see 1,1 Ga)
1,0	g	W	Southern edge of Kaapvaal craton subducted, forming Natal Metamorphic Province and mountain range of metamorphosed rocks and granites 1 000's of km long Natal/Cape Province, South Africa (see 490 Ma)
1,0	g	P	"Augen"-porphyry, Malmoe, Sweden
1,0	g	P	Dahlsland/Telemark orogeny, Scandinavia
1,0	g	P	A mountain has sunk to 5km depth, Copenhagen, Denmark
850 **Ma**	g	H	Completion of consolidation of several cratons to North American continent (see 1,9 Ga)
835	g	I	Ultrabasic igneous rocks, St.Paul, Mid-Atlantic
800	g	H	Formation of rift (mobile) zones where later the continents would separate from Gondwana (see 182 Ma)
800	g	AG	Ayers Rock not a sandstone monolith, but also consists of shales, mudstones and conglomerates (see 100 Ma)
750	g	AC	Rodinia super-continent breaks up into Proto-Laurasia and Proto-Gondwana super-continents, separated by *Proto-Tethys*, and Congo craton (1,1 Ga, 720, 700 Ma)
750	g	AG	Eruptions of the chain of volcanoes south of the Massif Central, Cap d'Agde, France
740	g	AH	Start of Pan-African mountain building (see 570 Ma)

	Subject Ref.	Source Ref.	
720 **Ma**	g	AC	Proto-Laurasia split into Laurentia, Siberia (NE of Laurentia, separated by *Paleo-asian ocean)*, Baltica (east of Laurentia, separated by *Iapetus ocean)* (750)
700	g	AB	During "Snowball Earth" drop stones transported by glaciers onto floating/melting ice sheets, Namibia
700	g	H,U	Rodinia super-continent breaking up into Ur with eastern Antarctica, Laurentia, Atlantica, Baltica (Europe), Siberia and dispersing globally, creating *Iapetus ocean* separating North America/Greenland, Gondwana and Baltica (Europe) (1,1 Ga, 700, 500, 380)
700	g	K	Seychelles granites rise, not as an island, but in the interior of Gondwana

650 Ma to 600 Ma Vendian Period

600	g	H	Metamorphosis of banded iron stones ends

600 Ma to 543 Ma Ediacaran Period

600	g	AC	Begin of Pannotia super-continent, largely around the poles, with a small strip near the equator connecting the polar masses (see 540 Ma)
600	g	U	Begin of formation of Gondwana by collision of Ur with eastern Atlantica super-continents (see 550, 520 Ma)
600	g	R,U	Malmesbury Sediments, Cape Province, South Africa
600	g	S	Otavi system, Namibia
600	g	S	Start of granite emplacements, which weakened the Gondwana plate, Cape, South Africa
570	g	AH	End of Pan-African mountain building (see 740 Ma)
550	g	U	Ur and Atlantica now welded together, Gondwana consolidated: Africa/South America/Australia/India Antarctica/Madagascar/Falkland Plateau (see 600 Ma)
550	g	W	End of Granulite facies metamorphing Archean granites into Charnockite group of gneissose rocks, but only in former Gondwana continents, Madras, India (2,5 Ga)

543 Ma to 490 Ma Cambrian Period

540	g	AC	End of Pannotia super-continent (see 600 Ma)
540	g	K	Granitic base of Table Mountain solidifies, Cape Town, South Africa (see 260 Ma)
525	g	H	Gondwana, Laurasia (N.America/Greenland/Scotland), Siberia, Baltica, Kazakh, China, all continents/ cratons near equator, mostly flooded by shallow seas (see 520 Ma)

	Subject Ref.	Source Ref.	
520 **Ma**	g	AC	Gondwana and Baltica are formed, formation of Laurentia near the equator, with the *Panthalassic ocean* to north and west, the *Iapetus ocean* in the south and the *Khanty ocean* in the east (600, 525 Ma)
510	g	S	End of granite emplacement, Cape, S.Africa (600 Ma)
500	g	U	Arabia added to Gondwana (see 380 Ma)
500	g	P	Start of formation of Natal Group sandstones, Natal, South Africa (see 350 Ma)
500	g	H	Micro-cratons of England and Scotland are separated for 100s of km by *Iapetus ocean*
500	g	H	North America/Greenland (Laurentia), Siberia (Angara), Scandinavia/Northern Europe (Baltica), *Iapetus* ocean development ends, separating these major plates (see 700, 460 Ma)
500	g	U	Rift between African and Falkland plates starts, forms Agulhas Sea between Africa and Antarctica (550 Ma)
500	g	W AJ	Great Unconformity: schists submerged by sea, covered by new sediments, Grand Canyon area, USA (see 1,7 Ga and 250 Ma)
500	g	Y	Chihuahuan desert, Mexico/Texas

490 Ma to 443 Ma Ordovician Period

490	g	W	1st sediments deposited on African continent, Cape/ Natal coast, South Africa (see 1,0 Ga)
480	g	U	Table Mountain sandstones deposited in Agulhas Sea, Cape Peninsula, South Africa
480	g	AC	Avalonia micro-continent breaks from Gondwana and drifts towards Laurentia, later forms US, Nova Scotia and England
470	g	H	Baltic Sea north of England (near N.Africa), Scotland near Greenland, separated by *Proto-Tethys* (380, 300)
470	g	H	1st Appalachian (Taconian) orogeny starts, creating base of Appalachians (see 420 and 395 Ma)
460	g	H	*Iapetus* narrows, Laurentia, Baltica close (700, 440)
450	g	AC	Siberia close to Euramerica, with the *Khanty ocean* separating them
450	g	I	Melt water channel in Sahara sandstone by ice cap of South Pole (plate has wandered 8 000km) (see 1,3 Ga)

443 Ma to 417 Ma Silurian Period

440	g	AC	Baltica collided with Laurentia (see 460, 430 Ma)
430	g	AC	Laurentia, Baltica and Avalonia merge to minor super-continent Euramerica or Laurussia, closing *Iapetus ocean* and North and South China crotons rift from Gondwana (see 440 Ma)

	Subject Ref.	Source Ref.	
420 **Ma**	g	H	Taconian orogeny ends (see 470 Ma)

417 Ma to 354 Ma Devonian Period

415	g	P	Start of red gneiss, metamorphosed ex older granites, Spessart, Germany (see 325 Ma)
>400	g	H	Samfrau orogeny along southern coast of Gondwana, adding the eastern part to Australia (see 2,1 Ga)
395	g	H	Caledonian orogeny Scotland and Scandinavia (350 Ma)
395	g	1	Canadian folding, intrusions
395	g	H	2nd Appalachian (Acadian) orogeny starts due to Laurentia, Greenland and Baltica fusing to Old Red Continent (=Laurasia), closing *Iapetus ocean* (see 500, 380 Ma)
390	g	P	Cu, Zn, Pb ores deposited, Rammelsberg, Harz, Germany
385	g	H	Laurasia and Gondwana possibly temporarily connected
380	g	H	*Iapetus* closed, England/Scotland, Northern/Southern Ireland united (see 700, 470 and 460 Ma)
380	g	H	Proto-Andean orogeny starts (see 200 Ma)
380	g	H	*Proto-Tethys* separates Gondwana and Old Red Continent and China/Siberia (see 700 and 395 Ma)
380	g	AC	Southern Europe separates from Gondwana, heading towards Euramerica across new *Rheic Ocean* (340 Ma)
380	g	H	Turkey, Arabia are part of Gondwana, Florida attached to North Africa/South America (see 500 Ma)
375	g	H	Hunsrueck slates deposited, Germany

354 Ma to 290 Ma Carboniferous Period

350	g	P	End of formation of Natal Group sandstones, Natal, South Africa (see 500 Ma)
350	g	P	Le Piton de la Fournaise, oldest still active volcano, Isle de La Reunion, Indian Ocean (see 250 and 65 ka)
350	g	H	Acadian/Caledonian orogenies end, USA/Europe (395 Ma)
340	g	AC	NW Africa collided with, South America moved north touching southeast Euramerica (see 380 Ma)
340	g	H	Limestone deposits ex fusulines, crinoids, bryozoan detritus creating 100m high reefs
325	g	P	Variscan orogeny, end of granite metamorphosed to red gneiss, Spessart, Germany (see 415 and 320 Ma)
325	g	H	Siberia and China separate (see 260 Ma)
320	g	H	3rd Appalachian (Alleghenian/Variscan) orogeny starts in Laurasia by collision of Laurasia and North Africa, causes Mauritanean/Atlas orogeny in North Africa (see 280 Ma)
312	g	P	Porphyry granite, Fichtelgebirge, Germany (290 Ma)

Subject	Subject Ref.	Source Ref.	
310 **Ma**	g	U	Subduction zone along southern margin of Gondwana creates Cape mountains and Karoo depression which later filled with Ecca sediments
300	g	U	Pangaea starts to form, most continents again consolidated (see 260 Ma)
300	g	A	Africa placed east-west, not north-south (see 80 Ma)
300	g	AC	North China craton collides with Siberia, closing most of the *Proto-Tethys* (see 470, 280 Ma)
300	g	AC	Kazakhstania and Baltica crotons collided, closing *Ural ocean* and starting the Uralian orogeny and completing Laurasia (see 260 Ma)
300	g	P	Hercynian orogeny: Harz, Massif Central, Pyrenees, Lake District, Western Europe (see 65 Ma)
300	g	U,5 R	Dwyka tillite, overlaid by sandstone (part of Karoo system), glacial striations when Gondwana drifted over South Pole, Nooitgedacht, South Africa (290 Ma)
300	g	1	Proto-Rocky Mountains start to rise (see 65 Ma)
290	g,e	U	Drifting north of Gondwana ends glaciation, rivers form swamps creating coal deposits, South Afr. (300)
290	g	AB	European plate near equator

290 Ma to 248 Ma Permian Period

290	g	P	Margin granite, Fichtelgebirge, Germany (312, 288 Ma)
290	g	P	Rhyolite, volcanic quartzite porphyry, Spessart, Germany
288	g	P	Central granite, Fichtelgebirge, Germany (290, 286 Ma)
286	g	P	Tin granite, Fichtelgebirge, Germany (see 288 Ma)
280	g	AC	The Cimerian craton starts to drift from Gondwana to Laurasia, closing the *Proto-Tethys* and opening the *Tethys* (see 300, 200 Ma)
280	g	AC	Australia at the South Pole
280	g	H	Alleghenian orogeny stops (see 320 and 80 Ma)
260	g	K	Table Mountain sandstone on granite base, was 3km high, now eroded to 1,5km, South Africa (see 540 Ma)
260	g	H	China, Siberia welded to Europe, create Ural mountain, completing Pangaea, 5km thick sediments (see 325, 300 and 205,2 Ma)
260	g	H	Cathay (=Southeast Asia) the only separate continent
260	g	H	"Zechstein Sea" up to 7 marine saline cycles from the North and evaporations, with 1km deep anhydrite, salt, copper shales and oil deposits Northern Germany/Baltic Sea/East Greenland (see 230 Ma)
260	g	7	Limestone (Karst) plateaux, started out as coral reefs in tropical sea, southern tip of Chile
250	g	P,U	Karoo Sea largely silted up, Ecca and Beaufort shales and sandstones, Fraserburg, South Africa (see 190 Ma)

Ma	Subject Ref.	Source Ref.	
250 **Ma**	g	5	Strong folding, Cape formations, South Africa
250	g	P	Oslo rift, similar to East African rift valley, Larvicite, rhombic porphyry, Oslo Fjord, Norway
250	g	W	Jutland covered by shallow warm ocean, precipitating salt deposits several km thick, overlaid by 4km thick loam/sand, then by a $CaCO_3$ cover, the top salt altered to gypsum, Moensted, Denmark (see 60 Ma)
250	g	7	Top layer of Grand Canyon, USA (see 500 and 5,5 Ma)
248,2	g,e	3	Huge lavas in Siberia, plume volcanism rising 3 000km to surface, lava fields 3km thick, cause acid rain

248,2 Ma to 205,7 Ma Triassic Period

Ma	Subject Ref.	Source Ref.	
240	g	W	Oldest dolomite caves, Nelspruit, South Africa
230	g	H	Shallow "Muschelkalk Meer" (Shelly Limestone Sea), part of the Tethys, covers same area as "Zechstein Sea", flooding from the South, depositing shelly limestones, keuper and red sandstones, Central Europe (see 260 and 2,0 Ma)
225	g	3	*Tethys* covering 65% of Earth's surface (like now), between Laurasia (Eurasia, N.America) and Gondwana at equator, later mostly disappeared into crust (190 Ma)
225	g	AB	Pangaea breaks up: Laurasia (Eurasia, North America) separate from Gondwana (South America, Africa, Australia, Antarctica) (see 205,2 Ma)
215	g	H	Palisades formation in a sill, New York, USA
215	g	H	Petrified Forest, Arizona, USA

205,7 Ma to 144,0 Ma Jurassic Period

Ma	Subject Ref.	Source Ref.	
205,2	g	AB	1st signs of Pangaea break-up into Laurasia (Eurasia, North America) and Gondwana (South America, Africa, India, Australia, Antarctica) (see 260, 175, 150 Ma)
205,2	g	AB	Intensive volcanism starts, Southern Africa (183 Ma)
200	g	AC	The Cimerian craton collided with Eurasia, closing the *Proto-Tethys* and opening the *Tethys* enclosed by Pangaea in the form of a "C" (see 280 Ma)
200	g	AB	Jura Sea, depositing huge sediments of shelly limestone, covers Central Europe (see 185 Ma)
200	g	V	Start of Gulf of Mexico, separating North and South America (see 160 Ma)
200	g	H	Andean orogeny starts by S.America subducting Nazca oceanic plate, crust 70km thick, still active (see 380, 50 and 16 Ma)
200	g	Q	Land surface completely covered by granite

Ma	Subject Ref.	Source Ref.	
195 **Ma**	g,e	W	Start of clay deposits under Paris, London, Oxford and most of France and England by a warm tropical sea (see 140 Ma)
190	g	H	Tethys separates Eurasia and Africa, leftovers are present Mediterranean, Black + Caspian Seas (225 Ma)
190	g	U	Karoo sand sea becomes sandstones, S.Africa (250 Ma)
185	g	P	"Jurassic Coast" formed, Devon / Dorset, England (200)
183	g	AH	Karoo dolerites intrude, 2M km^3 Drakensberg basalts erupt, 2km thick, now eroded to 1,8km covering Karoo sandstones, South Africa (see 205,2 Ma)
182	g	U	Begin of break-up of Gondwana (see 800, 140 Ma)
181	g	S	End of lava outpours, Drakensberge, South Africa
180	g	U	Mantle plumes cause Maluti Mountain to rise, S. Africa
180	g	7	Magma streams, Dry Valleys, Antarctic see 160 Ma)
180	g	Y	Massive dunes formed from eroding Appalachians turned into sandstone, Colorado Plateau, USA (see 160 Ma)
175	g	AC	Start of rift of Pangaea, resulting in formation of Laurasia and Gondwana (see 205,2 and 150 Ma)
170	g	H	Start of shallow maritime calcareous deposits (aragonite needles), their great mass forcing sea bed to sink 10km, Bahamas Bank, West Atlantic
170	g	5	Limestones form south of Massif Central, France (130)
165	g,e	Z	Start of violent period of breaking up of continents and climate changes (see 155 Ma)
160	g	A	New Guinea separates from Australia
160	g	A,I	North America separates in the form of many islands from Laurasia, starting North Atlantic (100, 80, 55)
160	g	1	Plateau lavas pour out, Antarctica (see 180, 120 Ma)
160	g	Y	Forests, rivers, swamps, inland seas with dinosaurs, crocodiles, giant seagoing lizards and huge sharks, Morrison Formation, Colorado Plateau, USA (180, 150)
160	g	I,V	Gulf of Mexico now established, near Cuba (see 200 Ma)
155	g	H	"Solnhofen limestone slates", Jura mountains, Southern Germany, Minette ores, Lorraine, France
155	g	H	Sierra Nevada orogeny, California, USA
155	g,e	Z	End of violent period of breaking up of continents and climate changes (see 165 Ma)
150	g	H	Pangaea ends, Gondwana a separate super-continent (see 205,2 and 175 Ma)
150	g	H	Penninian Sea starts between Africa and Eurasia as the Iberian and Penninian cratons drift between Europe and Africa (see 45 Ma)
150	g	H	"Dinosaur grave-yard", Morrison Formation, North America (see 160 Ma)
150	g	I	Earliest known earthquakes in California, USA (60 Ma)
145	g	AC	Gondwana begins to rift into continents (see 140 Ma)

144,0 Ma to 65,0 Ma Cretaceous Period

	Subject Ref.	Source Ref.	
140 **Ma**	g	U AC	Gondwana breaking up into Africa/South America and Antarctica/Australia/India/Madagascar, possibly due to mantle plume beneath Mozambique, creating the Southern Indian Ocean (see 182, 145, 120 and 50 Ma)
140	g	P	Elbsandstein mountain formed, Saxony, Germany
140	g	W	End of clay deposits under Paris, London, Oxford and most of France and England (see 195 Ma)
135	g	S	Diabase (dolerite) eruptions, Namibia
135	g	I	Age of rocks from sea floor, found by "Glomar Challenger" expedition, Pacific Ocean
130	g	H	Western alpine orogeny starts (see 80 and 40 Ma)
130	g	5	Limestone rocks change to dolostone (dolomite), due to interaction of water and magnesium, Montpellier le Vieux, France (see 170 and 65 Ma)
125	g	P	Fine-grained basalt, Southern Sweden
125	g	I	Northern Pacific floor was 3 000km south of the equator, drifted north, then south, then north again (see 65 and 55 Ma)
125	g	W	Seas repeatedly cover southwestern USA
120	g	U	India/Madagascar separate from Antarctica/Australia, Australia has reached its present place (see 140 Ma)
120	g	1	Plateau lava out-pour ends, Antarctica (see 160 Ma)
120	g	S,U	Start (mitochondrial DNA) of rifting between Africa and South America, eventually creating the South Atlantic, Falkland Plateau (as part of South America) separates from Africa (see 100 Ma)
120	g,e	AB	Antarctica already occupying the South Pole, but still ice-free (see 35 Ma)
110	g	AM	Begin of kimberlite intrusions, producing most of the diamond deposits, South Africa (90 Ma)
110	g	H	Tethys floods parts of England, France, North Germany, depositing chalk, Dover, Champagne, Isle of Ruegen
110	g	AM	Atlantic, rifting from south to north (160 Ma)
100	g	I,U	Volcanic Kimberlite diamond pipes reach surface due to erosion of surrounding rocks, South Africa (see 2,0 Ga and 90 Ma)
100	g	K	Uluru (= Ayers Rock) appears, remnant of vast sandstone plateau, Central Australia (see 800 Ma)
100	g	A	Ocean between North/South America and Eurasia/Africa has widened considerably (see 120 and 80 Ma)
100	g	AB	Breakup of Laurentia, western part of Svalbard now northern tip of North America, opening of Arctic Sea (see 17,5 Ma)
100	g	AG	Yellow Mountain formed, glaciers of Quaternary ice age shape granite pinnacles, Anhui, East China

	Subject Ref.	Source Ref.	
100 **Ma**	g	AC	South America separates from Africa, starting the South Atlantic
98	g	Q	Flooding of "Great Artesian Basin" ended, Australia (see 110 Ma)
95	g	AC	India/Madagascar rift from each other, India moving north at 15cm/a (a plate tectonic record !), Madagascar got stuck on the African plate (110 Ma)
95	g	H	Mowry Sea flooding from Caribbean to Artic, developing into the cretaceous Interior Seaway, N.America (67)
90	g	S	Diamond-bearing kimberlite pipe in volcanic caldera, Orapa, Lesotho (see 120 Ma)
90	g	AM	End of kimberlite intrusions, South Africa (110 Ma)
90	g	AM	Plateau lava out-pour ends, Antarctica (see 160 Ma)
85	g	H	Sea levels high, continents covered by shallow seas
85	g	AB	Western China covered by up to 35°C tropical sea
82	g	I,K	New Zealand separates from Australia/Antarctica Tasman Sea starts to open (see 80 and 70 Ma)
80	g	1	Europe, Russia, North America, North Africa, Australia, Arabia flooded
80	g	A	African axis from east-west to north-south (300 Ma)
80	g	AB	Driftwood on beaches of shallow sea petrified to fossil forest, since then land has risen over 400m, Natal South Coast, South Africa
80	g	H	Eastern alpine orogeny starts (see 130 and 40 Ma)
80	g	H,3 P	Chalk formations by protist fossils, coccoliths and algae, isle of Ruegen, Baltic Sea, Germany
80	g	1	Coal deposits in Siberia
80	g	7	New Caledonia separates from Australia (see 82 Ma)
80	g	A	North America consolidates, North/South America and Eurasia/Africa are closer again (see 160 and 100 Ma)
80	g	H	Appalachians now largely eroded (see 280 Ma)
75	g	H	Corsica, Sardinia, Sicily are minor cratons
75	g	Q	Western Interior Seaway (Mowry Sea) splits N.America
70	g	H	Africa, South America, India separated, Australia and Antarctic still connected (see 40 Ma)
70	g	1	Seychelles separate from drifting India (see 95 Ma)
70	g	K	Tasman Sea at present configuration (see 82 Ma)
70	g	Q	North Western Hawaiian Islands formed
70	g	I	Vast chert deposits created by skeletons of opalinida micro organisms, North Atlantic sea bed
70	g	V	Start of orogeny of Sierra Madre Oriental by sub-duction of Cocos plate, Mexico (see 40 Ma)
70	g,z	W	Giant frog "Devil Toad", 4,5kg, armored, not related to African, but to S.American ceratophrys, suggests that Madagascar still was, via much warmer than present Antarctica, part of Africa (see 110 Ma)
67	g	H	Closure of cretaceous Interior Seaway (see 95 Ma)

	Subject Ref.	Source Ref.	
65 **Ma**	g,e	AJ L	Deccan Traps, 2km thick, 500 000km^2, include 500 000km^3 of basalt, sulfuric acid rain, contributing to K/T extinction ?, India

65,0 Ma to 54,8 Ma Paleocene Epoch

65	g	G,K	Africa collides with Europe, forming the Atlas mountains, North Africa, Pyrenean orogeny "rejuvenated Hercynian chain" (see 320 and 300 Ma)
65	g	5	Les Causses limestone plateaux, south of Massif Central, France (see 130 and 10 Ma)
65	g	Q	Greenland rifts from Scotland/Scandinavia (see 60 Ma)
65	g	I	Movement of Northern Pacific floor reversed direction, drifting south (see 125 and 55 Ma)
65	g	W	Rocky Mountain orogeny starts, USA (see 300, 35 Ma)
60	g	A	Atlantic ocean narrower than now (see 20 Ma)
60	g	1	Renewed flooding of Europe (see 26 Ma)
60	g	H	Beringia land bridge in existence, rifting between Greenland, North America and Europe starts (65, 50)
60	g	W	Separation of Northern Europe and North America created layer-cake of related igneous rocks, Isle of Rhum, Scotland
60	g	5	Rhein-Graben, triple junction rift between Black Forest and Vosges, Germany/France
60	g	7	"Giant's Causeway", lava flows into the sea, instant cooling, 1 000s of hexagonal blocks, Northern Ireland
60	g	W	Bryozoan chalk with flint bands, Moensted, Sealand, Denmark (see 250 Ma)
60	g	1	Laramide orogeny, mountains rise 2km, later Grand Canyon developed there, Colorado, USA (see 45 Ma)
60	g	I	Earliest known strong earthquakes, California (150 Ma)
55	g	AC	Laurasia rifts into Laurentia and Eurasia, opening the North Atlantic (see 160 Ma)
55	g	1	Italy rotated 43° clockwise (see 45 Ma)
55	g	P	Volcano in Skagerrak Straits, youngest in Scandinavia, lighter than water Mo-clay deposits: ⅓ clay mineral smectite, ⅔ diatoma fossils, interspersed by 179 volcanic ash layers over few My, isle of Mors, Denmark
55	g	I	Northern Pacific floor drifts north again (125, 65 Ma)

54,8 Ma to 33,7 Ma Eocene Epoch

51	g	AG	Insect fossils in amber show less divergence from specimen from Africa or Madagascar than expected after assumed long separation, Cambay, India (95 Ma)
50	g	I	Philippines emerge due to tectonic plate movements
50	g	U	Australia separates from Antarctica (see 140 Ma)

	Subject Ref.	Source Ref.	
50 **Ma**	g	W	India collides with Asian plate, moving fastest ever at 20cm p/a because there is a hot spot underneath, causing start of Himalayan orogeny, having increased plate thickness to 100 km (see 5,0 Ma)
50	g	Q	Andes orogeny accelerates to 25mm/100a since then (see 200 and 16 Ma)
50	g	W	Volcano eruption creates St.Barthélemy Is., Caribbean
50	g	V	Uplifted Central Mexican Plateau (see 2,0 Ma)
50	g,e	Q	Beringia land bridge exposed due to dropped sea levels, Alaska (see 60 Ma)
45	g	H	Iberian and Penninian cratons wedged between African and Eurasian plates, Atlas and Pyrenees, Alps and Carpathians start to form, the Penninian Sea (part of Tethys) closed, some sea floor now on 4 477m Matter-horn mountain, Switzerland (see 150, 20 Ma)
45	g	1	Italy rotated 25° anti- clockwise (see 55 Ma)
45	g	H	Laramide orogeny ends, North America (see 60 Ma)
45	g	H	India collides with Indochina on the Eurasian plate (see 20 Ma)
45	g	3	South America an island, Pacific/Atlantic connected (see 3,5 and 3,0 Ma, 12 ka)
40	g	H	Atlantic ocean widens between Scandinavia and Green-land, rifting between N.America and Greenland stops
40	g	H	Alps reach nearly present form (see 130, 80, 8,0 Ma)
40	g	H	Start of Turgai Sea east of Ural, connecting Tethys and Arctic Sea (see 30 Ma)
40	g	H AC	Australia, moving north at 5cm/a, separates from Antarctic, finalizing the break-up of Gondwana (70)
40	g	1	Eastern Pacific floor develops
40	g	I	Limestone outcrops from ocean floor still rise, Cuba
40	g	V	Sierra Madre Oriental established, Mexico (see 70 Ma)
38,5	g	AM	Start of most recent volcanic eruptions, Southern Africa (see 35,7 Ma)
37	g	G	Aegean, Adriatic, Western Mediterranean seas formed
37	g	G	Volcanoes: Vesuvius, Etna, Stromboli, Italy, and Massif Central, France (see 12 Ma)
37	g	Q	Badlands clay stone deposits start, S.Dakota, USA (25)
36	g,z	I	Land bridge connects Cuba and South America, primates (new-world monkeys) migrate to Cuba
35,7	g	AM	End of most recent volcanic eruptions, Southern Africa (see 38,5 Ma)
35	g	AC	India starts to collide with Asia (see 20 Ma)
35	g	I	Fiji Islands appear
35	g	S,U	Drake Passage between Australia and Antarctica opened, starting circum-Antarctic oceanic circulation (7,5)
35	g	1	Central Rocky Mountains rising, North America (65 Ma)

	Subject Ref.	Source Ref.	
35 **Ma**	g,e	AB	Land bridges between Antarctica and South America and Australia disappeared, glaciers increased, cooling of surrounding seas increased the plankton, leading to development of whales and dolphins (120, 14 and 7,5)
34	g	D	Tasmania separate from Australia (see 43 ka)

33,7 Ma to 23,8 Ma Oligocene Epoch

30	g	U	Africa reaches its present geographic position (10 Ma)
30	g	W	East African "Graben" (rift) starts (see 27,5 Ma)
30	g	I	Ethiopian highlands created by volcanic eruptions (20)
30	g	H	European flooding reaches Russia and Himalayas, connecting via Turgai Straits with Arctic Ocean (40 Ma)
30	g	Q	Pacific plate with Kure Atoll travels over "hot spot" at 8cm p/a, Hawaii (see 5,6 Ma)
30	g	V	Start of Sierra Madre Occidental by extensive volcanic eruptions ,Mexico (see 20 Ma)
30	g	H	Orogeny of the Cascades (Mt.St.Helens), still in progress today, USA
27,5	g	AF	Arabia starts separating from Africa, creating the Red Sea and Afar Basin and Nubian and Somalian plates, extending into the Rift Valley of East Africa (see 30 Ma, 250 ka)
26	g	H	End of Turgai Sea east of Ural, connecting Tethys and Arctic Sea (see 30 and 24 Ma)
25	g	H	African plate stationary over mantle since then
25	g	AB	A rift creates start of Baikal Sea, largest liquid freshwater reservoir (20%) of 23 000km³,160 bar pressure, 1 637m deep, 673km long, 48km wide, Siberia
25	g	Q	Badlands deposits end, S.Dakota, USA (see 37 Ma)
25	g	AH	Cape Peninsula high mountains an island, South Africa
24	g	B	African plate collides with Eurasia, closing off E. Mediterranean Sea (see 10 Ma)
24	g	H	Global maritime regression: Europe, Turgai Straits dry again, Southern Russia (see 40 and 26 Ma)

23,8 Ma to 5,3 Ma Miocene Epoch

20	g	H	Start of Ethiopian and Kenyan "Domes", E.Africa (30)
20	g	G	Apennines start folding, Italy (see 45 Ma)
20	g	7	Isle of Madeira, volcanic stock 6km above ocean floor, 4km above sea level, South Atlantic
20	g	W	Fuerteventura Is. appears, Canary Is., South Atlantic (see 15 Ma)
20	g	A	Atlantic ocean in present form (see 60 Ma)
20	g	U	Uplift in East by 250m, in West by 150m, South Africa (see 5,0 and 1,4 Ma)

	Subject Ref.	Source Ref.	
20 **Ma**	g	K	Lake George Range rises, Australia
20	g	H	Start of Himalaya orogeny by Indian plate pushing underneath Tibet (see 35 and 15 Ma)
20	g	V	Sierra Madre Occidental in present form by erosion of lava and ash, Mexico (see 30 Ma)
<20	g	H	Afar triangle lifted as oceanic crust, Indian Ocean
18	g	H	Start of collision of Eurasia/Africa (see 14 Ma)
18	g	Z	Oldest recorded eruption of Yellowstone super-volcano, a 560km string of calderas across Idaho, Oregon and Nevada due to SW move of tectonic plate, USA (2,1 Ma)
17,5	g	W	Previously isolated Arctic Ocean, during a temperature maximum, now opened to Atlantic by Fram Straights between Greenland and Svalbard, North Atlantic (100)
17	g	7	Old bed of Orange River, diamonds washed downstream from Kimberley fields, South Africa
16	g	1	Main Andean orogeny (see 200 and 50 Ma)
16	g	AJ	175 000km^3 basalt flow, Columbia River Plateau, USA
15	g	L	Ethiopian/Kenyan "domes" by ±3km plate movements (20)
15	g	1	Zagros mountains rise, Iraq/Iran
15	g	W	Gran Canaria, Lanzerote appear, Canary Islands, South Atlantic (see 20 Ma)
15	g	5	Island of Borneo appears, Indonesia
15	g	H	Australian plate collides with Asian plate (20 Ma)
15	g	AM	India collides with Asia (see 20 and 5,0 Ma)
15	g,e	AH	Antarctica separates from Gondwana, drifts to South Pole, ice cap starts to form (see 5 Ma)
14	g	H	North Sea floods lower parts of Europe up to Cologne, creating extensive brown coal deposits, N.Germany
14	g	H	End of collision of Eurasia/Africa (see 18 Ma)
13	g	I,Q	Huge earthquakes, with intervals of ca. 2 000 years along Teton Valley create Teton Range, North America (see 12 ka)
12	g	W	Huge volcanic eruption of Massif Central, France (see 37 Ma, 900 ka)
12	g	V	Start of Baja California rifting, moving north, California/Mexico (see 6 Ma)
12	g	V	Arc of volcanic islands fused, Caribbean plate starts to move them towards present Panama
10	g	U	African plate in present position versus mantle (30)
10	g	5	Les Cirques limestones collapse, France (65, 6,0 Ma)
10	g	1	Western Mediterranean Sea closed off from oceans, deposited rock salt (see 24 and 5,0 Ma)
9,0	g	Q	Volcano at Atlantic mid-ocean rift forms Iceland
8,0	g	W	Mauritius and Reunion appear, Indian Ocean
8,0	g	H	Alpine orogeny ends (see 40 Ma)

	Subject Ref.	Source Ref.	
7,5 **Ma**	g,e	S	"Terminal Miocene Event", caused by the separation of Australia and South America from Antarctica, creating cold Benguela current, 40-70m sea level drop results in land bridge at Gibraltar, Mediterranean (35, 14)
6,0	g	N	Cirque de Navacelles formed, 285m deep and 500m wide limestone sinkhole, Massif Central, France (10 Ma)
6,0	g	Z	Collision of Pacific and North American plates causes rise of Alaska Range, highest point of North America with 6 194m Mt.McKinleay, Alaska
6,0	g	V	Baja California in present position, Mexico (12 Ma)
5,6	g	H	Kauai, oldest (volcanic) island of Hawaii, appeared and moved over "hot spot" at 5cm/annum (30, <1,0 Ma)
5,5	g	7	Colorado River starts Grand Canyon (see 250 Ma)
5,4	g	W	Land bridge closing Mediterranean by submarine mountain rising 70mm per 100 years, dropping sea levels >2km, happened several times, Gibraltar and Messina, creating 2 separate basins (7,5 and 5,0 Ma)

5,3 Ma to 1,8 Ma Pliocene Epoch

5,0	g	I,H	Mediterranean Sea again connected to oceans, salinity normalized, sea levels rise again (see 5,4 + 5,3 Ma)
5,0	g	H AM	Main Himalayan orogeny starts, caused by Indian plate colliding with Asian plate, still active at 5cm/a (see 15 Ma)
5,0	g	AB	Tectonic movements cause several islands to converge, create mountain ranges, New Zealand
5,0	g	AG	Galapagos Archipelago rises from sea floor due to still very active volcanic eruptions, South Pacific
5,0	g,e	U	100m uplift of western, 900m of eastern South Africa, cutting off moist sea winds results in formation of Kalahari Desert, South Africa/Namibia (20 and 1,4 Ma)
3,0	g	K	Mt.Kenya volcano starts to erupt, East Africa (750 ka)
3,0	g	W	Under-sea lava flow of 5 000 000km^2, larger than the entire USA, Ontong Plateau, Java, Indonesia (<3,0 Ma)
3,0	g,e	AB	North and South American plates collide, deviating warm equatorial current to become Gulf Stream, changing global climate, causes Arctic to be ice-free, creating glaciation elsewhere, Panama seaway closes, Isthmus of Panama (see 45 Ma and 12 ka)
<3,0	g	AJ	Ontong Java Plateau, 5 Mkm^2 of sea-bed lava, near Borneo (see 3,0 Ma)
2,1	g	Z	Explosion of Yellowstone super-volcano >2 000x the Mt.St.Helens explosion, leaving a hole 72km across, USA (see 18 and 2,0 Ma, 640 ka)
2,0	g	AB	River Main digs 100m deep valley in shelly limestone deposited by "Muschelkalk" Sea, Germany (230 Ma)

	Subject Ref.	Source Ref.	
2,0 **Ma**	g	V	Death Valley, a tectonic rift valley between two mountain ranges, 86m below sea level, maximum temperature 57°C, California, USA
2,0	g	Q	Hotspot under Yellowstone Park 200km deep, magma chamber in 8 - 16km depth, caldera 65 km across, Mammoth Hot Springs with 300+ geysers globally greatest concentration (see 40 ka), "Old Faithful" blows every 74 min, USA (see 2,1 Ma, 640 ka)
2,0	g	V	Yucatan peninsula emerges from ocean, Mexico (50 Ma)
2,0	g b,z	5	Ngorongoro volcano explodes, 18km crater with 100m walls, creating unique closed habitat, East Africa

1,8 Ma to 42,0 ka Lower Paleolithic Age

1,4	g	R	Coastline 100m higher than now South Africa (see 20 and 5,0 Ma, 25 ka)
<1,0	g	H	Hawaii Is., the youngest of the archipelago, appears (see 5,6 Ma, 700 ka)
900 **ka**	g	W	Eruption of group of volcanoes south of Massif Central, France (see 12 Ma)
750	g	I	Eruption of Kilimanjaro (5 895m), East Africa (3,0 Ma)
750	g	AF	Globally largest sand island, Fraser Is., Australia
700	g	P	Basalt "organ", exposed columns, St.Thibery, France
700	g	Q	Big Island created by volcanic action when drifting over a stationary "hot spot", Hawaii (5,6 + <1,0 Ma)
640	g	Z	Most recent explosions of Yellowstone super-volcano 1 000x the strength of the Mt.St.Helens explosion in 1980, USA (see 2,1 Ma, 70 ka)
500	g	7	Natural limestone bridge over the Ardeche, Pont d'Arc, Massif Central, France
450	g	AB	Volcanic appearance of Marion Is., South Atlantic
300	g	7	Mt.Shasta explodes, lava tubes, California, USA
250	g	Z	Ruapehu volcano starts, still active, New Zealand
250	g	H	Victoria Lake created as part of ongoing widening of the Rift Valley, East Africa (see 27,5 Ma)
250	g	AB	Eruption of Piton de la Fournaise, Reunion (see 350 Ma and 65 ka)
220	g	AB	Eruption of El Chichon, Mexico
200	g	AB	Heavy volcanic activity, Eifel mountain, Germany (11)
125	g,z	K	Coral reef atop a volcano rim rises from the sea, home of rhea (flight-less bird), giant tortoise, Aldabra Is., Seychelles, Indian Ocean
74	g,e	V,Q	Extreme eruption Mt.Toba, 100 x 30km crater, 48km high ash cloud, 96km long caldera, 3 000x stronger than Mt.St.Helens, "volcanic winter", Sumatra, Indonesia
70	g	Z	Most recent volcanic eruption, Yellowstone, USA (see 640 ka)

	Subject Ref.	Source Ref.	
65 **ka**	g	AB	Eruption of Piton de la Fournaise, Reunion (250 ka)
60	g	V	Borneo and Sumatra joined as Sunda, separated by 100km of open sea from Australia, Tasmania and Indonesia joined as Sahul
43	g	D	Tasmania is again part of Australia (34 Ma and 14 ka)

42,0 ka to 10 ka Upper Paleolithic Age

40	g	7	Uzar caldera, 2nd largest geyser field, Kamchatka, Siberia (see 2,0 Ma)
35	g,e	W	Super-lake Makgadikgadi, 100m deep, now dry salt pan due to tectonic movements, Botswana (see 5,0 Ma)
30	g	K	Start of erosion of a mountain of clay at Mt.Colombis, France (see 18 ka)
25	g	R	Coastline similar to now, South Africa (20 and 1,4 Ma)
25	g	V	Plinian pyroclastic eruption of Vesuvius, Italy (see 22,5 ka)
22,5	g	V	Plinian pyroclastic eruption of Vesuvius, Italy (see 25 and 17 ka)
21	g,e	AF	Bahamas limestone plateau mostly exposed, sea level 120m lower than at present (see 18 ka)
20	g	AB	Present sand dunes start to form, Natal, S.Africa
20	g,e	R	Coastline of Southern Africa 60m lower than now, rivers dig deep off-shore channels (see 25 ka)
18	g	K	Oldest of the "hatted ladies": = clay columns topped by a glacial rock, Mt.Colombis, France (see 30 ka)
18	g,e	AF	End of Bahamas limestone plateau exposure (see 21 ka)
18	g,e	Z	Due to low ice age oceans Japan's main island is connected by a land bridge to Asia, not to Japan (10 ka)
17	g	V	Plinian pyroclastic eruption of Vesuvius, Italy (see 22,5 and 15 ka)
15	g	V	Plinian pyroclastic eruption of Vesuvius, Italy (see 17 and 11,4 ka)
15	g	I	Southern crater of Ol Doinyo Lengai volcano erupts, 18km across, natro-carbonatite lava is 50% cooler than magmatic lavas, disintegrates in days, Tanzania
14	g	D	Tasmania finally separate from Australia (see 43 ka)
14	g	AB	Explosion of huge volcano, Laombok Is., Indonesia
12	g	W	North/South America are apart, oceans are connected, again, Panama (see 3,5 and 3,0 Ma)
12	g,e	Q	Glaciers carve canyons, Teton Range, Wyoming (13 Ma)
11,4	g	V	Plinian pyroclastic eruption of Vesuvius, Italy (see 15 and 8,0 ka)
11	g	P	Last volcanic eruption, Eifel, Germany (see 200 ka)
11	g,e	8	South coast of Arctic Sea near Iceland, Thames, Weser, Elbe tributaries of the Rhine in the area of the later North Sea (see 7,0 ka)

	Subject Ref.	Source Ref.	
11 **ka**	g,e	7	Beringia land bridge disintegrates, sea-levels 100m lower than now (see 20 ka)
10,5	g	AG	Start of Yoldia Sea ice reservoir (present Baltic Sea) (see 10,2 ka)
10,2	g	AG	End of Yoldia Sea ice reservoir due to amelioration of last ice age (see 10,5 and 8,9 ka)
10	g	8	Japan finally an archipelago (see 18 ka)

10,0 ka to 7,0 ka Mesolithic/Archaic Age

10,0	g	K	Puy de Dôme, part of a chain of volcanoes, Massif Central, France
10,0	g,e	H	Scandinavia starts rising after glaciers receded, so far by 100m (±1cm/a) in the center
10,0	g,e	J	Britain is now an island, North Sea and Channel are flooded (see 11 ka)
8,9	g	AG	Fresh water Ancylus Sea (present Baltic Sea) has replaced the Yoldia ice reservoir (see 10,2 ka)
8,0	g	V	Plinian pyroclastic eruption of Vesuvius, Italy (see 11,4 ka)
7,7	g	Z	600m deep crater lake, result of volcanic eruption, Mt.Mazama, High Cascades, Oregon, USA
7,0	g	W	Last active volcano, France
6,9	g,e	AG	Scandinavia keeps rising, blocking the connection between the Ancylus Sea and the oceans, turning it into a fresh water sea (see 8,2 and 5,0 ka)

Etymology of geological times

Cosmic Eon	my own term to cover the times before Earth solidified
Pre-Cambrian Eon	before Cambrian, originally thought to have 1st (oldest) fossils
Priscoan Era	now some call it Hadean refers to Hades,
Archean Era	oldest time era
Primary Time (now defunct)	**1st** geological time
Proterozoic Era	dawn of life era
Riphean Period	Riphean mountains of Roman authors
Vendian Period	originally included Ediacaran
Ediacaran Period	Ediacaran Hills, Australia
Phanerozoic Eon	fossil yielding eon
Paleozoic Era	ancient life era
Cambrian Period	Latin name of Wales
Ordovician Period	a Welsh tribe
Silurian Period	a Welsh tribe
Devonian Period	Devon, England
Carboniferous Period	coal bearing period
Permian Period	province of Perm, Russia
Secondary Time (now defunct)	**2nd** geological time
Mesozoic Era	middle life era
Triassic Period	named in German after 3 systems: Jurasic Lias/Keuper/Muschelkalk
Jurassic Period	Jura mountains, Germany/Switzerld.
Cretaceous Period	"Kalk" (German) = limestones
Cenozoic Era	Cenomanian chalks
Tertiary Time (now more or less defunct)	**3rd** geological time
Paleogene Period	old genological period
Paleocene Epoch	old geological epoch
Eocene Epoch	dawn of recent time epoch
Oligocene Epoch	less recent time epoch
Neogene Period	new geological time period
Miocene Epoch	middle recent time epoch
Pliocene Epoch	more recent time epoch
Quaternary Time (on the way out)	**4th** geological time
Pleistocene Epoch	most recent time epoch
Holocene Epoch	present time epoch
Paleolithic Age	old stone age
Mesolithic Age	middle stone age
Neolithic Age	younger stone age

Some geological common terms **(ref. U)**

For names of minerals and rocks see specialized literature

Amygdales	mineral deposits in gas bubbles of vesicular lava
Batholith	large body of intrusive igneous rock $>100km^2$
Caldera	volcanic "mouth"
Cenotes	sink holes near impact crater margins
Coccoliths	petrified plankton organisms
Continental	crust, 35km thick, more under mountain ranges, granitic
Craton	ancient core of continent, a micro continent, see Pluton
D''	(pronounced D double prime), transition zone between the Mantle and the CMB (Core-Mantle Boundary)
Diapirism	slow upward rise of less dense through denser material
Graben	elongated block of rocks lowered by faulting
Kaapvaal	ancient croton of African continent
Lithification	loose sediment is cemented into sedimentary rock
Matrix	finer grained material cementing larger parts in a rock
Metamorph.Belt	suture between cratons and continents, permanently weak
Moho	Mohorovicic Discontinuity, at base of Earth's crust
Oceanic Crust	5 - 7km thick, basalt and gabbro
Orogeny	rising mountains due to tectonic activity
Paleomagnetism	magnetism imprinted in rocks when they formed
Pluton	rock body $<100km^2$, see Craton
Pyroclastic	flow of lava and volcanic superheated gases
Shield volcano	flat bed of fluid lava
Spherule	spherical particle, often concentrically layered
Subduction	subsidence of a plate into the mantle
Supercontinent	amalgamation of several previously separate continents
Tectonics	continental drift plus sea-floor spreading
Terrane	region of similar geological formations and history
Unconformity:	older rocks atop younger ones, or igneous intrusion into country (older) rocks, or sedimentary rocks overlay metamorphosed rocks

Observations & Comments:

The obvious and usual contradictions between sources

Apparently, the movement of continents and cratons was cyclical and they changed position and adherence repeatedly.

Rodinia, surrounded by Iapetus Ocean, appears to have been similar to Pangaea, surrounded by Panthalassan Ocean, but is also claimed to be similar in composition to Gondwana

Laurentia: North America plus Greenland and Baltica

Laurasia: North America and Greenland plus Eurasia

Gondwana (or Rodinia) and Laurentia existed prior to the formation of Pangaea, Gondwana and Laurasia after Pangae

The Super-Continents and Super-Oceans

this mainly follows the Rogers-Unrug theory as given by ref.U, plus additional info from wikipedia (ref.AC)

3,0 **Ga**	g	U	**UR** super-continent starts to assemble: parts of southern Africa, Madagascar, India, western Australia, eastern Antarctica (see 1,5 Ga)
2,5	g	U	Start of **Arctica** super-continent: parts of northern Canada, eastern Siberia, Greenland (3,6 and 1,5 Ga)
2,0	g	U	**Atlantica** super-continent starts: parts of South America and West Africa (see 1,5 Ga)
1,9	g	AC	Formation of **Columbia or Nuna (Nena ?)** super-continent (see 1,8 and 1,6 Ga)
1,85	g	H	North America/Greenland nucleus of **Laurentia**, added Northern Ireland/Scotland, Scandinavia, Siberia
1,8	g	U	Start of **Columbia**, a speculative super-continent of unspecified components (see 1,9 and 1,5 Ga)
1,6	g	U	**Nena** super-continent of **Arctica**, Baltica, Ukraine, western N.America, eastern Antarctica (see 2,5 + 1,9 + 1,3 Ga)
1,5	g	U	Formation of **Ur**, **Arctica** and **Atlantica** super-continents complete (see 3,0 + 2,5 + 2,0 Ga)
1,5	g	U	End of **Columbia** speculative super-continent (1,8 Ga)
1,3	g	U	End of **Nena** super-continent (see 1,6 Ga)
1,1	g	AC	**Rodinia** super-continent forms (see 750 Ma)
1,1	g	U	**Rodinia** super-continent formed by collision of **Nena**, **Ur** and **Atlantica** super-continents (see 700 Ma)
1,1	g	H,U	Grenville orogeny, due to collision of Canadian shield with **Rodinia**, surrounded by ***Panthalassic*** *ocean* (700)
800 **Ma**	g	H	Formation of rift (mobile) zones where later the continents would separate from **Gondwana** (see 182 Ma)
750	g	AC	**Rodinia** super-continent breaks up into **Proto-Laurasia** and **Proto-Gondwana** super-continents, separated by ***Proto Tethys*** *ocean*, and Congo craton (see 1,1 Ga, 720, 700 Ma)
720	g	AC	**Proto-Laurasia** split into **Laurentia**, Siberia (northeast of **Laurentia)**, separated by ***Paleo-asian*** *ocean*, and Baltica (east of **Laurentia)**, separated by ***Iapetus*** *ocean* (see 750 Ma)
700	g	H,U	**Rodinia** super-continent breaking up into **Ur** with eastern Antarctica, **Laurentia**, **Atlantica**, Baltica (Europe), Siberia and dispersing globally, creating ***Iapetus*** *ocean* separating North America/Greenland, **Gondwana** and Baltica (Europe) (1,1 Ga, 700, 500, 380)
600	g	AC	Begin of **Pannotia** super-continent, largely around the poles, with a small strip near the equator connecting the polar masses (see 540 Ma)
600	g	U	Begin of formation of **Gondwana** by collision of **Ur** with eastern **Atlantica** super-continents (see 550, 520 Ma)
550	g	U	**Ur** and **Atlantica** now welded together, **Gondwana** consolidated: Africa/South America/Australia/India Antarctica/Madagascar/Falkland Plateau (see 600 Ma)
540	g	AC	End of **Pannotia** super-continent (see 600 Ma)

525	g	H	**Gondwana**, **Laurasia** (N.America/Greenland/Scotland), Siberia, Baltica, Kazakh, China, all continents/ cratons near equator, mostly flooded by shallow seas (see 520 Ma)
520	g	AC	**Gondwana** and Baltica are formed, formation of **Laurentia** near the equator, with the ***Panthalassic*** *ocean* to north and west, the ***Iapetus*** *ocean* in the south and the ***Khanty*** *ocean* in the east (600, 525 Ma)
500	g	H	Micro-cratons of England and Scotland are separated for 100s of km by ***Iapetus*** *ocean*
500	g	H	North America/Greenland (**Laurentia**), Siberia (Angara), Scandinavia/Northern Europe (Baltica), ***Iapetus*** ocean development ends, separating these major plates (see 700, 460 Ma)
470	g	H	Baltic Sea north of England (near N.Africa), Scotland near Greenland, separated by ***Proto-Tethys*** (380, 300)
460	g	H	***Iapetus*** narrows, **Laurentia** and Baltica close (see 700, 440 Ma)
450	g	AC	Siberia close to **Euramerica**, with the ***Khanty*** *ocean* separating them
440	g	AC	Baltica collided with **Laurentia** (see 460, 430 Ma)
430	g	AC	**Laurentia**, Baltica and Avalonia merge to minor super-continent **Euramerica or Laurussia**, closing ***Iapetus*** *ocean* and North and South China crotons rift from Gondwana (see 440 Ma)
395	g	H	2nd Appalachian (Acadian) orogeny starts due to **Laurentia**, Greenland and Baltica fusing to **Old Red** Continent **(= Laurasia)**, closing ***Iapetus*** *ocean* (see500, 380 Ma)
385	g	H	**Laurasia** and **Gondwana** possibly temporarily connected
380	g	H	***Iapetus*** closed, England/Scotland, Northern/Southern Ireland united (see 700, 470 and 460 Ma)
380	g	H	***Proto-Tethys*** separates **Gondwana** and **Old Red** Continent and China/Siberia (see 700 and 395 Ma)
380	g	AC	Southern Europe separates from **Gondwana**, heading towards **Euramerica** across new ***Rheic*** *Ocean* (340 Ma)
340	g	AC	NW Africa collided with, South America moved north touching southeast **Euramerica** (see 380 Ma)
300	g	U	**Pangaea** starts to form, most continents again consolidated (see 260 Ma)
300	g	AC	North China craton collides with Siberia, closing most of the ***Proto-Tethys*** (see 470, 280 Ma)
300	g	AC	Kazakhstania and Baltica crotons collided, closing ***Ural*** *ocean* and starting the Uralian orogeny and completing **Laurasia** (see 260 Ma)
280	g	AC	The Cimerian craton starts to drift from **Gondwana** to **Laurasia**, closing the ***Proto-Tethys*** and opening the ***Tethys*** (see 300, 200 Ma)
260	g	H	China, Siberia welded to Europe, create Ural mountain, completing **Pangaea**, 5km thick sediments (see 325, 300 and 205,2 Ma)

225	g	3	***Tethys*** covering 65% of Earth's surface (like now), between **Laurasia** (Eurasia, N.America) and **Gondwana** at equator, later mostly disappeared into crust (190 Ma)
205,2	g	AB	1st signs of **Pangaea** break-up into **Laurasia** (Eurasia, North America) and **Gondwana** (South America, Africa, India, Australia, Antarctica) (see 260, 175, 150 Ma)
200	g	AC	The Cimerian craton collided with **Eurasia**, closing the ***Proto-Tethys*** and opening the ***Tethys*** enclosed by **Pangaea** in the form of a C (280)
190	g	H	***Tethys*** separates Eurasia and Africa, leftovers are present Mediterranean, Black, Caspian Seas (225 Ma)
182	g	U	Begin of break-up of **Gondwana** (see 800, 140 Ma)
175	g	AC	Start of rift of **Pangaea**, resulting in formation of **Laurasia** and **Gondwana** (see 205,2 and 150 Ma)
160	g	A,I	North America separates in the form of many islands from **Laurasia**, starting North Atlantic (100, 80,55)
150	g	H	**Pangaea** ends, **Gondwana** a separate super-continent (see 205,2 and 175 Ma)
145	g	AC	**Gondwana** begins to rift into continents (see 140 Ma)
140	g	U AC	**Gondwana** breaking up into Africa/South America and Antarctica/Australia/India/Madagascar, possibly due to mantle plume beneath Mozambique, creating the Southern Indian Ocean (see 182, 145, 120 and 50 Ma)
110	g	H	***Tethys*** floods parts of England, France, North Germany, depositing chalk, Dover, Champagne, Isle of Ruegen
110	g	AC	India/Madagascar rift from Antarctica (see 95 Ma)
100	g	AB	Breakup of **Laurentia**, western part of Svalbard now northern tip of North America, opening of Arctic Sea (see 17,5 Ma)
100	g	AC	South America separates from Africa, starting the South Atlantic, rifting from south to north (160 Ma)
95	g	AC	India/Madagascar rift from each other, India moving north at 15cm/a (a plate tectonic record !), Madagascar got stuck on the African plate (110 Ma)
55	g	AC	**Laurasia** rifts into **Laurentia** and **Eurasia**, opening the North Atlantic (see 160 Ma)
40	g	H AC	Australia, moving north at 5cm/a, separates from Antarctic, finalizing the break-up of **Gondwana** (70)

Tectonics: Science or Theory ?

Alfred Wegener formulated his Theory of Tectonic Movements of the Earth's crust in 1912 and published "Die Entstehung (origin) der Kontinente und Ozeane" in 1915. My geography teacher studied under Wegener and taught us in the late 1930's all about this subject. We demolished a papier-mâché globe and fitted Africa and Europe next to South and North America. The fit of Africa and South America was near perfect, not only as to coastal lines, but also as to mountain ranges.
However, Wegener over-estimated the speed of movement (35cm instead of 2cm p.a.). At the time, his theory was ridiculed, because he could not explain the mechanics of these movements, and because he was a meteorologist and geophysicist, not a geologist ! In the meantime it has been discovered that the driving force for plate tectonics were magmatic plumes and "hot spots". At this stage, nothing was known about Gondwana and other super- continents, but in the 1950's/60's it became clear, that this was not just a theory. In the 1970's (?), a world conference was held in South Africa, where Gondwana was discussed in detail by the world's leading geologists, among them Prof.Du Toit of South Africa, a fervent supporter of Wegener. Amazingly, the Anglo-American geographic scientific community refused to accept this (because Wegener happened to be German, and WW2 was still too close ?), even so the driving forces of tectonics were identified by then. The 1970 edition of the Encyclopedia Britannica still insisted that this was just a theory, and there was no entry under Pangaea !

The Geological Structure of the Earth

extracted from B.Bryson, A short History……, 2003 ref.T
approximate thickness in km, measured from the surface

0 - 40km	crust, rocky
40 - 400	upper mantle, hot, viscous rocks
400 - 650	transition zone
650 - 2700	lower mantle
2700 - 2890	D'' layer
2890 - 5150	outer core, liquid
5150 - 6370	inner core, solid

Rocks of the World ref.AJ

inner core, solid NiFe
outer core, fluid NiFe
inner mantel = asthenosphere, semi-fluid rocks = magma
outer mantel, solid rocks
crust, solid, these 2 = lithosphere, consisting of plates and cratons, "swimming" on asthenosphere

e ecological: **atmosphere, glaciation, climate, ocean levels, water, lakes, river floods, Earth's axis/poles**

see also the References section for further notes

4,6 Ga to 3,8 Ga Priscoan Era

	Subject Ref.	Source Ref.	
4,53 **Ga**	c,g e	U F,Q	Earth struck a glancing blow by a Mars-sized object, which is mostly thrown into Earth's orbit, part falls back, vaporizing part of the mantle, rest forming Moon surface, tilted Earth's axis, now spins in a conical path for 26My, creating seasons and tides, increased revolutions, rotating NiFe nucleus creates magnetosphere, protecting atmosphere from solar wind (see 4,55 Ga)
4,404	g,e	W AM	Oldest zircon crystal in globally oldest sandstone deposits, proof of presence of water, Pilbara, Western Australia (see 4,252 and 3,0 Ga)
4,4	g,e	7,F	Rocky islands in magma ocean, crust probably has present average thickness of 35km, first water (see 4,6 and 3,9 Ga)
4,3	e	7	Water etc. expelled, this photo-dissociated to oxygen and hydrogen (see 4see 4,0 Ga)
4,25	c,e	W	Impactor space craft (2005) proves much ice in meteorites, but water differs from ours, oceans are green (iron content), denser atmosphere reddish, now believed water reached Earth from outer asteroid belt meteorites, deflected into Earth orbit by Jupiter (see 4,7 Ga -20 Ma)
4,0	e	Q	A day is less than 10 hours long (see 3,3 Ga)
4,0	e	3,U	1st atmosphere, O_2 level <0,1% of present, mainly CO_2 and some N_2 (see 4,3 Ga)
4,0	e	W	Moderate temperatures of ±90°C and absence of acids allow H and CO_2 to form methane (see 3,9 and 2,5 Ga)
4,0	e	P	Sun radiation only 70% of present, balanced by CO_2 greenhouse effect, temperature 50 - 80°C, atmospheric pressure 30 - 50 bar, today about 1 bar (see 2,5 Ga)
3,9	g,e	U	Oldest sedimentary banded iron rocks, indication of surface water, Amitsoq terrane, Isua Group, Greenland (see 4,4 and 2,0 Ga)
3,9	e,b	3,U	Laminated slime mats and proto-stromatolites formed by blue-green prokaryotes cyano-bacteria photo-synthesize CO_2 into C and O_2, reacted to $CaCO_3$, further reducing the CO_2 content of the atmosphere, Barberton, South Africa (see 4,0, 3,5 and 3,0 Ga)

3,8 Ga to 2,5 Ga Archean Era

	Subject Ref.	Source Ref.	
3,8 **Ga**	e	T,W	Oceans are acidic and shallow and contain almost the present volume of water
3,5	e,b	T,W S	Proto-stromatolites produce O_2 by photosynthesis, Sebakwia, Zimbabwe, Warrawoona, Western Australia and Pilbara, Australia (see 3,9 Ga)
3,45	e	AG	Earth's magnetic field exists, Barberton, S.Africa
3,3	e	AM	Probably 14 hrs/d (see 4,0 and 3,1 Ga)
3,1	e	U	Earth rotating faster, days shorter, more days per year (see 3,3 and 2,45 Ga)
2,95	e	U	Possibly 1st glaciation, South Africa
2,7	e	H	Huron, first known global glaciation (see 2,4 Ga)
2,7	e	W	Underwater volcanoes absorb most O_2, enriching oxygen-rich seabed minerals
2,6	g,e b	AH	Start of Transvaal stromatolitic dolostones, free oxygen generation, South Africa (see 2,4 Ga)
2,6	e	H	Heat production of the Earth only 37% of original, but double the present value
2,6	e	B	Earth has an ozone shield

2,5 Ga to 1,6 Ga Early Proterozoic Period

2,5	e	U	Evidence of global freezing (Snowball Earth theory, Kirschvink) except near underwater volcanoes (see 2,2 and 1,5 Ga)
2,5	e	AF	"Oxygen Revolution", some life starts to depend on oxygen
2,5	e	H	Global heat production double of present, leading to unstable crust
2,5	e	U	CO_2 atmosphere changes to one dominated by N_2, methane production partly compensates for this change, pressure near present
2,45	e	AM	19 hrs/d, 457 d/a, 14,5 lunar months (see 3,1 Ga, 620 Ma)
2,45	e	AM	Moon's recession from Earth was 1,24cm/a, now 3,82
2,4	g,e	AH	End of Transvaal stromatolitic dolostones, free oxygen generation, South Africa (see 2,6 Ga)
2,4	e	H	End of global Huron glaciation (see 2,7 Ga)
2,3	e,b	H	Start of period of abundant stromatolites, free oxygen (see 1,5 Ga and 580 Ma)
2,2	e	W	Global ice age, oceans frozen 800m deep (see 2,5 and 1,5 Ga, 900 Ma)
2,2	e	H	Apparent global glaciation, Canada, South Africa etc.
2,0	g,e	3,6 W	Banded Fe formation ends = free oxygen ±2% of present values (see 3,9 and 1,9 Ga, 580 Ma)

	Subject Ref.	Source Ref.	
2,0 **Ga**	g,e	W	Continents and oceans similar to present appearance but in different shapes and positions
1,9	g,e	U	Sedimentary rocks stained red by iron oxide, proof of significant free O_2, Kaapvaal craton, South Africa (see 2,0 Ga)

1,6 Ga to 650 Ma Riphean Period

1,5	e	U	Renewed global freeze (Snowball Earth theory) (2,5 Ga)
900 **Ma**	e	H	Gnejsoe glaciation, global except Antarctica (see 2,2 and 1,5 Ga and 750 Ma)
850	e	H	Start of series of global or regional glaciations with tillite deposits (see 600 Ma)
750	e	1	Sturtian glaciation (see 900 Ma)
720	e,b	L	Higher oxygen levels allow multi-cellular life (700)

650 Ma to 600 Ma Vendian Period

630	e	AB	CO_2 build-up globally, average temperature changes from -50° to +50°C (see 2,5 Ga, 850 Ma)
620	e	AM	21,9 hrs/d, 400 d/a, 13,1 lunar months (see 2,45 Ga, 400 Ma)
600	e	H	End of a series of global or regional glaciations with tillite deposits (see 850 Ma)

600 Ma to 543 Ma Ediacaran Period

580	e	1	Oxygen ±7% of present value (see 2,0 Ga, 500, 360 Ma)
580	e	H	Sea levels lower than at any time during the Paleozoic, very low in regard to continents (see 440 Ma)
580	e	1,H	Tillites proof Varangian global glaciation except in South America
543	e	3,6	Ediacaran glaciation (see 530 Ma)

543 Ma to 490 Ma Cambrian Period

530	e	7	Cambrian Warming (see 543 and 450 Ma)
500	e b,z	W	Ozone levels are now sufficient to protect terrestrial life incl. animals from UV radiation (see 580 Ma)

490 Ma to 443 Ma Ordovician Period

470	e	H	Equator dissects Canada and Angara (Siberia)
450	e	H	Temporary drop in sea levels due to global ice age (see 530 Ma)

443 Ma to 417 Ma Silurian Period

	Subject Ref.	Source Ref.	
440 **Ma**	e	S	Gondwana ice age, South Pole in central Africa, ice covering most of Africa and South America, but not Antarctica, Greenland tropical, sea levels low (see 580, 430, 360 Ma)
430	e	H	Melting of polar glaciers, sea levels high, warming South pole in southern Morocco (see 440, 380 Ma)
418	e,b	Y	O_2 levels probably higher than now, plants grew only 3cm tall, oldest wildfire recorded, England

417 Ma to 354 Ma Devonian Period

400	e	Q	Year has 400 days at 22 hours (see 620 and 120 Ma)
385	e	H	Devonian global warming (see 330 Ma)
380	e	H	South Pole in Parana basin, South America (440, 430)
360	e	H	Gondwana glaciation ends (see 440 Ma)
360	e b,z	S	O_2 levels 35% of atmosphere in Devonian/Carboniferous, allowing plants/animals to grow large quickly, South Africa (see 580 and 200 Ma)

354 Ma to 290 Ma Carboniferous Period

350	e,z	W	O_2 maximum of 30%, causing fish-like vertebrates to leave the oceans, developing into amphibians (tetrapods) (see 375, 360, 270 Ma)
340	e	H	Highest sea levels, shallow flooding of continents (see 580 Ma)
330	e	Q	Global warming (see 385, 240 Ma)
320	e	P	Start of Permo-Carboniferous ice age, covering Central/South Africa, Antarctica, parts of South America, Australia (see 270 Ma)
300	e	W	Ice cap of Gondwana over Southeast Africa, Antarctica, South India, Northern Australia, Western South America (see 290 Ma)
290	g,e	U	Drifting north of Gondwana ends glaciation, rivers form swamps creating coal deposits, South Afr. (300)

290 Ma to 248 Ma Permian Period

290	e,b	AB	Sparse vegetation of mainly ferns and conifers, arid and warm climate, Central Europe
285	e,z	Q	Marine animals in warm, shallow sea, Moab, Utah (150)
280	e	H	Sea levels rise again (see 250 Ma)
270	e	P	End of Permo-Carboniferous ice age, Gondwana (320 Ma)

	Subject Ref.	Source Ref.	
270 **Ma**	e,z	W	Saurians survived O_2 minimum of 15% by developing new breathing system, using air sacks hidden in hollow bones, inherited by present-day birds (see 350 Ma)
265	e	H	Extreme climatic and sea-level variations
250	e	H	Extreme temperature gradation between poles/equator
250	e	6	Reduced salinity, lower temperatures (sea and land), drop in sea levels (see 280, 100 Ma)
250	e	H	Start of Michigan River as precursor to the Mississippi River, USA
248,2	g,e	3	Huge lavas in Siberia, plume volcanism rising 3 000km to surface, lava fields 3km thick, cause acid rain
248,2	e,z	H	Permian extinction not a single but continuous event over several My, probably caused by cooling and low sea levels

248,2 Ma to 205,7 Ma Triassic Period

240	e	1	Triassic global warming, arid dessert climate (see 330, 215 and 130 Ma)
215	e	1	Warming of Gondwana reaches peak (see 240 Ma)
205,7	e,b	AB	Release of 8 000 Gt CO_2, causes global warming, algae explosion absorbs most maritime O_2,resulting in extinction of 80% of maritime flora, mid-Atlantic

205,7 Ma to 144,0 Ma Jurassic Period

205	e,b	AB	Number of tree species much reduced due to acid rain (see 205,7 Ma), instead pollen of pioneer plants: ferns, horsetails, mosses containing toxic carbon C_2H_4 (see 220, 206 Ma)
200	e	Q	Earth radius speculated to be 38% smaller
200	e	A	Equator runs along West African coast between North and South America (see 40 Ma)
200	e	Y	O_2 levels 10 - 13% of present (see 360, 65 and 50 Ma)
195	g,e	W	Start of clay deposits under Paris, London, Oxford and most of France and England by a warm tropical sea (see 140 Ma)
165	g,e	Z	Start of violent period of breaking up of continents and climate changes (see 155 Ma)
160	e,z	I	Marine plankton evolved, extracting CO_2 from atmosphere using C to form shells, releasing O_2
155	g,e	Z	End of violent period of breaking up of continents and climate changes (see 165 Ma)
150	e	S	Ice age of relatively short duration, South Africa
150	e	H	Sundance Sea floods large part of North America
150	e,b	Q	Semi-arid savanna, Moab, Utah, USA (see 285 Ma)

144,0 Ma to 65,0 Ma Cretaceous Period

	Subject Ref.	Source Ref.	
130 **Ma**	e	Q	Global warming (see 330, 240 Ma)
120	g,e	AB	Antarctica already occupying the South Pole, but still ice-free (see 35 Ma)
120	e	AB AM	Tidal friction slows down Earth's revolutions by 3,82s per 100ky, length of day only 23 hours (see 400 Ma)
110	e	Q	Australia starts to be flooded (see 98 Ma)
100	e	H	Sea levels and global temperatures very high, probably highest average temperatures since then (see 440, 250, 70 Ma)
70	e	H	Global temperatures and sea levels recede again (100)
65	g,e	AJ L	Deccan Traps, 2km thick, 500 000km^2, include 500 000km^3 of basalt, sulfuric acid rain, contributing to K/T extinction ?, India
65	e	T	Global iridium levels 300-500 times higher than normal
65	e	H	Iridium in thin clay band (border clay), Gubbio, Italy
65	e,b	H	Fern spores 99% of micro-flora before extinction, afterwards only 15-30%, most extinct plants with un-serrated leaves used to warm climates, suggesting strong cooling as cause of extinction
64,98 ±50ky	c,e	3,Q	12km diameter meteorite hit (see 160 Ma), 180km diameter crater half under Caribbean water, 3 000 ring cenotes along crater perimeter, globally 10x normal iridium levels in thin clay layer Yucatan, Mexico, (see 205,7 Ma)

65,0 Ma to 54,8 Ma Paleocene Epoch

65	e	S	O_2 levels 30% of atmosphere (see 200 and 50 Ma)
63	e	AB	Huge river system connecting Okavango Delta and Makgadikgadi Lake = Kalahari Basin, Botswana (see 55 and 5,0 Ma)
60	e	U	CO_2 concentration then was 3 500 parts, now 360 parts per million
55	e	U	Ancestral lake Makgadikgadi formed, Kalahari River captures Karoo River to form Orange River, S.Africa (see 63 and 5,0 Ma)
54,8	e	D,Y	Oceanic frozen methane "belch" causes global maximum temperature, destroying many maritime life forms, fresh-water ferns, crocodiles in Greenland, Arctic and Antarctica ice-free (see 40 and 14 Ma)

54,8 Ma to 33,7 Ma Eocene Epoch

	Subject Ref.	Source Ref.	
50 **Ma**	g,e	Q	Beringia land bridge exposed due to dropped sea levels, Alaska (see 60 Ma)
50	e	Y	O_2 levels 18% (see 200, 65 and 40 Ma)
47	e	AG	El Niño effects stronger than at present, Messel, Germany
40	e	H	Begin of period of 5 abrupt temperature drops with global transgression over most continents (see 31 Ma)
40	e	A	Equator near present position (see 200 Ma)
40	e	Y	O_2 levels reach 23% (see 50 Ma)
40	e	I	Global temperature back to normal (see 54,8 Ma)
40	e	H	Antarctic glaciation starts, psychrosphere (cold sea bottom layer), cold seas (see 54,8 and 34 Ma)
35	g,e	AB	Land bridges between Antarctica and South America and Australia disappeared, glaciers increased, cooling of surrounding seas increased the plankton, leading to development of whales and dolphins (120, 14 and 7,5)
34	e	7	Ice sheets start to form for 1st time, Antarctica (see 40 and 30 Ma)
33,7	e	AB	Eocene-Oligocene climate transition, severest since 65 Ma, CO_2 double current levels, rapidly falling, creating start of Antarctic ice sheet
33,7	e	D	Eocene/Oligocene boundary, glaciation maximum

33,7 Ma to 23,8 Ma Oligocene Epoch

31	e	H	End of period of 5 abrupt temperature drops, climate turns arid, sea levels recede, Antarctic ice cap develops (see 40 Ma)
30	c,e	W	Red giant Mira Ceti starts to have comet-like 13Ly long tail, 1st time seen now, speed 468k km/h, since then 40k tons of cosmic dust deposited annually on Earth, He^{-3} content 5 000 times higher than on Earth
30	e	U	Major expansion of ice sheet, Antarctica (34, 23 Ma)
23,8	e	D	Oligocene/Miocene boundary, global glaciations

23,8 Ma to 5,3 Ma Miocene Epoch

23	e	U	Antarctic ice sheet reaches coast line (30 and 6,0 Ma)
20	e	2	East Africa covered by forests (see 10 Ma)
15	g,e	AH	Antarctica separates from Gondwana, drifts to South Pole, ice cap starts to form (see 5 Ma)
15	e	W	500m deep fresh water lake kept liquid by pressure of 4km of ice, largest of 150 similar bodies connected by underground rivers, signs of microbial life ?, coldest place globally -80°C, Lake Vostok, Antarctica

	Subject Ref.	Source Ref.	
14 **Ma**	e	Y	North Pole ice cap similar to present (see 54,8 Ma)
14	e	U	Rapid global cooling, especially Antarctica, start of cold Benguela current, South Atlantic/Africa, causing arification of Namib desert, Namibia (see 7,5 Ma)
11,8	e	AB	Amazon river source now in Andes mountains, earlier sources in central mountains, South America
10	e	2 AL	East Africa covered by fragmented forests, alternating seasons of wet and dry (see 20 Ma)
7,5	g,e	S	"Terminal Miocene Event", caused by the separation of Australia and South America from Antarctica, creating cold Benguela current, 40-70m sea level drop results in land bridge at Gibraltar, Mediterranean (35, 14)
6,5	e,z	C	Fossil ape "Toumai", $350cm^3$ brain, close to final common ancestor of chimpanzees and hominids, lived at 400 $000km^2$ Lake Chad, West Africa
6,0	e	H	Warming and sea levels increase again (see 5,4 Ma)
6,0	e	S	Antarctica reaches present ice thickness (see 23 Ma)
5,4	e	H	Messinian Event = Mediterranean Sea isolated, dried out temporarily, accumulating ±6% of global sea salts, Antarctic glaciation extended, sea levels sink ±50m, at later glacial periods sea levels reduced by >100m against present levels (see 6,0 and 5,0 Ma)

5,3 Ma to 1,8 Ma Pliocene Epoch

5,0	g,e	U	100m uplift of western, 900m of eastern South Africa, cutting off moist sea winds results in formation of Kalahari Desert, South Africa/Namibia (see 20 Ma)
5,0	e	3	Dense forest becomes sparse, East Africa (see 4,0 Ma)
5,0	e	AB	Makgadikgadi Lake covering 80 000 km_2 and 30m deep, Botswana (see 63, 2,0 Ma, 35 ka)
5,0	e	AH	Ice cap reducing, higher sea levels, Antarctica (see 15, 6,0 Ma)
4,0	e	3	Sparse forest turns into savannah, East Africa (see 5,0 and 2,8 Ma)
4,0	e	H	Climax of global warming, glaciers melt, Antarctica
3,3	e	H	Cooling on northern hemisphere, start of oscillating present ice age cycles, alternating glacials every ±10ky and inter-glacials, at maximum glaciation 50% of oceans covered by shelf and drifting ice
3,0	g,e	AB	North and South American plates collide, deviating warm equatorial current to become Gulf Stream, changing global climate, causes Arctic to be ice-free, creating glaciation elsewhere, Panama seaway closes, Isthmus of Panama (see 45 Ma and 12 ka)
3,0	e	I	Siberian permafrost starts
2,9	e	AL	Arctic Sea freezes

	Subject Ref.	Source Ref.	
2,8 **Ma**	e	Q	Climate changes to more arid conditions, Africa (4,0)
2,6	e	P	Laurentide ice shield from Arctic Ocean to Mexico
2,0	e	AB	Kalahari Basin starts to dry up due to rivers changing course and less rainfall, Botswana (5,0 Ma, 10,0 ka)
2,0	e	AB	Antarctica starts to freeze over (see 400 ka)
2,0	e	U	Dramatic global cooling, ocean temperature lowest ever since start of Cenozoic Era
2,0	e	AF	Glaciers start spreading over Greenland (see 1,0 Ma)

1,8 Ma to 42,0 ka Lower Paleolithic Age

1,78	e	Q	Reversal of Earth magnetic field, dating Dmanisi excavations (see 780 ka)
1,0	e	AF	Glaciers merge into 1,7 Mkm^2 and 3km thick ice sheet, depressing central plateau by 1km, Greenland (2,0 Ma)
780 **ka**	e	P,Q	Most recent Matuyame-Brunhes polarity reversal of Earth's magnetic poles, Tahiti, Chili, Hawaii, Las Palmas (see 1,78 Ma and 30 ka)
740	e	U	"Dome C" ice drilling core records global temperatures to present, Antarctica (see 420 ka)
680	e	AC	Begin of a series of glacials/interglacials, Guenz (1st) glacial starts, Western Europe (3,3 Ma, 620 ka)
620	e	AC	End of Guenz glacial and start of Guenz-Mindel interglacial, Western Europe (see 680 and 455 ka)
500	e,z	Q	Hippopotamus larger than at present, indicating warm climate, England (see 24, 2,4 Ma, 6,0 ka)
455	e	AC	Guenz-Mindel interglacial ends, Mindel (2nd) glacial starts, Western Europe (see 620 and 340 ka)
420	e	U	Vostok ice drilling core reveals global temperatures to present, 4 periods of abrupt warming and gradual cooling, Antarctica (see 740 ka)
400	e	AB	Antarctica freeze-over is complete (see 2,0 Ma)
340	e	AC	Mindel (2nd) glaciation ends, Mindel-Riss interglacial starts, Western Europe (see 455 and 200 ka)
300	e	H	Illinoian glacials/interglacials start, North America (see 130 and 122 ka)
200	e	Z	Lake Megafezzan, the size of England, perennial rivers, Fezzan, Libya
200	e	AC	Mindel-Riss interglacial ends, Riss (3rd) glacial starts, Western Europe (see 340 and 130 ka)
195	e	W	Start of global ice age (see 165 and 135 ka)
165	e	W	Sea levels up to 125m lower than at present (195, 135)
135	e	W,V	End of global ice age, sea levels 6m higher than now (see 195 and 165 ka)
130	e	AC	Riss glacial ends, Riss-Wuerm interglacial starts, Western Europe (see 200 and 110 ka)
130	e	H	Illinoian glacials/interglacials end (see 300 ka)

	Subject Ref.	Source Ref.	
130 **ka**	e	7	Coral reefs provide early El Niño records up to the present, New Guinea
125	e	H	Sea level maximum (see 105, 82 ka)
125	e	W	**H.**sap.neanderthalensis lived in near-tropical climate, hunted elephant, rhino, aurochs, Northwest France
122	e	H	Wisconsin glacials/interglacials start, North America (see 300 ka)
120	e	P	Tsunami, caused by landslide, deposits sand 500m up on Mt.Kohala, Mauna Loa, Hawaii
120	e,z	Z	Woolly mammoth decline dramatically due to global warming, but survive (see 410 ka)
110	e	AC	Riss-Wuerm interglacial ends, Early Wuerm glaciation starts, Western Europe (see 130 and 75 ka)
105	e	H	Sea level high, but lower than 125 ka levels (see 125 and 82 ka)
100	e	AB	Baltic Sea, North Sea and low lying coastal Arctic permafrost strips exposed, seas have receded by 100m due to global cooling
92,5	e	H	Fluctuation of Earth circulation around the Sun as now, according to 92,5ky cycle (see 22 ka)
82	e	H	Sea level high, but lower than 105 ka levels (see 125 and 105 ka)
75	e	AC	Early Wuerm glaciation ends, Lower Paleolithic interglacial starts, Western Europe (see 110 and 30 ka)
74	g,e	V,Q	Extreme eruption Mt.Toba, 100 x 30km crater, 48km high ash cloud, 96km long caldera, 3 000x stronger than Mt.St.Helens, "volcanic winter", Sumatra, Indonesia
70	e,z	W	Giant kangaroos, wombat-like marsupials, gigantic emus starved to death due to extreme climate changes, Australia (see 40 ka)
55	e	P	Start of a global wet cycle (see 25 ka)
50	e	Y	Interruption of long term desertification, Sahara (30)

42,0 ka to 10 ka Upper Paleolithic Age

35	g,e	W	Super-lake Makgadikgadi, 100m deep, now dry salt pan due to tectonic movements, Botswana (see 5,0 and 2,0 Ma, 10 ka)
30	e	AC	Lower Paleolithic interglacial ends, Main Wuerm (4th) glacial starts, Western Europe (see 75 and 12 ka)
30	e	I	Probable reversal of Earth's geomagnetic field about every 2 500 years (see 780 ka)
30	e	Y	Maximum of long term desertification, Sahara (50 ka)
28	e	W	Cro-Magnon people living at a cave now 40m below the sea, Cap Morgiou, Provence, France
26,5	e	AB	Start of maximum extension of last Ice Age, northern and southern hemisphere simultaneously (see 19,5 ka)

ka	Subject Ref.	Source Ref.	
25 **ka**	e	P	End of a global wet cycle (see 55 ka)
23	e	AB	Intensity of solar radiation at minimum
23	e	AB	Start of cold polar air flows into Mediterranean basin more often, but not more strongly than now (19 ka)
22	e	AB	Ice cover looks like at present-day Greenland and Antarctica, Northern and Central Europe
22	e	H	Fluctuation of Earth axle position as now, according to 22ky cycle (see 92,5 ka)
21	g,e	AF	Bahamas limestone plateau mostly exposed, sea level 120m lower than at present (see 18 ka)
20	g,e	R	Coastline of Southern Africa 60m lower than now, rivers dig deep off-shore channels (see 25 ka)
20	e	AB	Minimum age of extreme dryness, indicated by unchanged levels of sand since then, Atacama dessert, Chile (see 11 ka)
20	e	H	European climatic zones moved south by 20°C, but Beringia between Siberia and Alaska ice-free (11 ka)
20	e	7	Glaciation in N.America reaches maximum extend to southern tip of Great Lakes, Arctic Ocean frozen from northern Britain to southern tip of Greenland (10)
20	e	W	Glaciers gouging out Yosemite Valley etc., leaving behind cold, wet, vegetation-less land and lakes, California (see 18 ka)
19,5	e	AB	End of maximum extension of last Ice Age, northern and southern hemisphere simultaneously (see 26,5 ka)
19	e	AB	End of cold polar air flows into Mediterranean basin more often, but not more strongly than now (23 ka)
18	g,e	AF	End of Bahamas limestone plateau exposure (see 21 ka)
18	g,e	Z	Due to low ice age oceans Japan's main island is connected by a land bridge to Asia, not to Japan (10 ka)
18	e	W	Ice sheets move south, carving out Great Lakes, USA (see 14,8 ka)
18	e	U	Sea level drops by 130m, Southern African coasts
18	e	AB	Sea temperatures and CO_2 started to rise after ice had started to melt (see 23 ka)
18	e	W	Climate now arctic tundra, California (20 and 14 ka)
.18	e	1,7 Y	Last major global glaciation: temperatures 2,3°C, sea level 80m lower than now, North Pole ice maximum Eastern Siberia, Alaska, Yukon ice-free (see 14 ka)
16	e	AB	Masula ice dam breaks and re-freezes repeatedly, causing devastating flooding, North America
15	e,z	AB	Victoria Lake dries up almost completely, the multi-colored bass survive in small but deep Kivu Lake, preserving the genes of the original 500 species, East Africa (see 150 ka)
14,8	e	H	Glaciers reach south of the Great Lakes, North America (see 18 ka)

	Subject Ref.	Source Ref.	
14 **ka**	e	4	Slow amelioration of global Ice Age (see 18 ka)
13	e	AB	Danube delta starts to form, Black Sea
12	g,e	Q	Glaciers carve canyons, Teton Range, Wyoming (13 Ma)
12	e	AC	Main Wuerm glaciation ends, Upper Paleolithic interglacial starts, Western Europe (see 30 and 8,0 ka)
12	e	W	Formation of Larsen B ice shelf, which has now collapsed, Antarctica (see 5,0 ka)
12	e	W	Start of Niagara Gorge and Falls, USA/Canada
11,65	c,e	P	Sirius B imploded, became a "white dwarf", surface 300x harder, interior density 3 000x higher than diamond, claimed to be "manna from Heaven", the red star of the Egyptians and to have caused end of ice age
11,5	e	W	Strong rains green tropical Sahara, 150 archeological sites, Africa (see 10,0 and 7,3 ka)
11	g,e	8	South coast of Arctic Sea near Iceland, Thames, Weser, Elbe tributaries of the Rhine in the area of the later North Sea (see 10,0 and 7,0 ka)
11	g,e	7	Beringia land bridge disintegrates, sea-levels 100m lower than now (see 20 ka)
11	e	P	Start of a global wet cycle (see 5,0 ka)
11	e	Q	Atacama dessert habitable, more moderate climate than now, since then permanent drought, now globally driest place, Andes, Chile (see 20 and 6,0 ka)
10,4	e	W	Monsoon winds proceed 800km north to Sahara, creating marshes and swamps in Nile valley, Egypt (7,3 + 5,5)
10	e	AB	Climatic changes caused Makgadikgadi Lake to dry out, leaving behind huge salt pans, Botswana (2,0 Ma, 35 ka)
10	e	AC	Upper Paleolithic interglacial ends, Late Wuerm glaciation starts, Western Europe (see 12 and 8,0 ka)
10	e	L,7	End of global glaciation, Amazon basin with only fragmented forests, glaciation only north of Great Lakes, North America (see 20 ka)
10	e	W	Climate changes to warm and arid, all glaciers melted, California (see 14 and 6,0 ka)

10,0 ka to 7,0 ka Mesolithic/Archaic Age

10,0	g,e	H	Scandinavia starts rising after glaciers receded, so far by 100m (±1cm/a) in the center
10,0	g,e	J	Britain is now an island, North Sea and Channel are flooded (see 11 ka)
10,0	e	Q	African paleo-monsoon shifts northwards, inundating North Africa, hippos live there (see 6,0 and 5,0 ka)
10,0	e	4	Sahara from tropical vegetation to savannah (see 11,5 and 7,3 ka)
10,0	e	4	Forests spread, sea levels rise

	Subject Ref.	Source Ref.	
10,0 **ka**	e	7	Antarctic glaciation up to 5km thick
10,0	e,a	Z	Start of Kiffian culture due to intervening moist period, creating a large freshwater lake, "Green Sahara" (see 8,0 ka)
8,5	e	8	Baltic Sea a fresh water basin (see 11 and 7,0 ka)
8,5	e	8	Average temperature 2,5°C lower than now, Centr. Europe
8,2	e	7	Ice dam collapses, causing massive floods, Canada
8,2	e	7	Shift in Gulf Stream, cooling of Greenland and Europe
8,2	e	AG	Start of continental warming, the fresh water of the Ancylus Sea rises and connects to the oceans and becomes salty (see 6,9 ka)
8,0	e	AC	Late Wuerm glaciation ends, present interglacial starts, Western Europe (see 10 and 5,0 ka)
8,0	e,m	AB	Large parts of present Baltic Sea inhabited by Germanic (??) peoples (see 6,0 and 5,0 ka)
8,0	e,a	Z	End of Kiffian culture and "Green Sahara" due to return of prolonged arid period (see 10,0 and 6,5 ka)
7,5	e	7	(Ice ?) wall breaks, Mediterranean is flooding Black Sea fresh water basin (Noah's Flood ?), Bosporus (see 7,1 and 6,5 ka)
7,3	e	4	Global warming to "Climatic Optimum" (see 6,0 ka)
7,3	e	W	Sahara turns to dessert, villages abandoned, monsoon winds reduced, Nile valley, Egypt (11,5, 10,4, 5,5)
7,2	e	8	Taiga (steppe) starts, Siberia
7,1	e	P	Tsunami caused by underwater landslide off Norway leaves sand layers on coasts around NE Atlantic
7,0	e	8	End of last Ice Age, Northern Sweden

7,0 ka to 5,0 ka Neolithic Age

7,0	e	8	Sea level rises 40m, North Sea and Baltic Sea are now salt water seas (see 11 and 8,5 ka)
7,0	e	H	Global temperatures higher than ever since then
6,9	g,e	AG	Scandinavia keeps rising, blocking the connection between the Ancylus Sea and the oceans, turning it into a fresh water sea (see 8,2 and 5,0 ka)
6,5	e,a	8	Babylonian report: "Great Flood", 1 man and his family and animals are saved (see 7,5 and 7,1 ka)
6,5	e,a	Z	Start of Tenerian culture due to end of arid period, again "Green Sahara" (see 8,0 and 5,0 ka)
6,0	e	4	End of "Climatic Optimum", slight global cooling (7,3)
6,0	e	W	Climate gets wet again, 1st closed canopy forests, California (see 10 ka)
6,0	e,z	Y	Hippos, needing water all year round, Sahara, Africa (see 10,0 ka)
6,0	e,m	AB	Burial sites, posts and ceramic shards, fossils of earlier habitation of present Baltic Sea (see 8,0 ka)

	Subject Ref.	Source Ref.	
5,5 **ka**	e	W	African Monsoon winds cease, creating fertile Nile valley, Sahara again dessert, Egypt (see 7,3 ka)
5,0	e	P	End of a global wet cycle (see 11 ka)
5,0	e	4	Global climates similar to now
5,0	e	W	Formation of Larsen ice shelf A, Antarctic (see 12 ka)
5,0	e	Q	African monsoon shifts back to south, creating present desert conditions in the Sahara (see 10,0 ka)
5,0	e	AC	Present interglacial still in operation, Western Europe (see 8,0 ka)
5,0	e	AG	Rising oceans flood land bridge between Sweden and Denmark, creating brackish water Baltic Sea (6,9 ka)
5,0	e,a	Z	End of Tenerian culture due to renewed arid period, the freshwater lake dried up (see 6,5 ka)

Table 1: Timeline of Glaciation (ref.AC)

Table 1: Timeline of Glaciation (ref.AC)								
Backwards Glacial Index	Names					Inter/Glacial	Period (ka)	Epoch
	Alpine	N. American	N. European	Great Britain	S. American			
				Flandrian		interglacial	present – 12	Holocene
1st	Würm	Wisconsin	Weichsel or Vistula	Devensian	Llanquihue	glacial period	12 – 110	Pleistocene
	Riss-Würm	Sangamonian	Eemian	Ipswichian		interglacial	110 – 130	
2nd	Riss	Illinoian	Saale	Wolstonian or Gipping	Santa María	glacial period	130 – 200	
	Mindel-Riss	Yarmouth	Holstein	Hoxnian		interglacial(s)	200 – 300/380	
3rd – 5th	Mindel	Kansan	Elsterian	Anglian	Río Llico	glacial period(s)	300/380 – 455	
	Günz-Mindel	Aftonian		Cromerian*		interglacial(s)	455 – 620	
7th	Günz	Nebraskan	Menapian	Beestonian	Caracol	glacial period	620 – 680	

Ecological/Cultural Timelines in Europe

see the Reference Section for combined climatic and cultural timelines, Western Europe

Sea Level Measurements

These must be viewed with circumspection, because there is no fixed point of reference for global changes. One could calculate the increase/ decrease in glacial ice cover, but the rising/sinking of tectonic plates (including the sea floors) has a much larger influence on sea levels over extended periods. Local readings fluctuate widely and cannot be used to infer global measurements. Often they show rises and falls simultaneously in different parts of the world, because of rising or sinking of continental plates.

CO_2 Parts per Million for the last 500 000 years

high values are supposed to indicate warming of the atmosphere, but there are indications contradicting this:

420 ka	280 parts
350	225
315	275
260	200
240	250
160	180
120	270
60	200
0,1	275
present	360

F Subject Lists Paleo-Biology:

b botanical: **flora, fungi, procaryotes, eucaryotes, monera**

see also the References section for further biological notes and some botanical terms at the end of this section

4,6 Ga to 3,8 Ga Priscoan Era

	Subject Ref.	Source Ref.	
4,5 **Ga**	c,b	P,W	Carbonaceous chondrite meteor contains 74 types of amino acids (8 used by Earthly proteins), strings of polyols sugar unknown on Earth, components of Earth life (left-handed amino, di-amino acids) came from space, maybe forming proteins, molecules, Murchison, Australia (see 4,0 Ga)
4,0	b	W	1st life forms prokaryotes: B.archaea, anaerobic, from hydrothermal vents such as at the mid-Atlantic ridge (see 3,9, and 3,5 Ga)
4,0	b	U	4 self-replicating molecules, precursors to RNA, DNA, all life evolves from LUCA (see 3,5 Ga)
4,0	b	U	Amino acids, nucleotides, sugars in left- and right-handed form, all life uses left-handed amino acids and right-handed nucleotides and sugars (see 4,5 Ga)
3,9	e,b	3,U	Laminated slime mats and proto-stromatolites formed by blue-green prokaryotes cyano-bacteria photo-synthesize CO_2 into C and O_2, reacted to $CaCO_3$, further reducing the CO_2 content of the atmosphere, Barberton, South Africa (see 4,0, 3,5 and 3,0 Ga)
3,9	b	AM	It is suggested that the Late Bombardment sterilized Earth, destroying any older life forms
3,85	b	F,P	1st life forms develop in shallow water, carbonates, fossils of single-cell thermophilic bacteria, Isua Group, Greenland (see 4,0 Ga)

3,8 Ga to 2,5 Ga Archean Era

3,6	b	H	Proposed anaerobic bacteria operating chemosynthesis, changing SO_4 to SO_3 structures, emitting O_2
3,5	e,b	W TS	Proto-stromatolites produce O_2 by photosynthesis, Sebakwia, Zimbabwe, Warrawoona, Western Australia and Pilbara, Australia (see 3,9 Ga)
3,5	b	AG	Stromatolite-like structures indicate live, Mars
3,5	b	P,6	Dividing B.archaea and proto-stromatolites, greenstone belt, Barberton, South Africa (see 4,0 Ga)
3,5	b	V	LUCA (Last Universal Common Ancestor) (see 4,0 Ga)

	Subject Ref.	Source Ref.	
3,5 **Ga**	b	K	T4 virus, a bacteriophage virus eating the E.coli (Escherichia) bacterium
3,0	b	I	Probable age of photosynthesis (see 3,9 Ga)
2,9	g,b	S	Carbonaceous kerogen (bitumen) of biological origin (Hallbauer), Witwatersrand, South Africa
2,9	b	AB	Proto-stromatolite fossils, Ulundi, South Africa
2,7	b	I	$CaCO_3$ produced by organisms similar to present blue-green algae (see 2,65 and 2,0 Ga)
2,65	b	U	Cyano-bacteria cause precipitation of $CaCO_3$ (lime-stone), later changed to dolostone, South Africa (see 2,7 Ga)
2,6	g,e b	AH	Start of Transvaal stromatolitic dolostones, free oxygen generation, South Africa (see 2,4 Ga)

2,5 Ga to 1,6 Ga Early Proterozoic Period

2,5	b	U	Cyano-bacteria reach peak
2,3	e,b	H	Start of period of abundant stromatolites, free oxygen (see 1,5 Ga and 580 Ma)
2,2	b	S	Possibly trace fossils of metazoans, Witwatersrand dolostones (dolomites), South Africa (see 1,0 Ga)
2,1	b	AG	250 metazoans, similar to small jellyfish, Gabon
2,0	b	I	About a dozen types of proto-bacteria similar to present blue-green algae, Lake Superior, Canada (2,7)
2,0	b	U	Symbiotic relationship between anaerobic cyano-bacteria and the mitochondrial-bearing respiring purple bacteria created chloroplasts within cells, ancestors of plants, fungi and animals
2,0	b	3	Aerobic eukaryotes depending on oxygen: single/multi-celled with nucleus, DNA, RNA, ATP, organelles (mito-chondria, chloro plasts, captured prokaryotes such as cyano-phyta (blue-green algae)
2,0	b	3	Grypania fossil plants
1,9	b	H	Appearance of varied bacteria and cyano-bacteria, Gunflint Cherts, Canada (see >1,4 Ga)
1,9	b	H	Stromatolites evolve, only complex life form until 1,5 Ga (see 1,5 Ga)

1,6 Ga to 650 Ma Riphean Period

1,5	b	3	Stromatolites form 100m high reefs which are still alive, Shark Bay, Australia (see 1,9 Ga, 10,0 ka)
1,5	b	AB	Start of sexual propagation to pass on and to advance the genetic information
>1,4	b	H	1st eukaryotic life forms (see 1,9 Ga)
1,4	b	W	Tappania fossil fungi, China/Australia (see 850 Ga)

	Subject Ref.	Source Ref.	
1,2 **Ga**	b	B	Terrestrial microfossils, Arizona
1,0	b	I	Blue-green and green algae, fungi (eukaryotes), Bitter Springs, Australia (see 440 Ma)
1,0	b	AB	Foraminifera have $CaCO_3$ shield with perforations for suction "feet" to adhere to sand particles
1,0	b	S	Trace fossils of metazoans, Katanga, Congo (2,2 Ga)
1,0	b	3	Chuaria, an eukaryote of 10mm diameter
850 **Ma**	b	P	Oldest fungus (previously oldest 380 Ma), no living order, Victoria Is., Canada (see 1,4 Ga)
850	b	H	Adaptive radiation of acritarchians (microscopic algae) (see 543 Ma)
800	b	H	Oldest protozoan predators
720	e,b	L	Higher oxygen levels allow multi-cellular life (700)
700	b,z	U	Multicellular organisms with tissue differentiation (see 800 and 720 Ma)
670	b,z	S,U	Fauna and flora similar to Ediacaran, including shelly cloudina (animal) and skeletonized calcareous algae fossils, 1st hard shells by bio-mineralization, maybe to deter predators, Kuibis, Namibia, China (see 650 and 600 Ma)

650 Ma to 600 Ma Vendian Period

650	b	I	Fossil maritime multi-cellular organisms (see 670 Ma)
600	b	H	Most acritarchians disappear (see 543 Ma)
600	b,z	V	Eukaryotes develop into metazoans, present-day choano-flagellants eukaryotes still produce proteins required for metazoans and animals (see 670 Ma)

600 Ma to 543 Ma Ediacaran Period

580	b	H	End of period of abundant stromatolites (see 2,3 Ga)
550	b,z	H	Archaeo-cyathids, similar to but unrelated to sponges, involved in forming reefs by calcareous algae, Ediacaran Hills, Australia (see 650, 600 Ma)
543	b,z	3,6	Ediacaran extinction, 70% of life extinct, especially single cell organisms, e.g. acritarchians (850 Ma)

543 Ma to 490 Ma Cambrian Period

540	b	AB	Life neither botanical nor zoological, consuming dissolved minerals via large surface
540	b,z	3	Sexual and food competition starts, "survival of the fittest", viruses (stripped-down cells) as parasites
530	b,z	7	"Cambrian explosion of life" (see 525 Ma)

	Subject Ref.	Source Ref.	
525 **Ma**	b,z	L	Possibly end of "Cambrian explosion of life", ±30 of present phyla found, no NEW body building plans since developed, all ecological niches occupied (530 Ma)
500	e b,z	W	Ozone levels are now sufficient to protect terrestrial life incl. animals from UV radiation (see 580 Ma)
500	b	V	1st terrestrial plants, neither leaves nor roots (450)
490 Ma	**to**	**443 Ma**	**Ordovician Period**
450	b	I,S	Terrestrial multi-cellular plant fossils: when plants migrated to land they had to develop structures to hold them up, tubes to transport liquids and water-proof but breezing skin (see 500 Ma)
450	b	H	Early terrestrial plants, non-vascular, without roots, leaves, but horizontal stems and upright shoots (415)
450	b	7,H	Higher vegetation colonizes land, limited to marshes and moors (see 500 Ma)
450	b	W	Protein of 2 000 atoms reconstructed, belonging to gluco-corticoide group, active in present-day humans
443 Ma	**to**	**417 Ma**	**Silurian Period**
440	b	G	Chlorophyta (green algae) appear (see 1,0 Ga)
435	b	3	Liverwort early terrestrial plant, fossil spores (220)
418	e,b	Y	O_2 levels probably higher than now, plants grew only 3cm tall, oldest wildfire recorded, England
417 Ma	**to**	**354 Ma**	**Devonian Period**
410	b	K,I H	Baragwanathia fossils, oldest vascular plants, dated by graptolites, still no roots but proto-leaves and spore receptacles, Yeo fossil site, Victoria, Australia (see 450 Ma)
400	b	G	Psilophytales, early vascular terrestrial plants lacking roots, leaves, Rhynie cherts, Scotland (see 370 and 345 Ma)
400	b	U	Dutoitia, 1st terrestrial plant fossil, South Africa
380	b	G	Rhodophyta (red algae) appear
380	b,z	H	Tabulata/stromatopora reef communes prosper, Canning basin, Australia and Bighorn Canyon, Montana (360 Ma)
375	b	Z	Appearance of 1st pollen grains and seeds
370	b	G	Psilophytales disappear (see 400 and 900 ka)
370	b	H	Continents partially covered by forests, higher plants: vascular stems, roots, seeds, leaves, photo-synthesis (see 360 Ma)
370	b	G	Lycopodiales appear: baerlap (lycopodium.clavatum) (see 350, 300 Ma) and club mosses (see 270, 210 Ma)

	Subject Ref.	Source Ref.	
370 **Ma**	b	H	Appearance of seeds, obviating the need of terrestrial plants to live near water/moors
365	b	G	Phaeophyta (brown algae) appear
360	e b,z	S	O_2 levels 35% of atmosphere in Devonian/Carboniferous, allowing plants/animals to grow large quickly, South Africa (see 580 and 200 Ma)
360	b	H	1st large trees and forests (see 370 Ma)
360	b,z	H	Tabulata/stromatopora reef communes extinct, Canning basin, Australia and Bighorn Canyon, Montana (380 Ma)

354 Ma to 290 Ma Carboniferous Period

350	b	K	Lichen, symbiosis of green/blue-green algae with fungi
350	b	U	Club mosses, lycopodiales, ancestral gymnosperms, South Africa (see 370, 300 Ma)
345	b	3	Rhynie cherts yield fossilized ferns, Scotland (400)
310	b	H	Calcareous algae contribute to reefs
300	b	H	Lycopodiales spore scale trees (sigillaria =vertical scales and lepidodendrales =rhombic scales) produced coal deposits, Europe, North America (370, 275 Ma)
300	b	H	Glossopteris, a seed fern in wet areas (see 270 Ma)
300	b	H	Cordaitales trees are gymnosperma in dry areas, producing coal deposits, Gondwana (see 350 Ma)
300	b	G	Charophyta (stoneworts)
300	b	W	10 000ha rain forest fossils in coalmine roof, tree-sized horsetails, 40m club mosses Illinois, USA (270)

290 Ma to 248 Ma Permian Period

290	e,b	AB	Sparse vegetation of mainly ferns and conifers, arid and warm climate, Central Europe
290	b	G	Sphenophyllales, oldest articulate plants, shrubs with triangular stems joined like bamboo (see 190 Ma)
290	b	G	Calamitales, like modern horsetails but tall trees (see 175 Ma)
290	b	G	Coenopteridales (spore ferns) (see 185 Ma)
290	b	G	Cordaitales, oldest gymnosperms (naked-seeded plants) high trees branched only at crown, fructification, lanceolate leaves (see 270, 185 Ma)
280	b	1	Protozoans changed dramatically (see 250 Ma)
275	b	G	Lepidodendrales (scale trees),seed-like cones, thin wooden stele, fibrous periderm (see 300, 185 Ma)
275	b	G	Pteridospermales (seed ferns) (see 190 Ma)
270	b	5,U	Coal forests, mostly glossopteris, cordaitales, ferns, horsetail, club mosses, Antarctica/New Guinea/ South Africa (see 300 Ma)

	Subject Ref.	Source Ref.	
270 **Ma**	b,z	U	Start of most complete fossil record of Gondwana, Karoo, South Africa (see 180 Ma)
250	b	7	Bacterial spores of this age found alive now
250	b	3	Protists several cm across (see 280 Ma)
250	b	G	Equisetales (horse-tails) (see 175 Ma
248,2	b,z	U,6	Permian Extinction: major extinction of 96% of all species, 90% of maritime (trilobites, all corals etc.), 80% of terrestrial life extinct, including glossopteris, therapsids
248,2 Ma	**to**	**205,7 Ma**	**Triassic Period**
225	b	G	Filicales appear, spore ferns (see 95 Ma)
225	b,z	3,H	Modern reef-building hexa-corals symbiotic with algae, phyto-plankton (dinoflagellates, nano-plankton)
220	b	G	Hepaticae (liverworts) (see 435 Ma)
220	b	G	Musci (mosses) (see 205 Ma)
220	b	G	Coniferales (conifers) appear (see 190 Ma)
210	b	U	Riverine forest: seed ferns, cycads and ginkgos, wetlands: seed ferns, club mosses and horsetails, open woodland: cycadeoids, ginkgo, conifers, Gondwana
210	b	G	Ginkgoales, proto-leafed tree, 1 species left, China (see 60 Ma)
210	b	U	Early gymnosperms, Molteno formation, South Africa
206	b	G	Cycadales (modern cycads) appear (see 190 Ma)
206	b	AB	Numerous species of trees leave pollen traces (205 Ma)
205,7	e,b	AB	Release of 8 000 Gt CO_2, causes global warming, algae explosion absorbs most maritime O_2,resulting in extinction of 80% of maritime flora, mid-Atlantic
205,7	c b,z	7,H	Triassic extinction (by comet impact, indicated by iridium abundance and a "fern spike" ?), mass extinction of marine species, mammal-like reptiles extinct, seed ferns disappear (see 215, 210, 140 Ma)
205,7 Ma	**to**	**144,0 Ma**	**Jurassic Period**
205	e,b	AB	Number of tree species much reduced due to acid rain (see 205,7 Ma), instead pollen of pioneer plants: ferns, horsetails, mosses containing toxic carbon C_2H_4 (see 220, 206 Ma)
200	b	P	Wollemi pine flourishes, Gondwana (see 2,0 Ma)
190	b	1	Conifers, cycads abundant (see 220 and 206 Ma)
190	b	G	Pteridospermales (seed ferns) extinct (see 275 Ma)
190	b	G	Sphenophyllales extinct (see 290 Ma)
185	b	G	Lepidodendrales (scale trees) disappear (see 275 Ma)
185	b	G	Calamitales (horse-tails) extinct (see 290, 175 Ma)
185	b	G	Cycadeoidales (cycads-like) appear (see 80 Ma)

	Subject Ref.	Source Ref.	
185 **Ma**	b	G	Coenopteridales (spore ferns), cordaitales (oldest gymnosperms) extinct (see 290 Ma)
180	b,z	U	End of fossil record of Gondwana, Karoo, S.Afr. (270)
175	b	G	Neocalamitales (horse-tails) appear (185, 140 Ma)
175	b	G	Pleuromeiales, short un-branched shrub with needle-like leaves, rootlets (see 125 Ma)
175	b	G	Caytoniales (gymnosperms), fern-like foliage, pollen-bearing shoots appear (see 105 Ma)
150	e,b	Q	Semi-arid savanna, Moab, Utah, USA (see 285 Ma)
144	b,z	H	Limited extinction of fauna and flora

144,0 Ma to 65,0 Ma Cretaceous Period

140	b	G	Neocalamitales (horse-tails) extinct (see 175 Ma)
140	b	G	Chrysophyta, non-vascular plants
130	b	G,7 I	Monocotyledons (1-seeded leaves) oldest angiosperms incl. buttercups, magnolia, followed by dicotyledons (2-seeded leaves), 3 basal lineages based on DNA: amborellaceae (probably woody), nymphaeaceae (water lilies), illiciaeceae (star anises) (125, 100 Ma)
125	b	C	Freshwater angiosperms, flower above water, cpl. stem, roots, leaves, reproductive organs, China (130 Ma)
125	b	G	Selaginellales, modern form of pleuromeiales (175 Ma)
120	b	K	Rare sub-species of eudicots now dominant, China
115	b,z	3	Flowering plants and flying insects in "co-evolution" (pollination), both becoming highly specialized
110	b,z	U	80 species of fauna and flora, including lemurs, are endemic to Madagascar
105	b	G	Caytoniales (gymnosperms) extinct (see 175 Ma)
100	b	G	Palms, laurus, cinnamonum appear
100	b	H	Diatoms and foraminifera present in the oceans
100	b	K	Idiospermum, thought extinct angiosperm, found living in Queensland, Australia
100	b	I	Magnoliids 1st non-basal angiosperm, petals evolve for angiosperms, starting their "great radiation" (130)
95	b	G	Filicales (spore ferns) prosper (see 225 Ma)
95	b,z	H	Sea weeds, rudist reef builders symbiotic with algae (see 85 Ma)
90	b,z	S	Oldest South African angiosperm and insect fossils
88	b	W	Predominance of angiosperms, Patagonia, Argentine
85	b,z	H	Rudists up to 1m long build reefs together with algae, at the expense of corals (see 95 Ma)
80	b	G	Cycadeoidales extinct (see 185 Ma)
80	b	3	Oldest amber, Indian Ocean
80	b	G	Isoetales, modern form of pleuromeiales (see 125 Ma)
80	b	H	So-called sea grass develops, not a grass
80	b,z	W	Bee with oldest orchid pollen, Costa Rica

	Subject Ref.	Source Ref.	
70 **Ma**	b	7	Welwitschia appears, lives more than 2 000 years, still existing, Namibia
70	b	H	Angiosperms now dominant over gymnosperms
65	e,b	H	Fern spores 99% of micro-flora before extinction, afterwards only 15-30%, most extinct plants with un-serrated leaves used to warm climates, suggesting strong cooling as cause of extinction

65,0 Ma to 54,8 Ma Paleocene Epoch

65	b	S	Diatoma (but not 92% of foraminifera) survived
65	b	Q	Myxomycetes fungus (slime mould) with fused swarm cells = sexual intercourse
65	b	K	Microbialithes = co-habitation of cyano-bacteria/ bacteria thought extinct, alive in 25m depth, Pacific
60	b	H	Appearance of the only still existing gingko species, China (see 210 Ma)
60	b	H	Grasses appear, need long recuperation after being grazed (see 50 Ma)

54,8 Ma to 33,7 Ma Eocene Epoch

50	b	G	Cacti, leguminosae, ficus, eucalyptus prosper
50	b	H	Grasses prosper, "inventing" continuous growth (60 Ma)
42	b	H	Rose plant and upright tree fossils, Colorado, USA
40	b	H	Lignite (brown coal) deposits with extensive plant fossil beds, Geisel Valley, Halle/S, Germany
37	b	H	50% of our extant plant genera in existence

33,7 Ma to 23,8 Ma Oligocene Epoch

30	b	K	Volvoxes (green algae) developing 2 different kinds of cells: ±16 germ cells, and ±2 000 somatic paddlers, developed from free-swimming chlamydomonas
30	b	R	Succulents thrive, Namibia
25	b	H	Compositae (herbs) and other low growing wood-free plants

23,8 Ma to 5,3 Ma Miocene Epoch

10	b,z	I,H	High salinity killed all life when Western Mediter-ranean Sea was closed off
8,0	b	W	Proto-bacteria with 270 (currently 300 million) base pairs defrosted, still alive, doubling every ½ hour, previous "record age" 300 ka, Antarctica

5,3 Ma to 1,8 Ma Pliocene Epoch

	Subject Ref.	Source Ref.	
5,0 **Ma**	b	G	Gnetales (gymnosperms) appear
2,0	g b,z	5	Ngorongoro volcano explodes, 18km crater with 100m walls, creating unique closed habitat, East Africa
2,0	b	P	Wollemi pine was considered extinct, but now found again in Australia (see 200 Ma)

1,8 Ma to 42,0 ka Lower Paleolithic Age

900 **ka**	b	G	Psilotales, modern form of psilophytales (see 370 Ma)
140	b	P	Tomato mosaic virus ToMV found alive, Greenland

42,0 ka to 10 ka Upper Paleolithic Age

14	b	W	Pine, spruce, hemlock and alder grow then, California, (see 18 and 7,542 ka)

10,0 ka to 7,0 ka Mesolithic/Archaic Age

10,0	b	W	Present stromatolites start, Sharks Bay, Australia (see 1,5 Ga)
7,542	b	AB	Still living spruce tree takes root, Sweden (14 ka)

Some common biological terms used in this listing:

bacteria	prokaryotes, cell division, need 1000x magnification to be seen
archaebacteria (archaea)	most primitive life form, most are thermophiles, originally living near ocean vents, energized by oxidation of hydrogen sulphide to sulphate etc.
eubacteria	evolved from archaea, developed photosynthesis and chlorophyll, dinitrification, N fixation
thermophiles	heat-loving bacteria
anaerobics	oxygen hating, thermophile bacteria
aerobics	oxygen needing bacteria
purple sulfur bact.	anaerobic photosynthesis without release of O_2, based on infra-red (heat), CO_2 and H_2SO_3
cyanobacteria	aerobic photosynthesis, O_2 production, based on red (light) radiation, $CaCO_3$ and H_2O
protozoans /protists	the following 2 groups together
prokaryotes	single cell organisms without nucleus, DNA, RNA, mitochondria, chloroplasts
eukaryotes	single cell organisms with nucleus, DNA, RNA etc. evolved from symbiosis of eubacteria and archaea
metazoans	multi-cellular organisms
virus	a stripped-down cell: a string of DNA or RNA covered by a protein shell, invades cells and turns them into factories to replicate itself, needs 1 000 000x magnification to be seen and hard to destroy, can infect normal protein cells, transforming them into prions
Prions	copies of normal body proteins that have become malformed (mis-folded), forming tiny filaments
deoxyribonucleic acid (DNA)	2m in each cell, 4 components: adenine, guanine, cytosine, thiamine
ribonucleic acid (RNA)	translate messages from DNA to cell proteins
genome	listing of genes in a body
proteome	library of information to create proteins
ions	charged molecules, moving at specific speeds
LUCA	Last Universal Common Ancestor) of protists, plants, fungi and animals
gymnosperms	non-flowering plants, uncovered (naked) seeds
angiosperms	flowering plants, flowers, covered seeds, pollen

The Plant Phyla:

extracted from: Geology for South African Students, G.N.G. Hamilton et al., 4th rev. ed., 1960, C.N.A., ref. R:

Phylum Thallophyta (single or group of cells not differentiated into tissues): include **Algae** (e.g. diatoms) and **Fungi** (e.g. mushrooms and slime moulds)
algae produce silica skeletons, which create diatomite or kieselguhr
diatoms from "Tripoli powder"
coccoliths: monocellular marine algae with many calcite plates, which accumulate as chalk beds
radiolaria: secreted silica shells that built cherts
charophytes: freshwater algae, stems having whorls ("leaflets")
stoneworts: freshwater charophyte algae

Phylum Bryophyta: includes the mosses and liverworts
liverworts: non-vascular plants related to mosses
bryozoans: colonial mono-cellular net-like structures
foraminifera: built chitin shells around them, reinforced with sand grains, others secrete $CaCo_3$ creating limestone, chalk deposits

Phylum Pteridophyta: mostly fern-like and includes extinct tree-ferns

Phylum Spermatophyta (seed producing): included are modern plants such as trees, grasses and flowering plants
gymnosperms: non-flowering plants
angiosperms: flowering plants

Notes:

the first 3 Plant Phyla are reproducing by spores

there have been substantial changes in classification, including the number of phyla, since the 1960's

pteridophyta: I noticed the mention of extinct tree-ferns: there are plenty in South Africa, or are these not the species referred to ?

hox (homoeo box) genes in fauna, 183 gene pairs controlling growth
wox genes in flora, 183 gene pairs controlling growth

there seems to be some confusion between B.archaea and proto-algae
1st of the algae species reported, some by the out-dated Encyclopedia Britannica are:

3,9 Ga blue-green
2,0 purple
1,0 blue-green and green
440 Ma green
380 red
365 brown

Definitions by ref.H

protozoans (single-cells)
- monera: prokaryotes (mono-cellular without nucleus) bacteria,
- protista: eukaryotes (mono-cellular, nucleus) blue/blue-green algae

metazoans (multi-cellular with tissue differentiation)
- plants produce their own food: multi-cellular (red, brown, green) algae without tissue differentiation, plus higher plants
- fungi absorb food from their environment
- animals digest their food

phyto-plankton: plants incl. diatoms
zoo-plankton: animals incl. radiolaria, foraminifera
nano-plankton: plants and animals <40μm

z zoological: **fauna, including hominids prior to Homo**

see also the References section for further biological notes

1,6 Ga to 650 Ma Riphean Period

	Subject Ref.	Source Ref.	
700 **Ma**	b,z	U	Multi-cellular organisms with tissue differentiation (see 720 Ma)
670	b,z	S,U	Fauna and flora similar to Ediacaran, including shelly cloudina (animal) and skeletonized calcareous algae fossils, 1st hard shells by bio-mineralization, maybe to deter predators, Kuibis, Namibia, China (600 Ma)
670	z	L	Proto-jellyfish, segmented worms, arthropods, corals = all soft-bodied, generally NOT precursors of present phyla, global distribution, Ediacaran Hills, South Australia

650 Ma to 600 Ma Vendian Period

650	z	U	Otavia, possibly proto-sponge, 1st animal fossil in Africa (see 600 and 550 Ma)
600	b,z	V	Eukaryotes develop into metazoans, present-day choano-flagellants eukaryotes still produce proteins required for metazoans and animals (see 670 Ma)

600 Ma to 543 Ma Ediacaran Period

600	z	U	Split of Ediacaran fauna and Cambrian true animals (see 670 Ma)
600	z	U	Sponge-like otavia, Otavi, Namibia (see 650, 550 Ma)
590	z	6	Soft-bodied 0,5m long multi-cell animals in deep seas
580	z	3	Fossils with bilateral symmetry, jellyfish with radial symmetry (floating but mostly anchored)
580	z	H	Marine arthropods, annelids (ring worms)
570	z	7	Multi-cellular animal embryos, China (see 500 Ma)
550	b,z	H	Archaeo-cyathids, similar to but unrelated to sponges, involved in forming reefs by calcareous algae, Ediacaran Hills, Australia (see 650, 600 Ma)
543	b,z	3,6	Ediacaran extinction, 70% of life extinct, especially single cell organisms, e.g. acritarchians (850 Ma)

543 Ma to 490 Ma Cambrian Period

	Subject Ref.	Source Ref.	
540 **Ma**	b,z	3	Sexual and food competition starts, "survival of the fittest", viruses (stripped-down cells) as parasites
530	b,z	7	"Cambrian explosion of life" (see 525 Ma)
530	z	3	Small shelly mollusk fossils, brachiopods, trilobites with eyes (the oldest visual system = thousands of calcite rods) and other arthropods, possibly from pre-Cambrian un-fossilized tiny shell-less animals (see 450 Ma)
530	z	G	Branching sponges, jellyfish, big arthropods, echinoderms: proto-crinoids (sea-lily), eleutherozoa (starfish, sea urchins), mollusks (see 500 and 290 Ma)
530	z	L	Pikaia, founder of chordata phyla (see 450 Ma)
525	b,z	L	Possibly end of "Cambrian explosion of life", 30 of present phyla found, no NEW body building plans since developed, all ecological niches occupied (530 Ma)
520	z	3,6	Burgess shale: all major marine groups incl. predators exist, but only in northern hemisphere, Canada
520	z	AB	Anomalocaris.canadensis, 60cm to 2m long, largest predator amongst extinct invertebrates
500	e b,z	W	Ozone levels are now sufficient to protect terrestrial life incl. animals from UV radiation (see 580 Ma)
500	z	G,Q	Star fish, 70kg, 2m long predators, sea-scorpions, sea-urchins, nautiloid cephalopods: catfish, octopus, cuttlefish, squid and nautilus (see 530 Ma)
500	z	Q	Nautilus (squid-like) now generally only 20cm long, but present Humbold squid up to 2m long (see 300 Ma)
500	z	W	Embryos of worm-like animals scanned by SRXTM tomography, yolk pyramids, Siberia/China (see 570 Ma)
500	z	Y	Spiny ancestors of marine worms among 1st sea animals
490	z	H	Cambrian mass-extinction of marine fauna

490 Ma to 443 Ma Ordovician Period

470	z	H	Brachiopods, crinoids, stromatolites: = timing fauna
450	z	P	Conodonts with eyes thrive, Cedarberge, South Africa and North America (see 530 Ma)
450	z	3	Corals (tabulate + rugose) (limey skeletons of polyps related to colonial jellyfish) add to Cambrian reefs
450	z	3,G	Graptolites, of uncertain relationship, colonies of polyps ?
450	z	P,3	Ancestor of modern fish, 15cm long, no vertebrae, no teeth, with scales, fins (see 530, 435 Ma)
443	z	3	Ordovician mass extinction: >½ marine species extinct

443 Ma to 417 Ma Silurian Period

Subject Ref.		Source Ref.	
435 **Ma**	z	4 G,H	Ostracoderms: small, armored jaw-less fish with outer carapace, cartilage internal skeleton North America (see 450, 420, 354 Ma)
425	z	W	Shell crayfish with young in breeding chamber, Herefordshire, UK (see 400 Ma)
425	z	7	Tracks of arthropods = first terrestrial animals, Western Australia (see 420, 400 Ma)
420	z	K	"Pneumodesmus" oldest millipede fossil, Rhynie chert, Scotland (see 425, 410 Ma)
420	z	H	Appearance of acanthodiae, 1st jawed fish (435, 354 Ma)

417 Ma to 354 Ma Devonian Period

410	z	W	Millipedes with up to 750 pairs of feet, 2m length, 50cm wide, largest arthropod ever, could kill animals up to deer-size (see 420, 400 Ma)
410	z	W	Eoactinistia.foreyi lung fish, Victoria, Australia (see 395 Ma)
409	z	K	Oldest shark skeleton, paired chest fin radii (until now unknown with cartilage fish), 20 My earlier than previously known, 50-75cm long, Canada (see 360 Ma)
400	z	AB	Arrow-tail crayfish fossils, they had blue blood (425)
400	z	V	Hax genes activated, reshaping fins into limbs in lobe-fin fish embryos, leading to fish with fingers on fins, later a fish walking on land (see 385 Ma)
400	z	AB	Fish 1st vertebrates, develop facility to communicate by sounds using a neural regulating group of cells unchanged since than in all vertebrates
400	z	W	Dunkleosteus.terrelli, an 11m, 4t armor-plated fish with a 5 000kg force of its jaws, the greatest ever (see 380 Ma)
400	z	H,7 I	Terrestrial fossils: proto-scorpions, millipedes evolve, spider webs first as shelter, later to catch insects once these had developed wings, Rhynie chert, Scotland (see 410, 320 Ma)
400	z	AF	Wing-less insect eggs are round and smooth (300 Ma)
397	z	AG	Fossilized footprints of 1st vertebrate tetrapod (365)
395	z	5,H	Coelacanths (actinista), the most primitive species of proto-modern lung fish, thought to be extinct since 80 Ma, found living off South Africa and Indonesia, live birth, limb-like fins, jaws, 100kg (410, 375 Ma)
385	z	V	Eusthenopteron lobe-fin fish had fins with 1 large and 2 smaller long bones, similar to present mammal limbs (see 400, 375 Ma

	Subject Ref.	Source Ref.	
385 **Ma**	z	H	Fringe-finned fish with limb-like fins, a sister group of lung fish (see 350 Ma)
380	b,z	H	Tabulata/stromatopora reef communes prosper, Canning basin, Australia and Bighorn Canyon, Montana (360 Ma)
380	z	AB	Materpiscis.attenboroughi, a 23cm placoderm armored fish, 1st live birth, sex with penetration, with fetus and umbilical cord, proving live births evolved as early as egg laying, 30 My earlier than previously known (see 400 Ma)
375	z	V,W Z	Ichthyostegalia, "missing link" between actinista (lung fish) and tetrapod (amphibians): body of 2m long lobe-fin fish with scales and fins, 20cm long flat skull, distinct neck, bones within fins relating to legs, arms and wrists, but neck, ribs, bones in pectoral fins like tetrapod, sub-tropical climate, Tiktaalik, Arctic Canada (see 395, 385 Ma)
365	z	V	Tetrapod vertebrates have fully developed limbs including toes, despite being aquatic (397, 360 Ma)
360	e b,z	S	O_2 levels 35% of atmosphere in Devonian/Carboniferous, allowing plants/animals to grow large quickly, South Africa (see 580 and 200 Ma)
360	b,z	H	Tabulata/stromatopora reef communes extinct, Canning basin, Australia and Bighorn Canyon, Montana (380 Ma)
360	z	W	Bothriolepis.africana, coelacanth, lamprey and a new placoderm fish species in fossil beds in marine sub-arctic shale, Grahamstown, S.Africa (see 345 Ma)
360	z	G,H	Predaceous mollusk-eating sharks (see 409, 300 Ma), 10m long placoderms (armored fish), rays, insect-like arthropods (see 300 Ma)
360	z	AF	Tetrapods, common ancestors of all vertebrates (see 365, 350 Ma)
354	z	G,H	Devonian mass extinction: 70% of marine species incl. jawless ostracoderms (435), jawed acanthodiae (420)

354 Ma to 290 Ma Carboniferous Period

350	e,z	W	O_2 maximum of 30%, causing fish-like vertebrates to leave the oceans, developing into amphibians (tetrapods) (see 375, 360, 270 Ma)
350	z	5	Rhipditia fish, relatives of the coelacanth, colonize land, developing tracheae/lungs, establishing 5-digit tetrapods ,developed into all subsequent vertebrates (see 360, 340 Ma)
350	z	H	Freshwater bivalves, New York State, USA
340	z	H	Amphibians the only terrestrial vertebrates, up to 6m long (see 350, 320 Ma)

	Subject Ref.	Source Ref.	
340 **Ma**	z	AB	Thuringothyris.mahlendorffae, 30 skeletons, oldest terrestrial vertebrates, mostly <1m high, proto-saurians, 12 species, some previously unknown, including seymouria, previously only found in USA (proving existence of contemporary connection), Tambach, Thueringer Wald, Germany (see 287 Ma)
325	z	H	Mass extinction of marine fauna (crinoids, ammonoids)
320	z	H	Winged insects (see 400, 300 Ma)
320	z	H	Oldest reptiles with amniote eggs, independent from aquatic reproduction (see 340, 300 Ma)
310	z	W	16 orders of reptiles start to evolve, turtles are 1 of 4 which survived to present (see 300 Ma)
300	z	3	Sea-lily forests, related to sea-urchins, 100s species
300	z	Q	Vampire squid, precursor to modern squids and octopuses, Monterey Canyon off California (500 Ma)
300	z	W	Sharks develop ability to rip apart prey larger than themselves (see 360 and 170 Ma)
300	z	AF	Insect eggs develop spikes and other means to anchor them on suitable bases (see 400, 290 Ma)
300	z	Q,Y	Odonates (dragonflies, damselflies) and cockroaches (see 320 Ma)
300	z	P,H	Reptiles are 1st vertebrates to live whole life on land, amniote eggs with tough membranes (310, 287 Ma)
300	z	3	Reptiles with almost solid bone heads (see 310 Ma)
300	z	7	Synapsids = mammal-like large terrestrial reptiles (see 260 Ma)
290	z	G	Most echinoderms disappear (see 530 Ma)

290 Ma to 248 Ma Permian Period

290	z	G	Pulmonata (air-breathing snails), spiders, 7 orders of winged insects up to 75cm wingspan, cockroaches (300)
290	z	G	Proto ray-finned fish (see 115 Ma)
290	z	AB	Gerobatrachus.hottoni missing link fossil between frog (200, 180 Ma) and salamander (100 Ma), fused ankle bones of salamander, wide skull of frog, backbone a mix of both
287	z	W	Eudibamus.cursoris, 1st bi-pedal proto-saurians, male and female dimetrodon with 2m dorsal sails, 250 brachiosaurs, 80cm proto-saurus (oldest quadruped terrestrial vertebrates) Tambach, Thueringer Wald, Germany (see 340 and 270 Ma)
285	e,z	Q	Marine animals in warm, shallow sea, Moab, Utah (150)
280	z	3	Dragonflies as big as seagulls, millipedes 2m long

	Subject Ref.	Source Ref.	
270 **Ma**	e,z	W	Saurians survived O_2 minimum of 15% by developing new breathing system, using air sacks hidden in hollow bones, inherited by present-day birds (see 350 Ma)
270	b,z	U	Start of most complete fossil record of Gondwana, Karoo, South Africa (see 180 Ma)
270	z	P	Locusts thrive in Richtersveld, Namibia
270	z	H,3	Therapsidae (mammal-like carnivorous reptiles) with advanced legs and jaws, able to tear apart their prey before swallowing, ectotherm (cold blooded), up to 3m: dimetrodon, anteosaur, pelycosaur with dorsal fins, possibly already endotherm (warm blooded) with a pelt (see 287 and 220 Ma)
265	z	U	Mesosaurus, small aquatic 1st reptile fossil found in South Africa (see 250 Ma)
260	z	U	Synapsid, anapsid, diapsid reptiles radiate, South Africa (see 300 Ma)
260	z	AF	Mammal-like impala-sized saber-toothed therapsid Tiarajudens.eccentricus, similar to a South African species, oldest known example of closely related terrestrial vertebrates in Gondwana , Southern Brazil
250	z	7,3	Brachiopods with "lids" (see 530 Ma)
250	z	3,G	Lung fish, many species, true bugs, beetles, stone-flies abundant
250	z	1	Reptiles spread, fish: large scales, cartilage skeletons, animated suspension since then
250	z	Q	Some reptiles returned to seas (see 265, 200 Ma)
250	z	G,7	Archosauria.lagosuchus, A.euparkeria, common ancestors of dinosaurs, crocodilians, flying reptiles, birds
250	z	AF	Start of ichthyosaur ("fish lizard") run (see 90 Ma)
250	z	3	Saurian egg with shell, Texas (see 300 Ma)
250	z	7	Cynodont (dog-toothed lizard), precursor to Gondwana mammals (see 210 Ma)
250	z	AM	Fossilized termite mounds, South Africa
248,2	b,z	U,6	Permian extinction: major extinction of 96% of all species, 90% of maritime (trilobites, all corals etc.), 80% of terrestrial life extinct, including glossopteris, therapsids
248,2	e,z	H	Permian extinction not a single but continuous event over several My, probably caused by cooling and low sea levels

248,2 Ma to 205,7 Ma Triassic Period

Ma	Subject Ref.	Source Ref.	
240 **Ma**	z	Z	Crocodilians spread
240	z	W	Pig-sized mammal-like lystrosaurs herbivore reptile survived Permian extinction together with some carnivore species, Gondwana (see 210 Ma)
240	z	AF	Giant ichthyosaur raptor, Augusta Mtns., Nevada, USA
240	z	AG	1m high dinosaur-like Asilisaurus.kongwe, 10My older than previous dinosaur fossils, Tanzania
230	z	H	Crocodilians as terrestrial reptiles (see 190 Ma)
225	b,z	3,H	Modern reef-building hexacorals symbiotic with algae, dinoflagellates, nano-plankton (see 160, 150 Ma)
225	z	7	Pro-sauropods, herbivore crocodiles, Madagascar (see 190, 170 Ma)
225	z	Q	Henodus.chelyops, a placodont marine reptile, wider than long, bony carapace, Europe (see 215 Ma)
225	z	I	Sinocondon, mammal-like, 1st modern jaw hinge evolved (see 210 Ma)
220	z	7	Long-tailed pterosaurs evolve globally, 120 species, possibly warm-blooded with fur (= hair), first vertebrates to fly (see 270, 144 Ma)
215	z	H	Hexa (= 6-sided) corals appear, recent species built coral reefs
215	z	Q	Giant ichthyosaurs, largest ever marine reptile, gave birth to live young (240 Ma), plesiosaurs (200 Ma), nothosaurs, probably 1st reptiles to hunt in the sea, placosaurs, maritime saurians with lungs (225 Ma) North America
210	z	Y	Efficia.okeefeae, a 2,5m ancestor of crocodiles, New Mexico, USA (see 250 Ma)
210	z	G	Fish-eating trematosaurs, rhynchosaurs, ponderous herbivores
210	z	I	Cpl. skeletons of cynodont (see 250 Ma) and lystrosaur (see 240 Ma), both therapsidae, Antarctica
210	z	H,I	Mammal-like reptiles develop to morganucodentids, shrew-sized 1st proto-mammals, larger cranium/brain, single lower jaw bone, molars more complicated, jaw bones in 1 piece, separate middle ear bones, 1 set of permanent teeth, hence producing mother milk (see 225, 200, 195, 190 Ma)
205,7	c b,z	7,H	Triassic extinction (by comet impact, indicated by iridium abundance and a "fern spike" ?), mass extinction of marine species, mammal-like reptiles extinct, seed ferns disappear (see 215, 210, 140 Ma)

205,7 Ma to 144,0 Ma Jurassic Period

	Subject Ref.	Source Ref.	
205 **Ma**	z	I	Toothed monotremes, modified molars for modified diet (see 190, 175 Ma)
200	z	3	2 types of dinosaurs: saurischian (lizard-hipped) and ornithischian (bird-hipped) (see 80 Ma)
200	z	1	Proto-mammals had 4-5x larger relative brains than reptiles, were 1st to have brain neo-cortex: higher cognitive functions (see 210, 195 Ma)
200	z	3	Marine reptiles: ichthyosaurs, plesiosaurs (are not dinosaurs) return from land to sea, give birth there (see 250, 190 Ma)
200	z	U	Shrew-sized 1st true mammals, alongside therapsid ancestors (140), South Africa (see 210, 190 Ma)
200	z	V	Frogs evolve (see 290, 180, 90 Ma)
195	z	G	Chelonia (turtles, tortoises) of unknown ancestry
195	z	I	Hadrocodium.wai, mouse-like proto-mammal with detached middle-ear bones, relatively large brain, China (see 190, 200 Ma)
190	z	G	Cuttlefish, 600 genera of ammonoids
190	z	H	Crocodilians now also marine reptiles (see 230 Ma)
190	z	G	Ichthyosaurs, allosaurs (carnivores), enormous 4-pedal amphibious dinosaurs, pterosaurs (flying reptiles with 11m wing span), 1m long snake-like animals (200)
190	z	P	Massospondylus.carinatus, a pro-sauropod, 6 eggs (oldest ever) with embryos, Golden Gate, South Africa (see 225, 170 Ma)
190	z	K	Elephant shrew and golden mole do not belong to insectivore branch of mammals, but to afrotheria, together with elephant, aardvark and hyrax (DNA), ancestor a tiny paper-clip sized proto-mammal, China
190	z	S	Erythrotherium and megazostrodon the 1st true mammals (see 210, 195 Ma)
190	z	S	4 main mammal groups: monotremes (205, 175), multi-tuberculates (175), marsupials (167, 100), placentals (see 167, 125 Ma) (see also Notes for details)
187	z	AG	Arcusaurus, 2m long dinosaur, Senekal, South Africa
185	z	Q	Temnodontosaurus, an ichthyosaur, eyes 20cm diameter, could dive 650m deep, Europe
180	b,z	U	End of fossil record of Gondwana, Karoo, S.Afr. (270)
180	z	H	Proto-frog, Argentine (see 200, 90 Ma)
180	z	K	Dinosaurs look like rhinos, with long necks and tails, High Atlas, Morocco
175	z	H,G	Herbivore multi-tuberculata mammals appear, the most abundant until their disappearance, developed independently from proto-mammals (see 190 and 60 Ma)

	Subject Ref.	Source Ref.	
175 **Ma**	z	W	Platypus, a monotreme mammal, 5 pairs of chromosomes determine its sex, most mammals only have 2 pairs, similarity to chromosomes of birds and mammals, which are thought to have evolved independently (205 Ma)
170	z	3	Modern sharks appear (see 300 Ma)
170	z	1	Brontosaurs (sauropoda) disappear (see 190, 225 Ma)
167	z	I	Ancestor of marsupial and placental mammals with tribosphenic teeth, Gondwana (see 190 Ma)
165	z	G	Oldest sturgeons appear
165	z	G	Hymenoptera (ants, bees, wasps, true flies, earwigs) appear (see 148 and 100 Ma)
165	z	G	Stegosaurs (plated, 4-pedal) (see 160, 150 Ma)
164	z	W	Castorocauda.lutrasimilis, a fishotter-like mammal, 60cm long crane, China
161	z	Z	Tuojiangosaurus, herbivore with long, tapering spikes from each shoulder, China
160	e,z	I	Plankton evolved, extracting CO_2 from atmosphere using C to form shells, releasing O_2 (225, 150)
160	z	Q	Huge fish and flying reptiles, Svalbard, N.Atlantic
160	z	Z	Burst of evolution of new species of saurians, leading up to horned ceratopians, armored stegosaurs and tyrannosaurs (see 165, 150 Ma)
160	z	W	"Dino Death Trap" with 100's of skeletons of proto-triceratops, proto-crocodilians, 5 small guanlong CGI (proto-Tyrannosaurus.rex) dinosaurs stacked on top of each other, toothed and tooth-less theropods (changed from carnivore to herbivores), trapped in a mud pit, Junggar Basin, NW China
160	z	Z	Epidendrosaurus, sparrow-sized theropod, smallest dinosaur excl. birds, disproportionately large hands and 3rd fingers, China
160	z	AB	Anchionis.huxleyi, chicken-sized oldest bird ancestor, long feathers over feet as well, suggesting 4-winged dinosaur, NE Liaoning Province, China (see 150 Ma)
155	z	7	Short-tailed pterosaurs evolve, prosper until 65 Ma
≥150	z	AF	Anchiornis, chicken-sized proto-bird, covered in symmetrical feathers unsuitable for flight, China
150	z	H	Braarrudisphaera.bigelowi, a calcareous nano-plankton species (see 64 Ma)
150	z	Y	Turiasaurus.riodevensis sauropod, 36,5m long, 45t (= mass of 6 male elephants), Spain
150	z	I,3	Young dromaeosaur (theropod) shares 100 anatomical features [wishbone, swiveling wrists etc.] with bird, primitive feathers for warmth, not flight, China
150	z	W	Europasaurus.holgeri, group of small-sized 6m long dinosaurs, Harz, Germany

	Subject Ref.	Source Ref.	
150 **Ma**	z	3,W	Archaeopteryx: dinosaur/bird, earliest feathers, teeth and feet like dinosaurs, Sonthofen, Germany (see 160 and 140 Ma)
150	z	W,Z	Maritime pliosaur, 16m long, size of a bus, Svalbard Island, Arctic Sea
150	z	AF	Grottenolm evolves, a cave dwelling lizard, blind, lungs and gills, Adriadic Mountains, Istria, Croatia
150	z	7	Fossilized horse-shoe crab, North America
150	z	1	Stegosaurs die out (see 165 Ma)
150	z	Q	Limbic brain system develops from rhinen-cephalon ("swelling brain") in mammals (see 100 Ma)
148	z	P	Termites appear, start social organization, cementing their nests, first villages, then cities (see 165, 100 and 40 Ma)
144	z	7	Long-tailed pterosaurs die out (see 220 Ma)
144	b,z	H	Limited extinction of fauna and flora

144,0 Ma to 65,0 Ma Cretaceous Period

144	z	Z	Proliferation of crocodilians, Gondwana
140	z	G	Sponge reefs, primitive skates, marine crocs, Central Europe
140	z	H	Last therapsidae disappear (see 200 Ma)
140	z	G	Pterodactylus (flying saurian), Central Europe
140	z	W	Pterodaustro (flying saurian), bird-like,1 000 tiny teeth, 2m wing span, 100s of fossils, Argentina
140	z	5	Proto-bird shenzhoiuraptor fossil: no teeth, very long tail, able to fly, China (see 160, 150 Ma)
135	z	Y	Psittacosaurs appear (see 100 Ma)
135	z	P,Q	Dakosaurus.andiniensis, a jumbo carnivorous marine reptile "Godzilla", distant relative of crocodiles, paddles instead of feet, rudder-like tail, Pacific Ocean (then a deep tropical bay), off Chili
130	z	Z	Amargasaurus, double row of bony spines, Argentina
130	z	P	Repenomanus.robustus mammal, 60cm long, 7kg, ate small psittacosaur, ripping like a crocodile, which changes our perception of saurian/mammal relation, also found Repenomanus.giganticus mammal, 90cm long, 13,6kg, Liaoning, China (see 125 Ma)
130	z	W	Proto mammal, 1st evidence of renewable teeth, Germany
128	z	K	Flying incivosaurus, buck- toothed, cross between dinosaur and rabbit, herbivore, part of carnivorous theropod family, China
125	z	P	100's of falcarius.utahensis, 1st transitional herbivore therizinosaur, bone structure of carnivore, body of herbivore, lost serrated teeth, Utah, USA

	Subject Ref.	Source Ref.	
125 **Ma**	z	Q,Y AF	Volcanic gases killed, and thick rain of volcanic ash preserved Dilong.paradoxus, a proto-tyrannosaur (160) with hair-like proto-feathers, adult psittacosaur (130) and 34 juveniles (day care?), Hyphalosaurus. lingyuanensis, aquatic predator, protopteryx (150), a theropod primitive bird with 3 types of feathers, probably evolved from reptile scales, China
125	z	I	Jeholodens, placental mammals, mobile shoulder girdle allows increased range of motion (see 165 Ma)
125	z	I	Eomaia.scansoria: furred proto- placental "dawn mother", tree-living, 50 My earlier than previously thought, ex Asia or Gondwana (see 190, 167 Ma)
120	z	I	Archaeoraptor.liaoningensis.sloan = a forgery, China
115	b,z	3	Flowering plants and flying insects in "co-evolution" (pollination), both becoming highly specialized
115	z	1	Fish with bony skeletons and small scales (290 Ma)
115	z	I	Micro-raptor gui, crow sized bird ancestor, feathers on all 4 limbs, maybe gliding, not flying, China
110	b,z	U	80 species of fauna and flora, including lemurs, are endemic to Madagascar (see 51 Ma)
110	z	7	River crocodile, 10t, (= 10-15x Nile crocs), Sahara
110	z	Q	11t kronosaurs and woolungasaurs, marine predators
110	z	z	Nigersaurus, a diplodocoid herbivore sauropod, 80% of skeleton with light-weight skull bones, paper-thin vertebrae, 600 teeth, muzzle like a lawn mower, Niger
105	z	AG	Pakasuchus kapilimai, a cat-like Gondwana crocodile, short head with differentiated teeth, only the tail armored, Tanzania
100	z	Z	Leatherback turtles evolve (see 80 Ma)
100	z	Z	Modern crocodilians evolve, including Nile crocodile, Africa, saltwater crocodile, SE Australasia, alligator, North America
100	z	K,P	Nothomyrmecia proto-ant, evolved from solitary tiphiid wasps, forced to organize to compete with termites, thought extinct, found living in Australia (165, 148)
100	z	G	Octopods appear, ichthyosaurs decline, various plesiosaurs, salamanders
100	z	Y	Psittacosaurs disappear (see 135 Ma)
100	z	3	Marsupials spread globally (see 190 Ma)
100	z	Q	Cerebral cortex developed (see 150 Ma)
100	z	I	DNA data says most modern mammal groups appear (60 Ma)
98	z	AB	2 new sauropod saurians (largest herbivores ever and up to 30t) and a 2m carnivore with 3 huge claws on each extremity, Queensland, Australia
97	z	Z	Spinosaurus, 15m long, with 2m long dorsal spines, largest terrestrial carnivore ever, North Africa

	Subject Ref.	Source Ref.	
96 **Ma**	z	AB	Polypterus.senegalus, a present fish family long thought extinct, has skin built up by 4 nano-structured alternating soft and hard layers, Senegal
95	b,z	H	Sea weeds, rudist reef builders symbiotic with algae (see 85 Ma)
95	z	W	Carcharodontosaurus.iguidensis (shark lizard), size of Tyrannosaurus.rex, teeth banana-sized, Morocco similar C.saharicus, a shallow sea covering the intervening land lead to 2 species, Niger
94	z	Q	Thalassomedon plessiosaurs, marine predators, 6m neck carried stones in stomach for ballast, North America
90	b,z	S	Oldest South African angiosperm and insect fossils
90	z	S	Frogs look like at present, South Africa (200, 180 Ma)
90	z	AF	End of ichthyosaur ("fish lizard") run (see 250 Ma)
90	z	I	Argentinosaurus, 39m long herbivore, South America
88	z	W	70% of skeleton of 33m futalognkosaurus, of the titanosaur family, also pterosaurs, megaraptors, Patagonia, Argentine (see 80 Ma)
85	b,z	H	Rudists up to 1m long build reefs together with algae, at the expense of corals (see 95 Ma)
85	z	H	Snakes appear, related to modern boa and python
85	z	AB	Gigantoraptor.erlianensis, bird-like dinosaur with a beak, small legs and probably feathers, 1,5t, 8m long, 5m high, 35x larger than closest relative caudipteryx, West China
85	z	H	Mammals (marsupials and placentals) exist
82	z	W	Mzamba Fossil Formation, petrified forest, ammonites, inoceramus (giant clams), etc., Natal, South Africa
82	z	Z	Carnotaurus "meat-eating bull", battering ram head with horns, short arms, long legs, small teeth, Patagonia, Argentine
82	z	I,K	Bats the only mammals to survive the separation of New Zealand from Australia, (mitochondrial DNA) (60, 47)
80	b,z	W	Bee with oldest orchid pollen, Costa Rica
80	z	Q	Green turtles, Pacific Ocean (see 100 Ma)
80	z	Z	Modern crocodiles evolve (see 240 Ma)
80	z	I	1 000's of titanosaurus egg clusters swamped by flood, aucasaurs attacked young, Auca Mahueva, Patagonia (see 88 Ma)
80	z	I	Fossilized killing by velociraptor (carnivore) of proto-ceratops (herbivore), Gobi Desert, Mongolia
80	z	U	Indication that birds evolved from small light-boned theropod saurischians (reptile-hipped), not from ornithischians (bird-hipped) (see 200, 70 Ma)
76	z	Z	Parasaurolophus.walkeri, herbivore saurian, N.America
75	z	P	8 albertosaurs found, hunted in icy conditions, Canada

	Subject Ref.	Source Ref.	
75 **Ma**	z	Z	Styracosaurus, nose spike, profusion of head horns, rhino-sized herbivore, Alberta, Canada
75	z	I	Duck-billed dinosaur, Baja California
75	z	Q	Mosasaurs, marine raptors, North America
70	g,z	W	Giant frog "Devil Toad", 4,5kg, armored, not related to African, but to S.American ceratophrys, suggests that Madagascar still was, via much warmer than present Antarctica, part of Africa (see 110 Ma)
70	z	U	Fossil beds, some of the fish fossils still show color spots on scales, Stompoor crater, South Africa
70	z	1	First butterflies
70	z	Q	Cluster of eggs and dinosaur pelvis with 2 un-laid eggs, closer to birds than reptiles, China (80 Ma)
70	z	Z	Deinocheirus, possibly ornithomimid saurus, with 2,45m extra long arms, 25cm claws, Mongolia (80 Ma)
70	z	Z	Masiakasaurus, Alsatian-sized carnivore, Madagascar
70	z	P	Bird and eggs fossils, Romania (see 80 and 60 Ma)
70	z	1	Archaic creodonta (carnivorous mammals) (see 45 Ma)
68	z	W	Molecular evidence of protein fragments of T.rex suggest relation to birds (see 160 Ma)
67	z	Z	Dracorex, herbivore pachycephalosaur with spiky head and snout, South Dakota, USA
67	z	7	"Sue", most cpl. skeleton of T.rex ever found, London
66	z	I	Coprolite of Tyrannosaurus.rex, Saskatchewan, Canada
66	z	W	Tyrannosaurus.rex not found in Africa
65	z	G	Ammonoids extinct, nautiloids almost extinct
65	z	H	Marine reptiles and triceratops the last major dinosaur groups to die out
65	z	L	Carnivore marsupials: lions, dogs, herbivore marsupials: rhino-like, ground sloth, giant kangaroo, tapir-like, giant capybara, also giant lizards, all extinct, Australia (see 50 Ma)
65	z	6	Cretaceous/Tertiary (K-T) boundary extinction of 60 to 70% of fauna species globally, incl. saurians

65,0 Ma to 54,8 Ma Paleocene Epoch

65	z	U	Of the many reptilian species only 3 groups survived: lizards/snakes, crocodiles/alligators and birds
65	z	L	400 to 500 species of mega fauna survived globally, but only 4 marsupial species, Australia
65	z	S	Toads, corals, nautiloids (but not ammonites) survived
65	z	3,H	Turtles, crocodiles and lizards just survived, but now adaptive radiation of birds and mammals
64	z	H	Calcareous nano-plankton disappears (see 150 Ma)

	Subject Ref.	Source Ref.	
63 **Ma**	z	7	Extinct hoofed archaic ungulates split into mesonychidae, early whales (55 Ma) and even-toed ungulates (see 30 Ma)
60	z	G	Nearly all modern bird species exist (see 70 Ma)
60	z	3	Diatryma, giant flightless carnivorous bird (40 Ma)
60	z	G	Multi-tuberculates extinct (see 175 Ma)
60	z	W	Indohyus, a badger-sized herbivore aquatic land mammal, thought to be common ancestor of whales and hippos, initiating return to the sea (see 55, 50 Ma)
60	z	P	Mammal with poison fangs, Canada
60	z	I	Fossils say most modern mammal groups appear (100 Ma)
60	z	V	Bats evolve, nocturnal, paper-thin wings, echolocation (see 82 and 47 Ma)
60	z	4	Plesiadapidae, proto-simian proto-anthropoid, Europe, North America
60	z	C,S I	Madagascar lemurs and tarsiers share common ancestor with lemurs, tarsiers survive in interior of SE Asian islands (see 57 Ma)
57	z	4,H S,L	Anthropoids, ancestor to Old World monkeys/primates/ hominoids, tree-living, hands and feet hominoid, split from proto-simians (tarsiers, bush babies, lemurs), Africa (see 60, 45, 35 Ma)
56	z	Z	Hyracotherium, a horse ancestor, (the 5-toed horses ?) North America (see 45 Ma)
55	z	I	Mammals now larger, up to pig size
55	z	Y	Gomphos.elkema, common ancestor of rodents and lagomorphs (rabbits, pikas, hares), Mongolia
55	z	I	Phosphatherium.escuilliei, oldest proboscidean (elephant group), fox-sized, no trunk, straight "mouth", Morocco (see 54 and 50 Ma)
55	z	W	Whales and hippos split from common ancestor, they are now not considered related (see 63, 60, 55 Ma)

54,8 Ma to 33,7 Ma Eocene Epoch

54,5	z	AB	Anthrasimias.gujaratensis, proto-anthropoid, very small teeth, 60 -80g, India (see 50, 47, 45, 30 Ma)
54	z	L	Proto-elephant, 1m high, swamp-living, (originally aquatic ?), Algiers (see 55 and 50 Ma)
53	z	H	Most of modern animal genera exist
50	z	I	Mola fish develops, weighs up to 2 000kg
50	z	AF	Eels develop (see 47 Ma)
50	z	AG	Chiloe-like marsupial rat, South America, common ancestor of all marsupials, Australia ?? (100, 65 Ma)
50	z	I	Pezosiren.portelli, quadruped, maritime ancestor of manatees

	Subject Ref.	Source Ref.	
50 **Ma**	z	7	Pakicetus = common ancestor of cetacea (whales/hippos and horses/pigs/cows/sheep): 4-pedal, hoofed, furry, co-living with marsupials, squirrel-sized anthropoids (54,5), Himalayas/ Pakistan (60, 55 Ma)
50	z	I	Indricotherium, elephant group, largest ever land mammal, mass of several elephants, no trunk, Asia (see 55 and 54 Ma)
50	z	I	Oldest whale with terrestrial habitat, Himalayas/ Pakistan (see 60, 55, 48 Ma)
48	z	7	Walking/swimming fresh water whale, 4-toed feet, hooves, indicating they re-migrated from land to sea (see 50 and 45 Ma)
47,5	z	AB	Whale with fetus in head-first position, indicates proto-whales rested and gave birth on land, Pakistan
47	z	W,3	Kopidodon.macrograthus, 1m long European fruit eater, crocodiles, fish, eels (50), ungulates, turtles, reptiles, snakes (85), birds, lemurs, marsupials, insects, oldest fully developed bats (47), semi-tropical forest shale pit, Messel, Germany
47	z	AB	Darwinius.marsillae, 95% complete female skeleton "Ida", perfectly fossilized missing link between pro-simians and anthropoids, absence of pro-simian and presence of anthropoid features, 3m long 1m high, opposable thumbs, 5-digit hands, semi-tropical forest shale pit, Messel, Germany (see 54,5 and 45, 30 Ma)
45	z	7	Whales are now true marine mammals (see 48 and 40 Ma)
45	z	I	Creodonta, omni/carnivorous mammals extinct (70 Ma)
45	z	H,3	Proto-horse, 5-toed horse ancestor, size of small dog, 4 toes in front, 3 at back, North America (56, 20 Ma)
45	z	I	Eosimia, anthropoid, grasping hands/feet, color vision (see 57 Ma)
42	z	Z	Icadyptes and another penguin species, during hot climate period, Ica, Peru (see 36 and 10 Ma)
40	z	P	Wars between termites and ants (how does one know that ??), ants develop formic acid as a weapon (148)
40	z	H	Diatryma flightless birds extinct (see 60 Ma)
40	z	P	Mekosuchinae fossils of modern-like freshwater crocodiles, Queensland, Australia
40	z	7	1st modern whales spread from Tethys Sea (see 45 Ma)
40	z	Q	Nearly complete skeleton of whale-like dorudon, with detached pelvis and little legs
40	z	H	Mammal families reach 100, almost present number
37	z	H	Medium severe extinction of Mesozoic mammals, North America
37	z	7	Proto-canidae, North America (see 8,0 and 5,0 Ma)

	Subject Ref.	Source Ref.	
37 **Ma**	z	AF	1 000's of Basilosaurus, a whale (!), 2 tiny webbed hind legs, Wadi Hitan, Egypt
36	g,z	I	Land bridge connects Cuba and South America, primates (new-world monkeys) migrate to Cuba (35 Ma)
36	z	Z	1,5m tall Icadyptes.salasi penguin, 30cm long thin beak, during hot climate, Peru (see 42 and 10 Ma)
35	z	3	Marsupials only mammals in Australia, cover all niches (see 1,9 Ma and 70 ka)
35	z	I	Some hyrax rhino size, others with legs like gazelles
35	z	H	Tithanotheroids, rhino family North America, (31 Ma)
35	z	L,S	New World monkeys split from anthropoids (see 36 Ma)
35	z	S	Aegyptopithecus, ape-like anthropoid, Egypt
35	z	L	Modern mammals with 4-5x larger relative brains than older ones
34	z	I	Catopithecus, anthropoid with same dentals as humans: 2 incisors, 1 canine, 2 premolars, 3 molars each half (see 30 Ma)
33,7	c,z	U	Major extinction of mammalians, possibly connected to 2 meteorite impacts, allowed development to modern mammals (see 35,5 and 31 Ma)

33,7 Ma to 23,8 Ma Oligocene Epoch

32	z	AB	Oldest proto-whales, proto-penguins, Waitaki Valley, New Zealand (see 25 Ma)
31	z	H	Tithanotheroids, rhino family, extinct, North America (see 35 Ma)
31	z	P	Oldest modern kolibri with feathers in Old World and 2 others slightly younger, Germany
31	z	V	Reported kolibri fossils may not be true humming birds
31	z	H	Further medium extinction of mammals, N.America (33,7)
30	z	H	Even-toed now outnumber odd-toed ungulates (see 63 Ma)
30	z	H	Saber-toothed cats appear (see 2,6 Ma)
30	z	H	Multi-tuberculata extinct (see 175 Ma)
30	z	AF	Glyptodonts appear, 2t armored mammals, Americas (see 10 ka)
30	z	4,S	Anthropoid "Proconsul", 150cm^3 brain, split into Old World monkeys and hominoids, Africa (34, 20 and 15)
27	z	I,3	Middle of Africa's "Dark Period", 2 272kg rhino-like largest arsinoitherium (31), 5 new proboscidea species (54), incl. 3 species of palaeo-mastodon (3,0), deinothere (1,0), gomphotherium (55) migrated to Eurasia, Chilca, Ethiopia

	Subject Ref.	Source Ref.	
25 **Ma**	z	AB	Proto-dolphin with shark-like teeth, proto-baleen whale similar to present blue whale, with teeth instead of baleens, huge eyes, only 3,5m long, Waitaki Valley, New Zealand (32, 15 and 5,0 Ma)
24	z	B	Lions, saber-toothed cats, hippos, hyenas, antelopes migrate from Eurasia to Africa, large African mammals mainly disappear (see 5,5 Ma)

23,8 Ma to 5,3 Ma Miocene Epoch

23	z	D	Caribbean corals extinct
20	z	AB	Vipers evolve with live births
20	z	3,H	Fanged venomous snakes, rats, mice, singing birds
20	z	Y	Pelicans appear in their present form
20	z	H	Para-hippus (leaf eater) changes to proto-hippus (grass eater), later to equus (horse) (45 and 4,0 Ma)
20	z	W	Pigs the only mammals to loose thermogenin gene due to warm climate, now piglets need warmth to survive
20	z	L	Apes migrate from Africa to Eurasia
20	z	S	Gibbons split off hominoid lineage (DNA), Asia (see 30, 15 Ma)
17	z	AF	Orangutans split from hominoid lineage, Asia (20, 15)
15	z	W	Megalodon, giant whale-eating shark, could swallow a rhino, 48t and 18m long, ancestor of Great White shark, only a tooth found, Zululand, S.Africa (1,0)
15	z	Q	Tiger sharks unchanged since then
15	z	V	200kg wingless Terror bird, Patagonia (see 2,0 Ma)
15	z	Z	Amazon dolphins, the largest of 4 river species, evolve from cetaceans before marine species appear, Amazon basin, South America (see 25 and 5,0 Ma)
15	z	I	Camels originate in North America (10, 6,0 Ma, 100 ka)
15	z	I,4 S	Ramapithecus "Man-Ape", split off hominoid line (DNA), 1st hominid (??), probably related to sivapithecus, ancestor of pongos (orangutans), Asia (20, 17, 10)
13	z	K	Proto-fur seals evolve from proto-bears (brown bears?)
12	z	7	Proto-duck/goose, 700kg, largest ever bird, not related to emu, ostrich, etc., Australia
10	b,z	I,H	High salinity killed all life when Western Mediterranean Sea was closed off
10	z	Z	Dominant theory held, that penguins evolved in Antarctica and moved to moderate climes much later (42, 36)
10	z	W	Recovered usable bone marrow of Rana.pueyoi, a frog species, Spain
10	z	I	Camels, horses, canidae migrate from North America to Eurasia (see 15 Ma)
10	z	G	Placental carnivores exterminate marsupials, S.America

	Subject Ref.	Source Ref.	
10 **Ma**	z	Q	Hawaiian monk seals, oldest of the pinnipedia sub-order, the only tropical seal, all others cold water
10	z	2	±20 species of apes in East Africa (see 15 Ma)
10	z	2,4 S,W	Chororapithecus.abyssinicus or Dryopithecines, man-like primates, knuckle walkers, ancestors of gorillas, chimpanzees, hominids, Africa and Eurasia (see 15, 9,5 and 7,0 Ma, 500 ka)
9,5	z	AF	Gorillas split off hominoid line (DNA), Africa (10 Ma)
8,0	z	K	700kg herbivore guinea pig, enemies: crocs, Venezuela
8,0	z	7	Epicyon, wolf-sized precursor of canidae, North America (see 37 and 5,0 Ma)
7,5	z	2	Ape species decline, monkeys prosper, East Africa
7,0	z	S,I AF	Chimpanzees split off hominid lineage, (DNA analysis), 1st African bipedal primate species (see 10 Ma)
6,9	z	T	Sahelanthropus.tschadensis hominid fossils, possibly should be Sahelpithecus, an early ape, West Africa
6,7	z	W	African and Asian elephants separate (see 2,6 Ma)
6,5	e,z	C	Fossil ape "Toumai", 350cm^3 brain, close to final common ancestor of chimpanzees and hominids, lived at 400 000km^2 Lake Chad, West Africa
6,5	z	AB	Assumed last common ancestor of chimpanzee and Homo, a species not yet discovered, East Africa (5,8, 4,4)
6,5	z	AL	Common ancestor of alcelaphinae (arid browser specialists, ±40 species since then) and aepycerotinae (generalists, few species) (see 5,5 Ma)
6,0	z	W	Argentavis.magnificus, 75kg, 7m wing span, largest flying bird ever, size of a Cessna 152, Argentine
6,0	z	AB	191 footprints of hitherto unknown and largest species of camels, oldest in Europe, Jumilla, Spain (see 10 Ma and 100 ka)
6,0	z	K	Barbary macaques, Morocco
6,0	z	5	Orrorin.tugenensis "Millennium Man", bipedal, 1,5m tall, lived in trees and on ground, omnivore, Tugen Hills, Kenya
5,8	z	AF	Ardipithecus.kadabba, fragmentary hominid bones, Ethiopia (see 4,4 Ma)
5,5	z	2	Alcelaphinae with only 1 antelope species, now there are 10, including wildebeest and blesbok, East Africa (see 24, 6,5 and 5,0 Ma)
5,5	z	I	Lower jaw and molar of hominid, East Africa

5,3 Ma to 1,8 Ma Pliocene Epoch

5,0	z	S	Hemphillian extinction almost annihilated grazing animals, horses reduced to 1 species, S.Africa (5,5)
5,0	z	7	Walrus-like dolphins (see 25, 15 Ma)

	Subject Ref.	Source Ref.	
5,0 **Ma**	z	W	35% of chimpanzees carry the M and N types of the HIV retrovirus, the O type is carried by gorillas, PtERV1 retro-virus infects primates but not Homo, this may explain why primates despite infection are immune to the HIV1 retrovirus (see 10,0 ka)
5,0	z	S	750kg carnivorous bear, relative of panda, South Africa (see 2,0 Ma)
5,0	z	7	Eucyron, fox-sized early canidae, later evolves into wolves, jackals, coyotes (see 8,0 and 1,5 Ma)
5,0	z	AB	Dipoides, proto-beavers, ⅓ size of present species,
5,0	z	AL AC	Dinofelis (false saber-toothed cat) appears, dominant prey later seems to be australopithecus, Eurasia (see 1,2 Ma)
5,0	z	2,4	Divergence of bipedal hominids and apes (chimpanzees), molecular evidence (see 1,5 Ma)
4,5	z	1,S	**Australopithecus**, bipedal ground dwelling hominid 2 genera, stone tools/implements, East Africa (4,1)
4,4	z	AF S	Ardipithecus ramidus female "Ardi", (related to **Au.** ?), 1,2m, 50kg, partially bipedal, not knuckle-walking but long arms, Aramis, Central Awash, Tim White 1994, Ethiopia 1997 (see 6,5 and 5,8 Ma)
4.1	z	P,C	**Au.**anamensis: small carnivore hunters, small brain, 1st confirmed bipedal, Mrs.Leakey 1995, Kenya (see 4,5 and 3,9 Ma)
4,0	z	5	Mammoths develop in Africa, later migrate to Siberia and North America (see 7,0 and 5,0 ka)
4,0	z	Z	Horses develop, via mesohippus, archeohippus, parahippus, hippidion, dinohippus and other species to equus, North America (see 20, 3,0 and 1,6 Ma)
3,9	z	P	**Au.**afarensis almost cpl. skeleton incl. ankle bones, complete tibia, thighbone, Afar, Ethiopia (4,1 + 1,8)
3,7	z	C,3 S	Fossilized footprints of 3 hominids, "1st Family", probably **Au.**afarensis, walked upright like **H.**habilis Mrs.Leakey 1976, Laetoli, Tanzania, East Africa
3,6	z	AG	**Au.**afarensis fossil bones in excellent condition, Afar, Ethiopia 2005
3,6	z	S	Oldest **Au.**afarensis fossil in South Africa, 1925
3,5	z	S	Fossil beds, almost all species found there are now extinct, Swartkrans, South Africa
3,5	z	S,C	"Little Foot", **Au.**afarensis, a complete skeleton may be found, excavations continue, R.Clarke 1994, Sterkfontein, South Africa
3,5	z	C	**Au.**bahrelghazali "Abel", M.Brunet 1995, Chad
3,4	z	AG	**Au.**afarensis used stones to scrape meat from animal bones, Dikika, Ethiopia (see 2,5 Ma)

	Subject Ref.	Source Ref.	
3,3 **Ma**	z	7	**Kenyanthropus**.platyops (rudolfensis ?), Lake Turkana, Kenya, Mrs.Leakey 1999 (see 3,0 and 2,4 Ma)
3,3	z	W	Very complete skeleton of 3 year old **Au.**afarensis "Selam", shoulders and arms like gorilla's, Ethiopia
3.18	z	S,C	"Lucy", herbivore **Au.**afarensis, 1-1,2m tall, brain 400cm^3 (chimpanzee 320-480cm^3, modern human 1 400cm^3), D.Johanson, R.Leakey, Y.Coppens 1974, Hadar, Ethiopia
3,0	z	W	5m tooth, thigh bones of 25 year old 6t mastodon, 3,5m high, Greece (see 27 Ma, 50 ka)
3,0	z	W	Start of Great Barrier Reef by corals, Australia
3,0	z	AB	Terrestrial fauna migrate in both directions but maritime fauna are divided after North and South American plates collide
3,0	z	Z	Equus (horse) emigrated from North America to Eurasia and Africa (see 4,0 and 2,0 Ma)
3,0	z	I	Gelada primates roam Africa and India, only 1 species survives, Ethiopia
3,0	z	1	Fossil skull differs from other **Au.**, possibly **K.**platyops ?, Lake Rudolph, East Africa (see 3,3 Ma)
3,0	z	S	**Au.**africanus 1,3m tall, walked upright, hands/feet human-like, mixed herbivore/carnivore, 480cm^3 brain
2,7	z	2	**Au.**aethiopicus, East Africa (see 2,4 Ma)
2,6	z	D	Separation of African savannah elephant from Laxodonta.cyclotis, a forest dweller (see 6,7 Ma)
2,6	z	4	Saber-toothed cats in Americas (see 30 Ma and 12 ka)
2,6	z,d	4,C	**Au.**africanus thought to have evolved to **Homo.**habilis, East Africa (see 1,9 and 1,6)
2,6	z,a	I	**Au.**aethiopicus (or **H.**habilis ?) make oldest fabricated stone tools =Oldovan pebble culture, 1997, Lokalelei, Kenya and Gona, Ethiopia
2,5	z	S,2	"Taungs Child", now known to be young **Au.**africanus boy 3-4 years old, probably killed by a raptor, R.Dart 1924, Taungs, South Africa
2,5	z	AG	2nd oldest use of stone tools by **Au.**afarensis to scrape meat from animal bones, Bouri, Ethiopia (see 3,4 Ma)
2,5	z	AF C	**Au.**garhi, cranium 450cm^3, better bipedal than other **Au.**, but typical **Au.** dentition, T.White 1999, Hata, l'Awash, Ethiopia
2,5	z	C	"Black Skull", **Au.**aethiopicus, East Africa
2,5	z	2	Expansion of hominid brain, Africa (3,18 and 3,0 Ma)
2,5	z,f	L	Meat eating by hominids, East Africa
2,4	z	G	Dwarf hippos, dwarf elephants, probably shortage of grazing, Mediterranean islands, Malta (see 95 ka)
2,4	z	C	**Au.**aethiopicus extinct, East Africa (see 2,7 Ma)
2,4	z	C	**K.**rudolfensis (platyops ?), Kenya, East Africa (see 3,3 and 1,7 Ma)

	Subject Ref.	Source Ref.	
2,15 **Ma**	z	S	"Miss Ples" (originally classified as Plesianthropus. transvaalensis) ,adult female **Au.**africanus, Dr.R.Broom 1990, Sterkfontein, South Africa
2,0	z	W	60cm tall mini Panda, now 1,2m, South China (5,0 Ma)
2,0	g b,z	5	Ngorongoro volcano explodes, 18km crater with 100m walls, creating unique closed habitat, East Africa
2,0	z	V	Terror Birds vanish, possibly due to land bridge between Americas, South America (see 15 Ma)
2,0	z	Z	Horses emigrate from North to South America (see 3,0 and 1,6 Ma, 10 ka)
2,0	z	C,S	**Paranthropus** ("almost human") hominid side line, probably evolved from **Au.**afarensis, genus with 2 species: **P.**robustus and **P.**bosei, East/South Africa (see 1,9 and 1,8 Ma)
1,9	z	G	Marsupials radiate like placentals, Australia (35 Ma)
1,9	z	C,2	**P.**robustus, 1,7m tall, brain 550cm^3, almost complete skull found, Drimolen, South Africa (2,0, 1,0 Ma)
1,865	z	AF AG	**Au.**sediba, almost cpl skeletons, boy and women, said to be new species, link between **Au.** and **H.**, small brain, long legs and arms **Au.**-like; pelvis, shape of teeth, long cranium **H.**-like, (R.Leakey not convinced) Berger 2008 Malapa, Maropeng, S.Africa
1,8	z	S	**Au.**afarensis disappear, Africa (see 3,9 Ma)

1,8 Ma to 42,0 ka Lower Paleolithic Age

1,8	z	S	**P.**bosei, (originally called zinjanthropus), even more robust than **P.**robustus, large brain, omnivore, sagittal crest along the top of skull, East Africa (see 2,0, 1,8 and 1,5 Ma)
1,8	z	C	**K.**rudolfensis, large brain, 1,4m tall, 25-45kg, Kenya (see 3,3, 2,4, 1,7 Ma)
1,8	z d,m	1,2 S	**H.**ergaster (possibly **H.**erectus ?) coexists with **AU.**, Swartkrans, South Africa (see 1,9 Ma)
1,78	z	I,S	Saber-tooth cat, rhino, horse, giant ostrich, short-necked giraffe, 10% are African species, found 1999, Dmanisi, Georgia, Caucasus
1,7	z	C	**K.**rudolfensis extinct, East Africa (3,3, 2,4, 1,8 Ma)
1,6	z	Z	Equus (horse) develops, N.America (2,0 Ma, 10,0 ka)
1,5	z	7	Wolf-like canidae (see 5,0 Ma and 400 ka)
1,5	z	AF	Bonobo (pygmy chimpanzee) separates from chimpanzee (see 5,0 Ma)
1,5	z	C	**P.**bosei extinct, East Africa (see 2,0, 1,9, 1,8 Ma)
1,2	z	AL AC	Dinofelis (false saber-toothed cat) disappears, dominant prey seemed to be **Au.**, Eurasia (5,0 Ma)
1,0	z	B	Deinothere (proboscides) extinct, Eurasia (see 27 Ma)

	Subject Ref.	Source Ref.	
1,0 **Ma**	z	Q	Megalodon extinct, cartilage skeletons like sharks, 5t, 15m long, teeth only fossils found (see 15 Ma)
1,0	z	2	3-toed horse, saber-toothed cat almost extinct, E.Afr
1,0	z	S	**P.**robustus disappears, Swartkrans, South Africa (1,9)
500 **ka**	e,z	Q	Hippopotamus larger than at present, indicating warm climate, England (see 24, 2,4 Ma, 6,0 ka)
500	z	W	Mus.cypriacus, differs from house mouse, Cyprus
500	z	4	Gigantopithecus fossil ape extinct, China (see 10 Ma)
500	z	W	Primitive ancestors of Dessert Bighorn sheep migrate from Asia via Beringia land bridge to America
450	z	I	Pithecanthropus fossil hominoid in France
410	z	Z	Woolly mammoth appear, northern Eurasia, America (120)
400	z	Q	Proto-elephant Paleoloxodon.antiquus found during excavation for Channel tunnel, France/UK (see 100 ka)
400	z	7	Wolves start living near humans, scavenging detritus (see 1,5 Ma, 14 ka)
275	z	AF	Darwin's fox separates from South American grey fox (see 120 ka)
200	z	P	Polar bears evolve from grizzly bears, Arctic
150	z	AB	Cichlidae (multi-colored bass) populate Victoria Lake, East Africa (see 15 ka)
130	z	W	Felis.silvestris.lybica (African wild cat) (9,0 ka)
125	g,z	K	Coral reef atop a volcano rim rises from the sea, home of rhea (flight-less bird), giant tortoise, Aldabra Is., Seychelles, Indian Ocean
120	e,z	Z	Woolly mammoth decline dramatically due to global warming, but survive (see 410 ka)
120	z	Q	Arctic foxes established as a species, Arctic (275 ka)
100	z	P	African lions migrate to Asia, now only in India (see 10,0 ka)
100	z	7	Grey wolves all over Asia (see 80 ka)
100	z	Y	Wolves migrate from Asia to Ethiopia, only 600 remain
100	z	7	Proto-dogs (see 14 ka)
100	z	W	Elephant-sized dromedary camel, El Kowm, Syria
100	z	I	Camels become extinct in California, migrated to Middle East and Africa (see 15 Ma)
100	z	Q	Proto-elephant Paleoloxodon.antiquus extinct (400 ka)
95	z	Q	Cow-sized stegodonts (extinct elephant ancestors prone to dwarfing) and giant rats, Flores Is., Indonesia (see 2,4 Ma)
90	z	I	Musk oxen migrate from Siberia to North America
90	z	Y	Only known complete skeleton of 18 months old extinct narrow-nosed rhino, 1st thought a donkey, then a pre-historic bear, La Peruyal, Spain
80	z	7	Grey wolves migrate from Asia to N. America (100 ka)

	Subject Ref.	Source Ref.	
70 **ka**	e,z	W	Giant kangaroos, wombat-like marsupials, gigantic emus starved to death due to extreme climate changes, Australia (see 46 ka)
50	z	7	Genyornis, flightless 200kg birds extinct, Australia
50	z	W	Mastodont fossils, Alaska (see 3,0 Ma and 13 ka)
46	z	AG	Major extinction of mega-fauna, probably by climate change and/or (controversially) humans, aborigines and settlers, Australia (see 70, 30 ka)

42,0 ka to 10 ka Upper Paleolithic Age

40	z	I	Oldest fossils of La Brea asphalt pit: saber-toothed cat, mammoth, camel, bison, wolf, giant ground sloth, pig, horse, Californian lion, antelope, rodents, tapir, 125 bird species Los Angeles, USA (see 5,0 ka)
40	z	I	Large carnivorous kangaroos, truck-sized wombat-likes, marsupial lions twice the size of leopards, Tasmania, Australia (see 46, 30 ka)
40	z	Z	Most complete mammoth ever found, a calf, NW Siberia, Russia (see 7,0 ka)
30	z	W	2m high, 3m long, 3t giant wombat, Australia (40 ka)
20	z	K	Cave paintings of Przewalski's Takhi (Mongolian wild) horse, only remaining wild horse species
15	e,z	AB	Victoria Lake dries up almost completely, the multi-colored bass survive in small but deep Kivu Lake, preserving the genes of the original 500 species, East Africa (see 150 ka)
15	z	Q	Extinct horse, cameloid, giant armadillo found in cenotes, Yucatan peninsula, Mexico
14	z,f	7 AG	Wolves domesticated to dogs, oldest dog bones in human remains, proving dogs were bred before humans settled (see 400 ka)
13	z	7	Mastodons extinct, Florida (see 50 ka)
12	z	7	Extinction of saber tooth cats in Americas (2,6 Ma)
12	z	I	Fossils of extinct goat, sheep, Grand Canyon, USA
12	z	AF	Goats and sheep domesticated
11	z	AF	Pigs domesticated
11	z,f	L	"Pleistocene Overkill" by invading Clovis people, extermination of 57 species of large mammals incl. mammoth, glyptodont, elephant, mastodon, N.America (see >30, 14 and 9,0 ka)
10	z	G	Many mammal groups disappear, due to global warming or human activities ?
10	z	AF	Glyptodonts disappear, 2t armored mammals, Americas (see 30 Ma)
10	z	3	Giant sloth, glyptodont extinct in South America

	Subject Ref.	Source Ref.	
10 **ka**	z	O	500kg cave bear (Ursus.spelaeus) extinct, bones of 50 000 found in a cave in the Austrian Alps, W.Europe
10	z	Z	Horses extinct in Americas (see 1,6 Ma)

10,0 ka to 7,0 ka Mesolithic/Archaic Age

10,0	z	7	Asian lions live in Balkans, Anatolia, Persia, Northern India (see 100 ka)
10,0	z	AF	Cats domesticated (see 9,0 ka)
10,0	z,d	K	Aids virus theory: sick monkey eaten by chimpanzee (immune, but carry the virus), this eaten by Africans (see 5,0 Ma)
9,0	z,f	W	Domestic cat established, Fertile Crescent (130 ka)
8,0	z	AF	Chicken domesticated
7,0	z	3	Last mammoths, Wrangell Island, Alaska (see 4,0 Ma)

7,0 ka to 5,0 ka Neolithic Age

6,0	e,z	Y	Hippos, needing water all year round, Sahara, Northern Africa (see 10,0 ka)
6,0	z	AF	Llamas and alpacas domesticated
5,5	z	AF	Horses domesticated by Botais, Kazakhstan
5,0	z	I	Youngest fossils of La Brea asphalt pit: saber-toothed cat, mammoth, camel, bison, wolf, giant ground sloth, pig, horse, Californian lion, antelope, rodents, tapir, 125 bird species, Los Angeles, USA (see 40 ka)
5,0	z	AF	Water buffalo and dromedary domesticated

The 4 Groups of Mammals

according to the Encyclopedia Britannica (ref. G)

multi-tuberculata	extinct, rodent-like
monotremes	only platypus and spiny anteater survive, egg-laying, have no nipples, secrete milk through hair glands
marsupials	dominant group within mammals 200 - 100 Ma, now only opossum in N.America, others in Australia, New Guinea, scrambled DNA of avian, reptilian and mammalian ancestry, rear young in pouch, have nipples
placentals	rear young in womb

4 Super Orders of Placental Mammals

according to the National Geographic Magazine, (ref. I):

based on DNA tests rather than on fossils:

euarchontoglires,	supra-primates: rodents and primates
afrotheria,	elephant, aardvark, hyrax, mantee, elephant shrew, tenrec, golden mole
laurasiatheria,	flying fox, free-tailed bat, llama, cow, whale, hippopotamus, pig, seal, cat, pangolin, tapir, rhinoceros, horse, mole, hedgehog, shrew
xenarthra,	armadillo, sloth, anteater

The Animal Phyla

extracted from: Geology for South African Students, G.N.G. Hamilton et al., 4th rev. ed., 1960, C.N.AU., ref. R:

Phylum Protozoa (1st life): single-celled jelly-like, similar to amoebae
Order **Foraminifera** built small external calcareous shells which make up large part of chalks
Order **Radiolaria** built lace-like siliceous skeletons
both form large part of abyssal ooze of the sea, still present

Phylum Porifera (pore bearing): this comprises the sponges, many of which have no skeleton, but in the chitinous framework of some is a supporting skeleton of siliceous spicules, which can fossilize

Phylum Coelenterata (hollow-bodied): includes the sea-anemones, jellyfish and corals, also the extinct group of **Graptolites**

Phylum Echinodermata (hedgehog-skinned) with 5-fold symmetry: includes starfish and sea-urchins **(Echinoids)** and the almost extinct group of sea-lilies **(Crinoids)** which have a long stem of disk-like calcareous joints

Phylum Annelida (ring-bodied): includes some of the worms, although themselves not fossilized, their burrows are some built calcareous tubes, which also occur as fossils

Phylum Brachiopoda (arm-legged): 2-valved, similar to shellfish, bilaterally symmetrical about a plane perpendicular to their valves, not about the plane dividing their valves

Phylum Mollusca (soft-bodied): **Lamellibranchiata** include all ordinary bivalved (symmetrical about a plane separating the valves) such as mussels, cockle and oysters
Gasteropoda (univalve mollusks) contain the spirally coiled shells, such as snails, welk and cowry
Cephalopoda include catfish, octopus, cuttlefish and nautilus, builds new compartments as it grows
extinct **Ammonites** usually have flat coils

Phylum Arthropoda (joined legs) all invertebrates with jointed limbs, 3 sections, including insects nand the class **Crustacea** (including lobsters and crabs) and the **Trilobites**, extinct since 250 Ma

Phylum Chordata (chorded) includes **Fish**, **Amphibians** such as frogs and newts, **Reptiles** (turtles, snakes, lizards, crocodiles), **Birds**, **Mammals**

Some terms used in this section

phyto-plankton: plants
zoo-plankton: animals
nano-plankton: plants and animals <40µm

hox (homoeo box)	genes in fauna, 183 gene pairs controlling growth
wox	genes in flora, 183 gene pairs controlling growth
placoderm	armor-plated fish
ostracoderms	armored jaw-less fish
arthropods	insects, spiders, mites, scorpions, crustaceans, centipedes, millipedes
anapsids	evolved into turtles
eurypsids	evolved into arthropods, fossils 2m long diapsids evolved into saurians
synapsids	mammal-like large terrestrial reptiles
therapsids	mammal-like reptiles
cynodonts	dog-toothed, gave rise to mammals
tetrapods	4-limbed terrestrial vertebrates
coprolites	fossilized feces
saurischians	lizard-hipped reptiles, according to recent claims some evolve to birds (!)
ornithischians	bird-hipped reptiles, as above
brachiosaurs	front legs sized as hind legs, 5 toes, herbivores
spinosaurs	dorsal spines/sails, incl. T.Rex, carnivores
archaeopteryx	ancient winged (saurischian reptile)
creodonts	carnivorous early mammal
anthropoids	ancestors to Old World monkeys/primates/hominoids
hominoids	proto-hominids, quadrupeds
hominin	suggested new name for hominoids
hominids	proto-homo, bipedal

Notes: ref.AF (Tim White)

AR.=Ardipithecus: primitive biped, foot between tree dweller (big toe opposed to other toes) and fully bipedal (our big toe), teeth reduced, woodlands habitat

Au.= Australopithecus: still small-brained, fully bipedal, no longer restricted to woodlands, ranging from Tschad to Ethiopia and south to Transvaal

Au.anamensis and **Au.**afarensis are merely a continuing development without exact

G Subject Lists Anthropology:

When checking these lists for mistakes, please watch out for (maybe) correct times at or near - but on the wrong side of - a boundary

d development of Homo: **1st appearances, characteristics, ethnic lines, extinctions**

Please note that I have listed the archaic ***H.****sapiens as* ***H.****sapiens or* ***H.****sap. and the modern* ***H.****sapiens as* ***H.****sapiens sapiens or* ***H.****sap.sap. Neanderthals are shown as* ***H.****sap.neanderthalensis, a classification which is under dispute, some preferring* ***H.****neanderthalensis*

Please check *Notes* at end of section

5,3 Ma to 1,8 Ma Pliocene Epoch

	Subject Ref.	Source Ref.	
2,6 **Ma**	z,d	4,C S	**Australopithecus**.africanus thought to have evolved to **Homo**.habilis, East Africa (see 1,9 and 1,6)
2,1	d	W	Speculated appearance of **H.**erectus, East Africa (1,9)
1,9	d	Q	Oldest **H.**habilis fossils, Koobi Fora, Kenya (2,6 Ma)
1,9	d	W	**H.**habilis, lived with **H.**erectus (largely carnivore) for 500ky, who would have evolved independently from him (Mrs. Leakey), Kenya (see 2,1 and 1,78 Ma)

1,8 Ma to 42,0 ka Lower Paleolithic Age

	Subject Ref.	Source Ref.	
1,8	z d,m	1,2 S	**H.**ergaster (possibly **H.**erectus ?) coexists with **AU.**, Swartkrans, South Africa (see 1,9 Ma)
1,78	d,m	C,D	Group of **H.**erectus, 1st "Out-of-Africa pioneers", tiny brow ridge, short nose, huge canines, 1st smallest brain yet, 2nd much larger (2 species or male/female difference was larger than), primitive tools, 1999, Dmanisi, Georgia, Caucasus (2,1 and 2,0 and 1,9 Ma)
1,78	d,f	Q	**H.**erectus switches to being carnivore because of seasonal cold weather, Dmanisi, Georgia (1,9 + 1,44)
1,7	d,a f	S	**H.**erectus, 1 100cm^3 brain, used (but could not make) fire, hunted in teams, East Africa (1,6 Ma, 300 ka)
1,6	d	I	**H.**habilis extinct in Africa (see 2,6 Ma)
1,6	d	H	**H.**erectus, originally classified as a Pithecanthropus (see 700 Ma)
1,55	d	W	**H.**erectus small skull, female ? (Mrs.Leakey), Kenya
1,54	d,a	C,I S	**H.**erectus "Turkana Boy", super-bipedal, 1,3-1,6m tall, 12 years, 850cm^3 brain, small teeth, Proto-Acheulean tools, first weapons, R.Leakey 1984, Kenya

	Subject Ref.	Source Ref.	
1,44 **Ma**	d f	W	Part of upper jaw with some teeth, skull of **H.**erectus, largely herbivore (Mrs.Leakey), Kenya (see 1,78 Ma)
1,2	d,m	W,Z	**H.**antecessor, (**H.**erectus ?), 1st **H.** fossil in Europe, Atapuerca, Spain (see 780 and 700 ka)
1,0	d	AG	Suggested divergence date for claimed "X-Woman" **H.** species, possible relation of **H.**antecessor ? (see 1,2 Ma and <48 ka)
780 **ka**	d	N	**H.**antecessor (**H.**erectus ?), cannibalism on 6 hominids, Atapuerca, Spain (see 1,2 Ma)
700	d	AB	Hominid fossil, attributed to Pithecanthropus.erectus (old name for **H.**erectus), claimed to be "a twin" of "Java Man", Germany
700	d	Z	Ancestral **H.**sapiens and **H.**sapiens.neanderthalensis start to split (see 500 and 370 ka)
600	d	AF	**H.**erectus skull, Bodo, Central Awash, Ethiopia 1976
500	d	V	Last common ancestor of **H.**sapiens.neanderthalensis and **H.**sapiens (see 700 and 370 ka)
500	d	3,4	**H.**sapiens, East Africa (see 400, 200 ka)
410	d	Q	**H.**erectus extinct, China (see 300, 100 ka)
370	d	Z	Estimated lineage separation of **H.**sapiens and **H.**sapiens.neanderthalensis, based on genetic data (see 700 and 500 ka)
300	d	2	**H.**erectus disappears in Africa (see 1,7 Ma, 410 ka)
260	d,m	V	1,68m tall, 78,5kg female **H.**sapiens, largest known such fossil, also most northern and eastern human habitation, Jinniushan, Chinese/Korean border
259	d,m	S	Skull of **H.**sapiens, upright gait, pronounced brow ridges, "Florisbad Man", Florisbad, South Africa
230	d,m	Z	**H.**sapiens.neanderthalensis only counted about 15 000, hunting and gathering in Eurasia from Atlantic to Siberia, central Eurasia to Mediterranean (45, 28 ka)
200	d	S	3 calcified footprints by **H.**sapiens, Nahoon Point, East London, South Africa (see 500 Ma)
200	d	V	1st **H.**sap.sap. probable, **H.**sapiens likely disappears, East and South Africa (500, 195, 160, 150, 100 ka)
200	d,a	I	Fossils of **H.**sapiens.neanderthalensis: snout-like jaws, 100 000 worked stones, bones of rhinoceros, elephant, archaic cow, near Perpignan, France (230)
195	d	V,Y	Oldest fossils of **H.**sap.sap., previously thought to be 135 ky old, Omo Kibish I + II, Ethiopia (200, 160 ka)
160	d	V	**H.**sap.sap. fossils, Herto Ethiopia
157	d	AF	Skull of **H.**sapiens.sapiens, 1 450cm^3 crane (larger than present average), Herto, Ethiopia 1997
150	d	V,7	1st **H.**sap.sap. women "Black Eve", identified by mtDNA and DNA in X chromosome already in its present form, today found in San people and 2 African tribes having similar languages, South and East Africa (200, 59 ka)

	Subject Ref.	Source Ref.	
120 **ka**	d	?	**H.**sap.sap. split into Negroids (see 30,0 ka) and Non-Negroids (see 100, 70, 50 and 35 ka)
100	d	S	**H.**erectus extinct in Eurasia (see 410 ka)
100	d	K	When leaving Africa on 1st major exodus, **H.**sap.sap. had to lighten his black skin color to produce the necessary vitamin D (see 120 ka)
100	d,m	4	**H.**sapiens last fossils in China (see 200 ka)
95	d,a	Q	Claimed new species **H.**floresiensis, hunters, used fire and stone tools, Flores Is., Indonesia (see 18 and 12 ka and *Notes*)
70	d	Q	Only about 2 000 (?) people survived worldwide in aftermath of Mt.Toba explosion (see 74 and 35 ka)
70	d	4	Non-Negroids split (based on mtDNA) into a northern group of Caucasoids/Mongoloids and a southern group of SE Asians/Pacific Islanders, and New Guineans/ Australians (see 120, 50, 35 ka)
62	d,m	T 7,D	Aboriginals settled, extinct **H.**sap.sap. genetic lineage Lake Mungo, South Australia (50 and 45 ka)
60	d	V	Hyoid bone of **H.**sap.neanderthalensis suggests ability of speech, Kebara cave, Mt.Karmel, Israel (see 43 ka)
60	d,m	W	M130 Y chromosome, suggests arrival of 1st **H.**sap.sap., India
60	d,m	V	Major migration of **H.**sap.sap. from Africa to Near East, ancestors to all non-Negroids (see 100 ka)
60	d,a	V	"Great Leap Forward": tools are getting more refined, food is exploited more efficiently and art develops, indicating a change in conceptual thought by a more modern language, a distinct genetic change (see also *Notes* at end of this section)(see 50, 35 ka)
59	d	V	Khoi-San the oldest **H.**sap.sap. survivors but not the 1st, have more ancient evolutionary DNA than any other people, their language !Xu, probably the oldest, has 141 sounds, Southern Africa (see 200, 150 ka)
59	d	V,Q	Genetic analysis has traced the Y chromosome of all present **H.**sap.sap. males back to one "Adam" in Africa, M96 chromosomes of Negroids (see 150 ka)
52	d	K	**H.**sap.sap. "Cro-Magnon" brought "deletion at 508 gene of CF" (cystic fibrosis) to Western Europe (40 ka)
50	d	V	M168 Y chromosome found in all Non-Negroids (70, 40)
<48	d	AG	"X-Woman", a child, claimed to be new **H.** species, (another Hobbit?) based on mitochondrial DNA, Denisova, Siberia (see 1,0 Ma)
45	d	2	**H.**sap.neanderthalensis disappears in Middle East (28)
45	d,m	Q	M89 Y chromosome marks a major migration out of Africa, mostly found in Middle East (see 12 ka)

	Subject Ref.	Source Ref.	
43 **ka**	d	Z	Fossils of 9 **H.**sapiens.neanderthalensis had skulls and long bones smashed to gain brain and marrow tissue, faint traces of DNA genes MC1R and FOXP2 indicate red hair and pale skin, capacity for speech, El Sidron, Asturia, Northern Spain (see 60 ka)

42,0 ka to 10 ka Upper Paleolithic Age

40	d	E	6 gene groups ex Cro-Magnon live in Europe (7,0 ka)
40	d	V	M9 Y chromosome in Eurasian people (see 50, ka)
40	d,a	K	Cro-Magnon people (**H.**sap.sap.) had the modern lowered larynx enabling distinct speech, Southern Europe (see 50 and 15 ka)
38	d	W	1st **H.**sap.neanderthalensis genome to be deciphered by 454 Life Sciences, USA/Max Planck Institute, Germany
37	d	P	Penultimate genetic mutation of human brain, effecting 70% of global population (see 6,0 ka)
35	d	?	Northern group of Non-Negroids splits into Caucasoids and Mongoloids (see 70, 15 and 12 ka)
35	d	?	Southern group of Non-Negroids splits into SE Asians/ Pacific Islanders (see 70 and 8,0 ka) and New Guineans/Australians (see 70 and 12 ka)
35	d	Q	Major population expansion started, Altai Mountains, Central Asia (see 60 ka)
35	d,m	K	Ainos with Caucasian racial characteristics (related to Cro-Magnon ? = my speculation), Japan (32, 9,5)
30	d	Q	M173 Y chromosome found in most Western Europeans, M20 Y chromosome originated in Iran/India
28	d	4	Last **H.**sap.neanderthalensis extinct, Gibraltar, Spain (see 230 and 45 ka)
25	d	4	Mongoloid fossils, China (see 35 ka)
25	d	K	Khoi-San people in South Africa, 85 000 still survive now (see 10,0 ka)
24,5	d	T	Skeleton of **H.**sap.sap. 4 year old child with some ancient features (**H.**sap.neanderthalensis ?), Portugal
20	d	?	Split of New Guineans and Australians (see 35 ka)
18	d	Q,P	7 tiny bodies of **H.**floresiensis, (a tribe of "pygmies" **H.**sap.sap ?), including a 91cm tall 22,7kg female, brain <30% of modern humans, skull similar to Dmanisi people (?), nicknamed "Hobbits", speculation that children were born normal size but stopped growing, Flores Is., Indonesia (1,78 Ma, 95, 12 and 6,5 ka)
15	d	?	Mongoloids split into NE Asians and Amerindians (see 35, 10,0 ka)
12	d	?	Hamitic/Semitic peoples split from Caucasoids (35 ka)
12	d	Q	Massive eruption ends "**H.**floresiensis" (see 95, 18 ka)
12	d	Q	M172 Y chromosome found mainly in Middle East (45 ka)

10,0 ka to 7,0 ka Mesolithic/Archaic Age

	Subject Ref.	Source Ref.	
10,0 **ka**	z,d	K	Aids virus theory: sick monkey eaten by chimpanzee (immune, but carry the virus), this eaten by Africans (see 5,0 Ma)
10,0	d	V	M3 Y chromosome in Amerindians (see 15 ka)
10,0	d,f	S	Khoi-San (Bushmen) split from Negroids, San people maintain hunter-gatherer style, Khoikhoi adopting pastoral ways, Southern Africa (see 25 ka)
9,5	d,m	7,P	Skull form of "Kennewick Man" indicates Caucasian origin (?),possible Aino link (?), Washington State, USA (see 35, 32 ka)
8,0	d	?	Split of SE Asians and Pacific Islanders (see 35 ka)
8,0	d	AB	Mutation creates 1st blue eyes for **H.**sap.sap.

7,0 ka to 5,0 ka Neolithic Age

7,0	d	E	One gene group ex Cro-Magnon in Near East (40, 9,5 ka)
6,5	d	4	Pygmies separate from Negroids, West African rain forests (see 30, 18 ka)
6,0	d	P	Last genetic mutation of human brain, effecting 30% of global population (see 37 ka)

Queries on extinctions of the various hominin species

How and why did the various species of **Australopithecus** and **Homo** disappear in pre- historic times ?
Were they wiped out by climate changes ?, or by their successors ?
How come then, that at present, and for millions of years, at least 3 large cats (lion, leopard, cheetah) and at least 3 types of dog-like predators (hyena, jackal and wild dog) are living side by side with each other in East and southern Africa ? (let's not forget we belong to the animal kingdom !)
Maybe we can find the answer in historic times:
During the late classical and early medieval period numerous Germanic and Turk tribes migrated throughout Europe and found new places to settle, the Vandals even in Tunisia !
However, within a few centuries they all had mostly disappeared, not by being killed off by subsequent conquerors, but by intermingling with the native populace
This appears to me a logical explanation for the disappearance of the various (sub-)species of **AU.** and **H.**, since climate change during this period was not excessive

Disappearance of **H.**sapiens.neanderthalensis: different number of chromosomes than **H.**sap.sap. making common offspring infertile ?
It is thought that **H.**sapiens.neanderthalensis at the height of their distribution over almost all of Eurasia did not number more than 15 000

Notes:

there are more genetic differences between horse and zebra than between **Homo** and chimpanzee

The Controversy of Human Development

There are many theories how early Homo.habilis evolved to Homo.sapiens.sapiens, and I only list here the more realistic looking ones:

from **AU.**africanus via **H.**habilis (2,6 Ma) to **H.**erectus (2,1 Ma), **H.**ergaster (1,8 Ma) to **H.**sapiens (500 ka), to **H.**sap. sapiens (200 ka)

as above, but **H.**ergaster not considered to be a separate species, but rather a primitive form of **H.**erectus, both lines in Africa

another variety: **H.**erectus developed to Java Man (1,8 Ma) and Peking Man (670 ka) in Asia and to **H.**heidelbergensis (800 ka) and **H.**neanderthalensis (500 ka) in Europe

2 branches of **H.**erectus are postulated by some for Europe and Asia, the European branch said to be ancestors to **H.**neanderthalensis, *but **H.**neanderthalensis was more likely a **H.**sapiens.neanderthalensis*

H.antecessor (1,2 Ma), claimed to be ancestor to **H.**sapiens (500 ka) and **H.**sapiens.neanderthalensis (500 ka), would have existed 500 years without fossils, *was more likely a **H.**erectus or **H.**sapiens*

H.florensis: (see 95 and 18 and 12 ka), Flores Is., Indonesia claimed to be an extinct **H.** species nicknamed "Hobbits" (Dean Falk), speculation: children were born of normal size but stopped growing, newest speculation: small size of woman's skull caused by microcephaly (skull abnormally small due to abnormal brain development) (Robert Martin), now considered an abnormal **H.**sap.sap., caused by food deficiencies and isolation

It is claimed, that **H.**sap.sap. now evolves 100x faster than before, recent genetic changes in specific areas and/or populations represent 7% of genome, caused by dietary changes and infectious deceases. This included a gene allowing adults to digest milk, another allowing genetic resistance to malaria for some Africans

Nature reported: in 2000 Meave and Louise Leakey discovered 2 partial skulls in Kenya, of which the **H.**erectus was older than the **H.**habilis
my comment: this is in line with the fact that both species lived side by side for 500 000 years (see listing)

Do new species develop gradually or in "jumps" (allopatric speciation) ?

Climatic changes seem to play a major part either way. (ref. AL)

Ploetz, Weltgeschichte (ref. AI)

This shows the overlapping (and confusing) timing of the evolution from hominins to humans, as well as the difficulties to classify the fossils correctly, as evidenced by the differences in terminology between this reference and others, as shown in my listing, eg. Paranthropus.aethiopicus and **AU.**aethiopicus
Kenyanthropus.rudolfensis and **H.**rudolfensis
Pithecanthropus.erectus and **H.**erectus

6,4 Ma - 6,2 Ma Sahelanthropus
6,0 Ma Ma Orrorin.tugensis
5,8 Ma - 5,2 Ma Ar.ramidus.kadabba
4,4 Ma Ma Ar.ramidus
3,5 Ma - 3,3 Ma Kenyanthropus.platyops
2,7 Ma - 1,9 Ma Paranthropus.aethiopicus
2,2 Ma - 1,3 Ma Paranthropus.bosei
1,9 Ma - 1,2 Ma Paranthropus.robustus

4,1 Ma - 3,9 Ma AU.anamensis
3,8 Ma - 2,9 Ma AU.afarensis
3,6 Ma - 3,0 Ma AU.bahrelghazali
3,0 Ma - 2,4 Ma AU.africanus
2,5 Ma 2,5 Ma AU.garhi

2,4 Ma - 1,8 Ma H.rudolfensis
2,0 Ma - 1,5 Ma H.habilis
1,8 Ma - 1,1 Ma H.ergaster
1,1 Ma - 200 ka H.erectus
700 ka - 400 ka H.antecessor
600 ka - 200 ka H.heidelbergensis

300 ka Start of Late H.erectus = ante-Neanderthal (Swanscombe, Steinheim) (see 200 ka)
200 Start of proto-Neanderthal (Krapina) (see 120 ka)
120 Start of classical Neanderthal (see 30 ka)
30 End of classical Neanderthal (see 120 ka)

Development of the modern human races:

The queries and contradictions between the various sources of information and theories regarding the development of the human races are illustrated by this list, extracted from this subj. listing

This extract includes all source references marked "?" in the above listings, which are my own time estimates, and I hope that the experts will come forward with more realistic dates

It remains unclear, what role exactly epigenetic switches and trans-generational mutations played in these developments

120 **ka**	d	?	**H.**sap.sap. split into Negroids (see 30 ka) and Non-Negroids (see 100, 70, 50 and 35 ka)
70	d	4	Non-Negroids split (based on mtDNA) into a northern group of Caucasoids/Mongoloids and a southern group of SE Asians/Pacific Islanders, and New Guineans/ Australians (see 120, 50 and 35 ka)
35	d	?	Northern group of Non-Negroids splits into Caucasoids and Mongoloids (see 70, 15 and 12 ka)
35	d	?	Southern group of Non-Negroids splits into SE Asians/ Pacific Islanders (see 70 and 8,0 ka) and New Guineans/Australians (see 70 and 12 ka)
20	d	?	Split of New Guineans and Australians (see 35 ka)
15	d	?	Mongoloids split into NE Asians and Amerindians (see 35 and 10,0 ka)
12	d	?	Hamitic/Semitic peoples split from Caucasoids (35 ka)
10,0	d,f	S	Khoi-San (Bushmen) split from Negroids, Southern Africa (see 25 ka)
8,0	d	?	Split of SE Asians and Pacific Islanders (see 35 ka)
6,5	d	4	Pygmies separate from Negroids, West African rain forests (see 30 and 18 ka)

It has been claimed that the human races only appeared <20 ka, when genes involved in skin pigmentation appeared, causing <10 ka development of blue eyes

Separation of Mongoloids from Negroids could have happened rather early in Africa before **H.**sap.sap. left for Eurasia, the new race splitting into southbound Khoi-San (yellow-brown skin, almost narrow eyes) and northbound Mongoloids: *my suggestion*

The Genographic Project

The reference V = genographic project lists in the 60 ka time-slot:

> The tree of human genetic diversity has, at its root, "Adam" - the common male ancestor of every living man. Because he lived in Africa some 60 000 years ago, all humans must have lived there until at least that time

I would suggest, with due respect, that this is not logical. If the theories about the decimation of **H.**sap.sap. at about 70 ka are correct (which appears probable), then all presently living **H.**sap.sap. would be descendants of one surviving small group, whereas the descendants of all the other groups died out, not necessarily then, but sometimes between 200 ka and much later. In my opinion it is not correct to equate this 60 ka time slot with the 1st emigration of **H.**sap.sap. from Africa, which appears to have happened sometime around 110 ka

The genome investigation (see ref. V) revealed that all current humans are descendants of a small group of **H.**sapiens.sapiens which lived near Lake Baikal in the Altai Mountains in southern Russia about 60 ka, while no other groups have living descendants. Most experts attribute this fact to the explosion of Mt.Toba 74 ka in Sumatra, Indonesia.

This implies, that all the other groups were wiped out more or less simultaneously. Against this stands, in my opinion, the fact that there appear to be no major extinctions of any animal or plant groups at this time (74 ka)

All the genome information really proves is that all other human groups, at some time between then and now, died out without offspring. If they all did disappear at about the same time, it looks more likely to me that this did not happen due to any natural disaster, but because of something within the human species, such as a virus which was deadly or turned people infertile. An isolated group living in a mountain range would stand the best chance to be spared by such an epidemic

There is also the problem of a rather large time discrepancy between the Mt.Toba explosion of 74 ka and the oldest genome times from about 60 ka

m migrations: **migrations, ethnic/linguistic separations**

see also Notes at the end of this Section

5,3 Ma to 1,8 Ma Pliocene Epoch

	Subject Ref.	Source Ref.	
2,0 **Ma**	m	I	**H.**habilis reaches Sterkfontein cave, South Africa
2,0	m	C	Possibly 1st "Out-of-Africa" migration by **H.**habilis or **H.**erectus (see 1,78 Ma)
1,9	m,a	T	**H.**erectus leaves Africa with primitive Oldovan tools (see 1,7 Ma)

1,8 Ma to 42,0 ka Lower Paleolithic Age

	Subject Ref.	Source Ref.	
1,8	z d,m	1,2 S	**H.**ergaster (possibly **H.**erectus ?) coexists with **AU.**, Swartkrans, South Africa (see 1,9 Ma)
1,8	m	Q	**H.**erectus, Mojokerto, Java, Indonesia (see 1,7 Ma)
1,78	d,m	C,D	Group of **H.**erectus, 1st "Out-of-Africa pioneers", tiny brow ridge, short nose, huge canines, 1st smallest brain yet, 2nd much larger (2 species or male/female difference was larger than), primitive tools, 1999, Dmanisi, Georgia, Caucasus (2,1 and 2,0 and 1,9 Ma)
1,7	m	S	Re-dated **H.**erectus, Java, Indonesia (1,8 Ma, 800 ka)
1,7	m,a	Q	Oldest stone tools by **H.**erectus in East Asia, Nihewan, China (see 1,9 and 1,5 Ma)
1,5	m	I	**H.**erectus reaches Swartkrans, South Africa
1,5	m,a	Q	Oldest stone tools of **H.**erectus in Europe, Orce Ravine, Spain (see 1,7 and 1,1 Ma)
1,2	d,m	W,Z	**H.**antecessor, (**H.**erectus ?), 1st **H.** fossil in Europe, Atapuerca, Spain (see 780 and 700 ka)
840 **ka**	m	Q	Tools of **H.**erectus, Soa Basin, Flores Is., Indonesia
800	m	I	**H.**erectus reaches Ceprano, Italy
800	m	C	**H.**heidelbergensis, (I suggest **H.**erectus), Europe
700	m	I	**H.**erectus "Java Man" reaches Trinil, Java
670	m	Q	**H.**erectus "Peking Man", China (see 460 ka)
500	m	4,S	"Boxgrove Man", oldest **H.**erectus in England
460	m	V,I	**H.**erectus.pekinensis "Peking Man"in caves, Choukoutien, China (see 670 and 220 ka)
400	m	P	**H.**sapiens in Middle East (see 500 ka)
365	m	K	**H.**sapiens skull, had a brain tumor, Southern Germany
300	m	T	Only ancient human fossil (**H.**erectus or **H.**sapiens ?) ever found in India
300	m	S	**H.**sapiens "Saldanha Man", Saldanha Bay, South Africa

	Subject Ref.	Source Ref.	
300 **ka**	m,a	AB P	Sangoan Industry (culture) stone artifacts, antelope teeth ,considered 1st expansion into tropical climes by **H.**sap., Port Edward, Natal and Mapungubwe National Park, Limpopo, South Africa(see 120 ka)
260	d,m	V	1,68m tall, 78,5kg female **H.**sapiens, largest known such fossil, also most northern and eastern human habitation, Jinniushan, Chinese/Korean border
259	d,m	S	Skull of **H.**sapiens, upright gait, pronounced brow ridges, "Florisbad Man", Florisbad, South Africa
230	d,m	Z	**H.**sapiens.neanderthalensis only counted about 15 000, hunting and gathering in Eurasia from Atlantic to Siberia, central Eurasia to Mediterranean (45, 28 ka)
225	m	1	**H.**sapiens, Swanscombe, UK and Stuttgart, Germany
220	m	V	Last of **H.**erectus.pekinensis in caves, China (460 ka)
220	m	3	"Petralona Skull" of **H.**sapiens, Greece
160	m	Z	**H.**sap.sap. child, Jebel Irhoud, Morocco (see 200 ka)
140	m,f	AG	Start of **H.**sap.sap. 1st temporary occupation cycle, determined by Optically Stimulated Luminescence (OSL) and Thermo-Luminescence (TL), shell fishing, Blombos Cave, South Africa (see 70 ka)
130	m	Z	**H.**sap.sap. lived in Fezzan, Libya (see 70 ka)
130	m	T	**H.**sap.sap. fossils, Klasiesrivier, South Africa
100	d,m	4	**H.**sapiens last fossils in China (see 200 ka)
100	m	2	"True" **H.**sap.neanderthalensis in Southern Europe and Middle East
100	m	V	1st fossils (a skull) of **H.**sap.sap. outside Africa, Qafzeh cave, Palestine (see 90, 60 ka)
90	m	V	1st wave of African emigrants extinct, Near East (100)
70	m	Z	People left arid Fezzan, Libya (see 130, 5,0 ka)
62	d,m	T 7,D	Aboriginals settled, extinct **H.**sap.sap. genetic lineage, Lake Mungo, South Australia (50, 45 ka)
60	d,m	W	M130 Y chromosome, suggests arrival of 1st **H.**sap.sap., India
60	d,m	V	Major migration of **H.**sap.sap. from Africa to Near East, ancestors to all non-Negroids (see 100 ka)
50	m	Q	**H.**sap.sap., Malakunanja, Australia (see 62 and 40 ka)
50	m	P	Negroids (I suggest: relatives of Australian aboriginals) settle Nicobar and Andaman Is., Indian Ocean (see 62 ka)

Note: *arrival dates of Amerindians in Americas prior to 17,5 ka have been marked by (?) pending clarification, see Notes at end of section*

50	m,a	P	Stone tools and charcoal, Topper, S.Carolina, USA (?)
48	m	P	Humans at Serra da Capivara National Park, Brazil (?)

	Subject Ref.	Source Ref.	
45 **ka**	d,m	Q	M89 Y chromosome marks a major migration out of Africa, mostly found in Middle East (see 12 ka)
45	m	V	**H.**sap.sap. reached southeastern Australia (62, 40 ka)
42,0 ka	**to**	**10 ka**	**Upper Paleolithic Age**
40	m	Z	**H.**sap.sap. arrives, northern Eurasia
40	m	4	Aboriginals (**H.**sap.sap.) reach Indonesia on foot, 130m sea level drop has created a land bridge: Sahul (New Guinea, Australia, Tasmania) (62, 50, 45, 38, 32 ka)
40	m	Q	**H.**sap.sap. at Niah Cave, Borneo
40	m	Z	Earliest fossil of **H.**sap.sap. "Cro-Magnon" in Europe (see 52 ka)
40	m	V	Earliest tools found at Bobongara Point, New Guinea
38	m	D	**H.**sap.sap. settles Tasmania (see 40 ka)
37	m	AC	**H.**sap.sap. settles Pesteracu oasis, Romania
36	m	W	Skull of **H.**sap.sap. claimed to be contemporaneous with similar Cro-Magnon people of France, 1st such fossil since 70 ka, Hofmeyr, South Africa
35	d,m	K	Ainos with Caucasian racial characteristics (related to Cro-Magnon ? = my speculation), Japan (32, 9,5)
35	m	4	**H.**sap.sap. in China and Siberia (see 17,5 ka)
33	m	P	Human skull bones, Chimalhuacan, Mexico (?)
33	m,a	P	Stone and bone tools, San Luis Potosi, Mexico (?)
32	m	4	Colonization of Micronesia starts from New Guinea (40)
32	m	4	**H.**sap.sap. reaches Japan (see 35 ka)
30	m	4	Most southerly point in Asia reached prior to the end of the last Ice Age by **H.**sap.sap., Tasmania (as part of Australia)
30	m	P	The "Pie del Diablo" (Devil's Foot) is a human foot impression size 34 in volcanic ash, Mexico (?)
30	m	7,8	Preliminary mitochondrial DNA research suggests possible human presence in Americas (?) (see >30 ka)
27	m	4	San people and Khoikhoi in arid Namibia (see 20 ka)
24	m	I	Male human skull, Los Angeles (?)
20	m	5	1st human habitation by San people in the Drakensberge mountains, South Africa (see 27 ka)
19,9	m	Z	**H.**sap.sap. at Gibraltar, Spain
18	m		Ainu, 1st inhabitants, arrive from Asia, Hokkaido, Japan (see 15 and 7,0 ka)
18	m	7	Stone tools similar to Solutrean culture of France, Cactus Hill, Virginia (?)
17,5	m	V	1st migration of Paleo-Amerindians from Siberia to Alaska via Beringia, Arctic (timing hotly debated) (see 35, 17, 14,3 and 14 ka)
17	m	I	Laguna skull, date uncertain as locale was disturbed, California, USA

	Subject Ref.	Source Ref.	
17 **ka**	m	7	Paleo-Amerindians reach Alaska (see 17,5 ka)
16	m	4,V	Paleo-Amerindian rock shelter, date now accepted, Meadowcroft, Pennsylvania, USA
15	m	5	Paleo-Amerindians migrate to Alaska, related to Jomon, an ancient people in Japan (see 18 ka)
15	m	I	Paleo-Amerindians possibly in California
14,6	m,a	Q	Anvil stone, Big Eddy, Missouri, USA
14,3	m	AG	700 Amerindian coprolites dated by DNA, confirming agreement with Siberian population, Oregon, USA (see 17,5 ka)
14	m,a	I	Unifacial tools, chopper, burin from pre-projection point stage, with extinct sloths, cameloids, Ayacucho, Peru
14	m,a	7	Ivory tools/weapons made from Pleistocene horse, Aucilla, Florida
14	m	7	Main migration by Paleo-Amerindians from NE Asia to Alaska via Beringia land bridge (see 17,5 ka)
14	m	7	Paleo-Amerindian habitation, date now accepted, Monte Verde, southern Chile
13	m	P	1st habitation, Richtersveld, Namibia
13	m	Q	Paleo-Amerindian female, Santa Rosa Is., California
13	m	7	"Luzia" skull, near Rio de Janeiro, Brazil
11	m	7	Charlotte Is., Canada, is inhabited
11	m	4	Paleo-Amerindians reach Mexico
11	m	7	Skeleton of woman, Arch Lake, New Mexico, USA
11	m,f	H	Amerindians arrive in North America via Beringia, advancing 16km/a, with their sophisticated weapons they could have eliminated many species of the larger animals (see >30 ka)
11	m	4	Andes densely populated by hunters/gatherers

10,0 ka to 7,0 ka Mesolithic/Archaic Age

10,0	m	AG	Human skeleton 60% complete, Mexico
10,0	m,a	7	Spray-painted hands, Cuevas de las Manes, Patagonia (see 20 and 8,3 ka)
9,5	d,m	7,P	Skull form of "Kennewick Man" indicates Caucasian origin (?), possible Aino link (?), Washington State, USA (see 35, 32 ka)
9,5	m	5	Cyclades, Aegean Sea, are inhabited
9,0	m	I	Female skull "La Brea Woman", Los Angeles
8,3	m	7	The final destination of Amerindians reached, modern man has conquered the whole world, Tierra del Fuego, southern tip of Argentine (see 10,0 ka)
8,0	e,m	AB	Large parts of present Baltic Sea inhabited by Germanic (??) peoples (see 6,0 and 5,0 ka)
8,0	m	4	Amazon basin populated, Brazil

	Subject Ref.	Source Ref.	
8,0 **ka**	m,a	8	Northern immigrants, rectangular houses, neolithic tools, no ceramics, Jericho, Palestine (see 9,2 ka)
8,0	m,p	8	Hamites from Southern Arabia migrate to Egypt and Ethiopia, create 1st Egyptian empire (see 6,0 ka)
7,5	m	4	Mesolithic hunter-gatherers in Scandinavia, Britain
7,5	m	P	Spessart mountain populated, Germany

7,0 ka to 5,0 ka Neolithic Age

7,0	m	K	Migrations/exchanges by boats between China and Hokkaido, Japan (see 18 ka)
6,0	e,m	AB	Burial sites, posts and ceramic shards, fossils of earlier habitation of present Baltic Sea (see 8,0 ka)
5,1	m	G	Sumerians ex Iran, neither Indo-Europeans nor Semites (possibly Hamites ?)
5,0	m	Y	Inuit migration from Siberia to Greenland, Arctic
5,0	m	Q	Bantu speaking Negroes start displacing Pygmies and Khoi-San people, spreading south from their homeland, Nigeria/Cameroon
5,0	m	5	Indo-European proto-Greeks reach Greek islands
5,0	m,a	7,8	Indo-European language group: the Proto-Europeans in S.Germany, Danube valley, E.Europe, S.Russia, the proto-Indians/Iranians in the Ukraine (see 8,0 ka)

Notes:

Arrival of Amerindians: It appears at this stage, that the 1st of many waves arrived not before 17,5 ka in Alaska, but I have left numerous reports of earlier dates (particularly in respect of their arrival at southerly destinations and in S.America) unchanged, marked by a (?), pending further clarification of new finds which indicate the possibility, that 50 - 30 000 years ago humans were living in Central and South America

New claim: All non-Africans spread from India after arriving from Africa

Huge time differences for **H.**sap.sap. to have left Africa: 100 or 60 ka ? I believe the 100 ka time to be more likely for a 1st exodus, but there were many waves of migration

H.sapiens neanderthalensis is only found in Middle East and Europe and **H.**sapiens only in Africa and Eurasia

The Genographic Project of National Geographic Magazine

Interesting reading about this *project* at
http://www.genographic/nationalgeographic.com/genographic/index.html

a arts: art, religion, culture, speech, writing, fire, tools, materials, building, commerce and industry

see also the References Section and the end of this listing for further notes

Note: *the Oldowan technique of tool making is referred to by many references as Acheulean. I have changed these to Proto-Acheulean to differentiate them from the European Acheulean from about 500 ka*

5,3 Ma to 1,8 Ma Pliocene Epoch

	Subject Ref.	Source Ref.	
2,6 **Ma**	z,a	I	**Au.**aethiopicus (or **H.**habilis ?) make oldest fabricated stone tools =Oldovan pebble culture, 1997, Lokalelei, Kenya and Gona, Ethiopia
2,4	a	S,P	**H.**habilis used Oldovan tools, 1st to build shelters, Broca's area of skull suggests rudimentary/articulate speech, East Africa (see 1,6 Ma)
1,9	m,a	T	**H.**erectus leaves Africa with primitive Oldovan tools (see 1,7 Ma)

1,8 Ma to 42,0 ka Lower Paleolithic Age

	Subject Ref.	Source Ref.	
1,7	d,a f	S	**H.**erectus, 1 100cm^3 brain, used (but could not make) fire, hunted in teams, East Africa (1,6 Ma, 300 ka)
1,7	m,a	Q	Oldest stone tools by **H.**erectus in East Asia, Nihewan, China (see 1,9 and 1,5 Ma)
1,7	a,f	T	**H.**erectus female with deformed bones and growths due to hyper-vitaminosis, caused by eating the livers of carnivores, had been cared for, Lake Turkana, Kenya
1,6	a	AI	**H.**erectus, Proto-Acheulean tools, up to 30km between place of origin and of use, East Africa (see 1,1 Ma)
1,6	a	2,4	**H.**erectus with partial language, use of fire, East and South Africa (see 2,4 and 1,7 Ma)
1,54	d,a	C,I S	**H.**erectus "Turkana Boy", super-bipedal, 1,3-1,6m tall, 12 years, 850cm^3 brain, small teeth, Proto-Acheulean tools, first weapons, R.Leakey 1984, Kenya
1,5	m,a	Q	Oldest stone tools of **H.**erectus in Europe, Orce Ravine, Spain (see 1,7 and 1,1 Ma)
1,5	a	AC	Proto-Acheulean culture of **H.**erectus and his Oldovan tools, Ubeidija, Israel
1,5	a	T	**H.**erectus makes 1st sophisticated Proto-Acheulean stone tools in huge numbers, mostly used for ceremonial purposes, Oldovan, East Africa (see 1,2 Ma)

	Subject Ref.	Source Ref.	
1,2 **Ma**	a	T	Proto-Acheulean tool "factory", Olorgesailie, Kenya (see 1,5 Ma and 200 ka)
1,1	a	AI	Oldovan tools but no hand axes, Guadiz-Baza, Spain (see 1,5 Ma)
1,1	a	AI	Standardized basic forms of hand axes, up to 80km between place of origin and of use, East Africa (see 1,6 Ma and 29 ka)
700 **ka**	a	AB	Proto-Acheulean artifacts of **H.**erectus living near pools of standing water, Saldanha Bay, S.Africa
600	a	AC	Hand axes, **H.**erectus, Western Europe
500	a	AC O	Proto (Lower)-Acheulean culture of **H.**erectus or **H.**sapiens starts, core and flake tools, Western Europe (see 350 ka)
420	a	AC	Ashe wood spear tip, Clacton-on-Sea, UK
400	a	O	Use (not making) of fire by **H.**erectus, China)
400	a	K,N	**H.**sapiens, 8 wooden throwing spears, Helmstedt, superb condition, Schoeningen, Germany
380	a	4,8	1st human structure, use of fire by **H.**sap., France
350	a	AC O	Old (Middle) Acheulean culture of **H.**sap. starts: flaking hand axes with wooden baton, Western Europe (see 500, 250 ka)
350	a	K	Sharpened rose quartz Acheulean axe head found with 27 **H.**sap. skeletons, Attapuerca, Spain and Mapungubwe National Park, Limpopo, South Africa
300	m,a	AB P	Sangoan Industry (culture) stone artifacts, antelope teeth ,considered 1st expansion into tropical climes by **H.**sap., Port Edward, Natal and Mapungubwe National Park, Limpopo, South Africa(see 120 ka)
300	a	AC	More than 30 bodies thrown down a pit, Sima de los Hueses, Sierra de Atapuerca, Spain
250	a	O	Old (Middle) Acheulean culture/tools of **H.**sapiens, Western Europe (see 500, 350, and 170 ka)
230	a	V	Start of Mousterian culture of **H.**sap.neanderthalensis, later probably used by **H.**sapiens, Southern France and Northern Spain (see 200 ka)
200	d,a	I	Fossils of **H.**sapiens.neanderthalensis: snout-like jaws, 100 000 worked stones, bones of rhinoceros, elephant, archaic cow, near Perpignan, France (230)
200	a	T	End of tool "factory", Olorgesailie, Kenya (1,2 Ma)
200	a	4	Oldest wooden tool, England
200	a	N	Double-sided **H.**sapiens Acheulean stone axe, start of flint production to create sparks for fires and use for weapons, Pataud, France (see 180, 35 ka)
180	a	C	1st inhabitants (who?) worked pebbles, Soleihac, France
180	a	N	Double-sided stone axe re-cut, Pataud, France (200 ka)
170	a	AC O	Late (Upper) Acheulean culture, Western Europe (see 350 and 75 ka)

	Subject Ref.	Source Ref.	
164 **ka**	a	AB	Fire is occasionally used to manufacture weapons and tools from silcrete, which, when heated, allows easy splitting, Southern Africa (see 72 ka)
164	a,f	W	Oldest coastal habitation by **H.**sap.sap., shellfish, brilliant red hematite, Pinnacle Point, South Africa
140	a	U AG	Clay tablets with engraved red ochre bands, earliest evidence of cognitive abilities and 1st use of symbols by **H.**sap.sap., Blombos Cave, Cape Province, S.Africa
120	a	1	**H.**sap.neanderthalensis used stone and wood for tools, buried dead, used skins, Europe and Asia (see 100 ka)
120	a	W	Hut of **H.**sap.neanderthalensis, Ukraine
120	a	AC	Sangoan culture, South/East/Central Africa (300 ka)
100	a	AG	End of 1st occupation cycle, ochre working tools, Blombos Cave, S.Africa (see 140, 80 ka)
100	a	V	Oldest rock paintings by Khoi-San, Apollo cave, Namibia (see 27 ka)
100	a	O	Mousterian culture of **H.**sap.neanderthalensis: flake tools improved, inserted in wood/bone handles, Western Europe (see 120, 30 ka)
95	d,a	Q	Claimed new species **H.**floresiensis, hunters, used fire and stone tools, Flores Is., Indonesia (see 18 and 12 ka and *Notes*)
82	a	AB	Nassarius shells, perforated, with color enhancements are the oldest known examples of human jewelry, Grotte des Pigeons, Taforalt, Morocco (see 75 ka)
80	a	AG	2nd occupation cycle, bone tools, ochre engravings, Blombos Cave, South Africa (see 100, 73 ka)
80	a	N	Stone scraper by **H.**sap.neanderthalensis, France
77	a	5	Engraved human designs, Western Europe
75	a	P	Oldest jewelry found: beads made from shells, Blombos cave, South Africa (see 82 and 43 ka)
75	a	AC	Upper Acheulean culture, Western Europe (see 170, 28)
75	a	O	Levalloisian culture of **H.**sap.neanderthalensis, Western Europe (see 43 ka)
73	a	AG	3rd occupation cycle, bone tools, engraved ochre, Blombos Cave, South Africa (see 80 ka)
73	a	AG	Pressure flaking technique found 55 ky earlier than in Europe (transferred by emigrants or invented twice ?), Blombos Cave, South Africa (see 20 ka)
72	a	AB	Fire is routinely used to manufacture weapons and tools from silcrete, which, when heated, allows easy splitting, Southern Africa (see 164 ka)

	Subject Ref.	Source Ref.	
60 **ka**	d,a	V	"Great Leap Forward": tools are getting more refined, food is exploited more efficiently and art develops, indicating a change in conceptual thought by a more modern language, a distinct genetic change (see also *Notes* at the end of this section)(see 50, 35 ka)
60	a	AC	Fauresmith culture, South Africa (see 38 ka)
60	a	V	**H.**sap.neanderthalensis cave community cared for severely injured member, Shanidar, Iran

Note: *arrival dates of Amerindians in Americas prior to 17,5 ka have been marked by (?) pending clarification, see Notes at end of section*

50	m,a	P	Stone tools and charcoal, Topper, S.Carolina, USA (?)
50	a	4	**H.**sap.sap. has fluent speech, art, symbolic thought, complex religious beliefs, body ornaments (60, 40 ka)
45	a	4	Musical instrument (flute), North Africa (see 40 ka)
43	a	P	2nd oldest jewelry: perforated teeth and egg shells, Balkans (see 75 and 40 ka)
43	a	2	Chatelperronian (= Old Perigordian) culture, use of **H.**sap.sap. culture by **H.**sap.neanderthalensis, ritual burials, no sexual mix between these groups, France (see 23 ka)
43	a	7,8 AC	Levalloisian (Chatelperronian) culture of **H.**sap. neanderthalensis, maybe later used by **H.**sap.sap., narrow blades, eyed needles, carving, engraving bones and antlers (see 75 ka)

42,0 ka to 10 ka Upper Paleolithic Age

42	a	7,8 AC	Levalloisian (Chatelperronian) culture of **H.**sap. neanderthalensis, maybe later used by **H.**sap.sap., narrow blades, eyed needles, carving, engraving bones and antlers (see 75 and 42, 41,5 and 40,5 ka)
42	a	P	**H.**sap.neanderthalensis in lowest of 3 levels in a cave, Chatelperron, Massif Central, France
41,5	a	P	**H.**sap.sap. in 2nd lowest cave level
40,5	a	P	**H.**sap.neanderthalensis in top cave level
40	d,a	K	Cro-Magnon people (**H.**sap.sap.) had the modern lowered larynx enabling distinct speech (see 50 and 15 ka)
40	a	P	3rd oldest jewelry, ostrich egg shell beads, Kenya (43)
40	a	AB	Flutes found (**H.**sap.sap. or **H.**sap.neanderthalensis ?), Ulm, Germany (see 45 ka)
40	a	Y	Sturdy shoes said to have been developed (see 26 ka)
38	a	AC	Stilbay culture, South Africa (see 60 ka)
35	a	N	Flint production by Cro-Magnon people to create sparks for fire and use for weapons, France (see 200 ka)

	Subject Ref.	Source Ref.	
35 **ka**	a	AB	6cm female ivory statue "Venus", earliest example of 3-dimensual figurative art, exaggerated sexual attributes, parts of 25 items found, Tuebingen, Germany (see 25 ka)
35	a	AC	Mammoth figurine, 2007, Vogelherd, Germany
33	m,a	P	Stone and bone tools, San Luis Potosi, Mexico (?)
33	a	7 AC	Amongst oldest rock paintings/engravings of cave lion, horse, cave bear, rhino, leopard, bison, mammoth, monkey, correct perspective (my comment: compare lack of this in Middle Ages !), Chauvet Cave, France (11)
32	a	7	"Lion Man", artifacts of Aurignacian culture made from mammoth ivory, Southern Germany
32	a	5	Start of gigantic rock engravings, Aurignacian art, cave of Cussac, Dordogne, France
30	a	V	End of Mousterian culture of **H.**sap.neanderthalensis, Southern France, Northern Spain (see 100 ka)
29	a	AI	Standardized basic forms of hand axes, up to 200km between place of origin and of use ,Western Europe (see 1,1 Ma)
28	a	V,8 AC	Aurignacian culture by **H.**sap.sap. spreads from Middle East to Western Europe (see 75, 23 ka)
27	a	5,S	Paintings on portable stones, oldest Khoi-San rock paintings, Hundsberg, Namibia and South Africa (see 100, and 15 ka)
26	a	Y	Sturdy shoes almost certain to be in use (40 + 10,5)
25	a	4	Evidence of self-awareness in **H.**sap.sap., Europe
25	a	I	Artifacts similar to Mousterian near Beirut, Lebanon
25	a	4	"Venus of Willendorf", Austria (see 35 ka)
24	a	4	Burial with hooded jacket and beads, near Moscow
23	a	N,O AC	Gravettian (=Late Perigordian) culture starts, pressure flaking produces thin blades, 1st straight-backed knife, awl to perforate skins for clothing, more modern tools, nets, spear slingshots, textiles, La Gravotte, Cussac cave, Dordogne, France (see 28, 20 and 11,5 ka)
22	a	I	Ground stone tools, Hoabinhian culture, Australia (14)
20	a	AG	Oldest boomerang found, Poland (see 16 ka)
20	a	Z	Red hand-prints, Gibraltar, Spain (see 12 and 10,0 ka)
20	a	AC	Start of Solutrean culture, Western Europe (23, 15 ka)
20	a	N	Bronze laurel-leaf shaped spearhead, bones of 100 000 horses, Solutré, France
20	a	7	Spiritual use of Lascaux cave, Massif Central, France (see 16 ka)
20	a	P,Y	457 fossilized footprints, from toddler-size to 2m tall adult, in calcareous clay, Willandra Lake, NSW, Australia
18	a	AB	Oldest pottery made, Yuchanyan cave, South China

	Subject Ref.	Source Ref.	
16 **ka**	a	7	Magdalenian high art, cave paintings of Lascaux, France and Altamira, Spain (see 20, 10 ka)
16	a	5	Huts of grass or skins by San people, Namibia
16	a	O AC	Early (Proto)-Magdalenian culture starts: needles with eyes, barbed spearheads, boomerangs, France (see 20 and 11,5 ka)
15	a	7	Solutrean culture fades, France (see 20 ka)
15	a	4	San Bushmen rock paintings, Kalahari, Namibia (27 ka)
15	a	3	Hut made of mammoth bones and hides, Ukraine
15	a	N	Clay sculptures of bison, Tuc-d'Audoubert Cave, France
15	a	P	Start of Basque language, (my speculation: since not related to any known one, maybe ex unknown Cro-Magnon language ?), SW France and NW Spain (see 40 ka)
15	a,p	AB	Earliest maps (cartography) (?) (see 8,2 ka)
<15	a	W	Brahmin's chants in unknown language, sound similar to bird song, claimed to have been used before human speech evolved, India
14,7	a	AG	3 human skulls used as drinking vessels, SW England
14,6	m,a	Q	Anvil stone, Big Eddy, Missouri, USA
14	m,a	I	Unifacial tools, chopper, burin from pre-projection point stage, with extinct sloths, cameloids, Ayacucho, Peru
14	m,a	7	Ivory tools/weapons made from Pleistocene horse, Aucilla, Florida
14	a	N	Magdalenian spear slingshot, wood or bone, Mas-d'Azil, copies found at Bedeilhac and Arndy, Pyrenees, France
14	a	7	Bone needle, Broken Mammoth, Alaska
14	a	I	Hoabinhian culture lasted 6 - 8 000 years, Spirit Cave, Thailand (see 22, 12 ka)
13,5	a	Q	Oldest artifacts of Clovis people, Texas, USA
13	a	Q	Unfinished spear head, Big Eddy, Missouri, USA
13	a	7	Woven sandals found, Canada (see 10,5 and 7,5 ka)
12	a	I	Jomon pottery, (stone and fired-clay pots), Japan, linked to Hoabinhian culture ?, or Wei Shui River and lower Yellow River culture ?, China (14 and 7,2 ka)
12	a	Q	Stencils of hands, shamanistic symbols, probably related to Australian aboriginals, jungle caves, Borneo (see 20 and 10,0 ka)
12	a	O	Rock paintings of horses, grotto of Pech-Merle, France
12	a,p	4	Permanent villages of several 1 000s, permanent stone and wood huts, mortars, grindstones, Levant uplands
11,5	a	V AC	End of Neo-Magdalenian, start of Late Gravettian culture, Western Europe (see 16 ka)
11	a	K	Dug-out boats appear, Middle East (see 8,0 ka)
11	a	4	Cave art ends in Europe (see 33 ka)
11	a	Q	Iberian immigrants create Nuragic culture, Sardinia
10,5	a	Y	Oldest (?) sandal, Rock Cave, Oregon, USA (26, 13 ka)

	Subject Ref.	Source Ref.	
10,5 **ka**	a	AB	Start of all-male 10 x 20m cemetery with earliest of 65 graves, hills of Nazareth, Palestine (see 8,75 ka)
10,5	a	AG	England's oldest house (suggest a shelter, locals were hunters/gatherers !), Scarborough, England

10,0 ka to 7,0 ka Mesolithic/Archaic Age

10,0	a	AG	Concrete (suggest mortar) used in buildings, Anatolia
10,0	e,a	Z	Start of Kiffian culture due to intervening moist period, creating a large freshwater lake, "Green" Sahara (see 8,0 ka)
10,0	m,a	7	Spray-painted hands, Cuevas de las Manes, Patagonia (see 12 ka)
10,0	a	4	Microliths (small stone tools), Western Europe
10,0	a	4	Copper working, Middle East (see 7,6 ka)
10,0	a	K	Murujuga, largest Aboriginal art site, 250 000 petroglyphs, Australia
10,0	a	N,W	Weaving, "pottery" made of stone, stone tablets with engraved primitive pictures and symbols (no writing), Jerf, Syria
9,9	a	K	Sun-dried (not fired) pottery, China/Middle East (9,5)
9,6	a	AC	Pre-Ceramic A, Middle East (see 9,4 ka)
9,5	a	I	Oldest level of settlement, Fritz Hugh Sound, British Columbia, Canada (see 9,0 ka)
9,5	a	O	Pre-pottery village, clay bins, houses with windows, double doors and 1m thick walls, Hacilar, Anatolia
9,5	a	K	Pottery is now fired in kilns, China/Middle East (9,9)
9,5	a,p	7	9km long coastal town: remains of 200m long building, 45m wide, near Surat, Gulf of Cambay, India (9,0 ka)
9,4	a	AC	Start of Pre-Ceramic B, Middle East (9,6 and 8,5 ka)
9,2	a,p	8	Jericho oldest fortified town, no pottery, mesolithic stone/bone tools, round huts, Palestine (10,0 + 8,0)
9,0	a	I	Oldest level of settlement, Onion Portage, Alaska (see 9,5 ka)
9,0	a	V	Warriors and villagers threw about 15 000 weapons and articles like a deer antler axe into sacred Ljubljanica River, Slovenia
9,0	a	AB	3 human skulls with shell eyes and reconstructed noses and faces, Israel
9,0	a,f p	4	Multi-roomed/storied houses as status symbols in mixed agricultural/trading villages, Middle East
8,75	a	AB	End of all-male 10 x 20m cemetery with latest of 65 graves, hills of Nazareth, Palestine (see 10,5 ka)
8,5	a	K	Textiles, cords, cloths commercially made, Middle East
8,5	a	W	Early engraved seals of soft material, Iraq (5,0 ka)

	Subject Ref.	Source Ref.	
8,5 **ka**	a	Y	Possible age of rock paintings, Colorado, USA (8,0 ka)
8,5	a,f	AC	End of Pre-Ceramic B, raising sheep and goats, Cyprus (see 9,4 ka)
8,3	a	V	Start of culture based on obsidian trade with Iran, Syria and Levant, Catal Hueyuek, Turkey (see 7,5 ka)
8,0	e,a	Z	End of Kiffian culture and "Green Sahara" due to return of prolonged arid period (see 10,0 and 6,5 ka)
8,0	m,a	8	Northern immigrants, rectangular houses, neolithic tools, no ceramics, Jericho, Palestine (see 9,2 ka)
8,0	a	Q	Jade earrings, Mongolia
8,0	a	Q	Nomadic hunters/gatherers made tools, created rock art, Moab, Utah, USA (see 8,5 ka)
8,0	a,f	5	Oldest boat found, Black Sea (see 11 and 7,5 ka)
7,8	a	8	Cyprus population is isolated, farming, burial (see 7,2 and 8,5 ka)
7,6	a	K	Copper mines, metal is cold-hammered, Iraq (see 10,0 and 7,5 ka)
7,5	a	K	Distillation of alcohol, Middle East
7,5	a	I	Smelting, melting, alloying, casting of metals, Middle East (see 7,6 ka)
7,5	a	V	End of culture based on obsidian trade with Iran, Syria and Levant, Catal Hueyuek, Turkey
7,5	a	AG	Oldest (?) sandal, made of plant fibers, Missouri, USA (see 13 ka)
7,5	a,f	K	Boats are now built with planks, Middle East (8,0 ka)
7,3	a	4	"Bandkeramik", Balkans, spreading to Central Europe (see 6,5 ka)
7,2	a	8	"Bandkeramik" (?) of proto-Japanese Jomon culture (see 12 and 7,5 and 7,1 ka)
7,2	a,f	AC	Irrigated agriculture, ceramics, Cyprus (see 7,8 ka)
7,1	a	W	King Gilgamesh praise song in verses (which language and type of writing ?), Babylonian report: "Great Flood", 1 man and his family and animals are saved, Uruk, Iraq (see 7,5 and 6,5 ka)

7,0 ka to 5,0 ka Neolithic Age

7,0	a	Q	20 graves with alabaster items, Cairo, Egypt
7,0	a	W	Agate, carnelian, chalcedony, chrysoprase, jasper and rock crystal, all varieties of quartz, employed as ornaments, Egypt (see 6,4 and 6,0 and 5,0 ka)
7,0	a	M	Mud bricks in use, Iraq
7,0	a	K	Copper mine workings, Catal, Turkey (7,6 and 6,8 ka)
7,0	a	AB	Oldest "Pfahlbauten" (huts on stilts) on the shores of Alpine lakes and moors, Western Europe
7,0	a		Longhouse, burnt clay bottle, Goseck, Germany
7,0	a	AC	Cardial and Linear pottery, Western Europe

	Subject Ref.	Source Ref.	
6,8 **ka**	a	AC	Chalcolithic culture, copper metallurgy, Near East (see 7,0 and 5,8 ka)
6,7	a	N	Start of megalithic culture in Europe (menhirs, tombs, cairns), tumulus (megalithic tomb), Bongon, Bretagne Denmark, Portugal (see 6,5 and 5,2 ka)
6,5	e,a	8	Babylonian report: "Great Flood", 1 man and his family and animals are saved (see 7,5 and 7,1 ka)
6,5	e,a	Z	Start of Tenerian culture due to end of arid period, again "Green Sahara" (see 8,0 and 5,0 ka)
6,5	a	K	Megalithic graves, Isle of Ruegen, Northern Germany (see 6,7 and 5,7 ka)
6,5	a	P	Sicilians mine obsidian on Lipari Is., Italy
6,5	a	4	End of "Bandkeramik", Central Europe (see 7,3 ka)
6,5	a	K	Furniture fabrication, building of bridges starts, Middle East
6,5	a	W	Bronze (copper/tin alloy) usage starts, Egypt
6,5	a	G	Trade contacts between Middle East and Egypt (5,2 ka)
6,4	a	W	Turquoise mined, Sinai peninsula, Egypt (7,0 and 6,0)
6,0	a	W,V	Gold seen as something valuable, oldest worked gold objects, golden artifacts in Thracian royal tombs, Thracian civilization, Varna, Bulgaria (see 5,1 ka)
6,0	a	AG	A basalt figurine of a culture of herders, oldest statue ever found in Jordan
6,0	a	4	Potter's wheel, weaving loom invented, Middle East
6,0	a	M	Pottery figurines: cult objects or children's toys ?, Iraq
6,0	a	O	Rock painting of cattle drive, Tassili-n-Ajjer, Sahara
6,0	a	W	Turquoise, olivine, chrysocolla, amazonite, jade, green fluorite and malachite, these green minerals used ritually, Egypt (see 7,0, 6,4 and 5,0 ka)
6,0	a	AB	Counting based on fingers and toes leads to systems using 5, 10 and 20 to count farmed animals (5,1 ka)
6,0	a	Z	"Cup Mark" art (hollows within hollows), Preseli Hills, Wales, UK
6,0	a	Z	200 graves of Kiffian and Tenerian cultures, Gobero, "Green" Sahara, Niger (see 6,5 and 8,0 ka)
6,0	a	W	Best preserved mummy of young woman "Miss Chile", Atacama, Chile (see 11 ka)
6,0	a,f	K	20 000 flint stone axes, adzes, saws found, hunters/gatherers become farmers, Ruegen, North Germany
6,0	a	M	Pre-dynastic period, Hierakonpolis statues by hamitic people, Egypt (see 5,6 and 5,2 ka)
5,8	a	AC	Chalcolithic culture, copper metallurgy, Western Europe (see 7,0 and 6,8 ka)
5,7	a	J	Long barrows (chieftain's tombs) near Stonehenge and West Kennet near Avebury, England (see 6,5 ka)

	Subject Ref.	Source Ref.	
5,6 **ka**	a	P,M	Gerzean period, all elements of dynastic art, large rectangular tomb of an early ruler of Hierakonpolis, earliest known superstructure, wooden table, head of cow carved in flint, Edfu, Egypt (see 6,0 and 5,2 ka)
5,5	a	4	Sumerian civilization 1st to use cart wheels, Iraq
5,5	a	G	Woven skirt with beads, Eridu, Iraq
5,5	a	K	1st mention of gold in the Vedas (Indian holy script)
5,5	a	K	Caravans are operating, Middle East
5,5	a	I	Gonorrhea first observed, Middle East
5,5	a	W	Cemetery with 33 middle and lower class graves, largest brewery, Tall-al-Farkla, Egypt
5,5	a	I	Clay tablets with Oroto-Elamite writing, Iran
5,5	a	W	King Enmerkar said to have invented cuneiform writing in message to Iran to buy lapis lazuli, Uruk, Iraq (see 5,4 and 5,3 ka)
5,5	a	W	Local writing, not deciphered, Harrappa, Indus valley
5,5	a	AG	Pig or cow leather shoe, including laces, Armenia
5,5	a	AK	Mosaic Standard, "picture book" of this civilization, also 1 000s of human sacrifices in a royal tomb, oldest structural stone arches, below a 2,5m clay layer indicating a huge deluge, Ur, Sumeria, Irak
5,4	a	W	Lapis lazuli from Afghanistan in use, Egypt (5,5 ka)
5,3	a	M,4 W	Proto-literate period, "Start of History", writing, originally 800+ pictographs, 5 000 cuneiform clay tablets, Great Temple, Uruk, Iraq (5,5 and 5,2 ka)
5,3	a	W	Spoken Sumerian with known pronunciation survived until 4 ka, written cuneiform language until 75 AD (see 5,5 ka)
5.3	a,f	P,7	"Oetzi", hunter/gatherer buried in glacier, arrow head in his back, 1,6m tall, 46 years, charcoal tattoos, oldest copper axe found in Europe, flint dagger, unfinished longbow, tinder fungus and iron pyrites/ flints for sparks, tool to sharpen flint, bran of einkorn wheat, Eisack Valley, South Tyrol, Italy
5,2	a	4	Megalithic tomb of 200 000t of stones, world's oldest roofed structure, 85m long, 13m high, 10m wide with small opening to let in the sun to the floor during the winter solstice only, Newgrange, Ireland (see 6,7 and 6,5 ka)
5,2	a	5	Underground village of 50 inhabitants, Skara Brae, Orkney Islands, Scotland
5,2	a	5	1st European culture starts in Crete, metallurgy, ceramics, marble extraction in the Cyclades
5,2	a	Q,Y	Phoenicians sell cedar timber from Lebanon to Egypt (see 6,5 ka)
5,2	a	Q	Bone tags, bearing some of the oldest writing known, Abydos, Egypt (see 5,5 and 5,3 ka)

Subject	Subject Ref.	Source Ref.	
5,1 **ka**	a	4,G	Hieroglyphic pictographs, stone buildings, Memphis, Egypt
5,1	a	K	Gold medal of sun god Aton, used before silver, Egypt (see 6,0 ka)
5,1	a,p	K	Gold mines, golden treasures in royal graves, temple accountants used decimal and hexadecimal arithmetic, invented modern capitalism, credit, Ur, Sumer/Iraq (see 6,0 ka)
5,04	a	Z	Aubrey Holes burial pits, contemporaneous with ditch-and-bank monument, Stonehenge, England
5,0	e,a	Z	End of Tenerian culture due to renewed arid period, the freshwater lake dried up (see 6,5 and 5,0 ka)
5,0	m,a	7,8	Indo-European language group: the Proto-Europeans in S.Germany, Danube valley, E.Europe, S.Russia and the proto-Indians/Iranians in the Ukraine
5,0	a	K	Proto-Indo-European language splits into about a dozen groups: Germanic, Celtic, Slavonic, Greek, Italic, Thraco-Illyrian, etc. and the Indo-Iranian group
5,0	a,f	Z	When Sahara rains stopped the people stayed, starting livestock farming, later oasis agriculture, (Garamantian civilization), rock engravings, Fezzan, Libya (see 70 ka)
5,0	a	I	Oldest mummy in wooden coffin, only 2nd ever found untouched by thieves, Saqqara, Egypt
5,0	a,f	Q	14 planked boats in mud-brick graves, oldest ever found, Abydos, Egypt
5,0	a	W	Galena, rock crystal, garnet, hematite, lapis lazuli beads, seals and pigments, Egypt (7,0 and 6,0 ka)
5,0	a	W	Gypsum is heated to form Plaster of Paris, Egypt
5,0	a	W	Meteoric nickel-iron worked, Egypt
5,0	a	W	Cylinder seals now made of harder materials, engraved by rotating bow drills, Iraq (see 8,5 ka)
5,0	a	W	Healers wrote clay tablet prescriptions, using caraway and thyme, Iraq
5,0	a	1	Chinese culture well advanced
5,0	a	C	"Tantaval Man" burial sites, France
5,0	a	Z	20x larger henge than Stonehenge, Durrington Walls, UK
5,0	a	AG	Double circle of megaliths, 10 000t shingles tumulus, 50m long, 8m high, inside 29 stones engraved with spirals, concentric circles, great broken 300t menhir, 25m high, Bretagne, France

Table 2: The Principal prehistoric cultures of the Old World (ref. AC)							
	Prehistoric Europe		History of Africa & African archaeology		Near Eastern archaeology & History of Asia		
Period & Climate	Western Europe	Central Europe and Eastern Europe	North Africa, West Africa and Sahara	Central Africa, South and East Africa	Middle East	South Asia, and Central Asia	East Asia and South-East Asia
5000 BP	Enclosed villages first megaliths	Chalcolithic of Central Europe		Beginning of the Hunter-gatherer art of South Africa	Bronze Age		
6000 BP	Lower Neolithic	Danubian Neolithic	Mediterranean and Egyptian Neolithic	Beginning of Neolithic in East Africa	Chalcolithic (copper metallurgy)	Neolithic of Iran	Neolithic of Yang-Shao rice-growing (?)
7000 BP	Cardial and Linear Pottery (agriculture, stock-rearing, Pottery) Tardenoisian cultures	Starčevo and Vinča culture agriculture, stock-rearing (pigs, bovine, sheep)	Neolithic of the Sahara/Sahel		Irrigated agriculture ceramic Cyprus	Irrigation	Cultivation of millet pig rearing
8000 BP	Sauveterrian cultures (gathering of legumes)	Neolithic in Greece and the Eastern Mediterranean Sesklo and Choirokoitia	Ceramic		Neolithic with ceramic raising sheep & goats end of pre-ceramic B aceramic Cyprus	Pre-ceramic of Iran Afghanistan and Baluchistan	Neolithic of northern China
9000 BP		Backed point culture		Wiltonian	Pre-ceramic B Pre-ceramic A Neolithic in Turkey (wheat, barley)		Hunter gatherers of Jōmon (ancient Japan)
10,000 BP	Azilian and Asiloid cultures		Capsian		Goats domestication Zagros in Iran First towns Near East at Aşıklı Höyük and Jericho		Hoabinhian of Southeast Asia
11,000 BP	Late Gravettian	Late Gravettian plains complex Mezine Kostienk		Magosian	Natufian	Khandivili	
12,000 BP Holocene	Magdalenian Solutrean		Ibero-	Lupemban culture	Kebarian		Pre-Jōmon ceramic

began glacial ended (12,000 BP) glacial at its coldest (20,000 BP)	Epigravettian	Epigravettian	maurusian Sebilian		Athlitian		(Japan)
20,000 BP	Gravettian Aurignacian (art)	Pavlovian Aurignacian (art)			Aurignacian (art)		Sơn Vi culture (northern Vietnam)
30,000 BP	Châtelperronian	Szeletian	Aterian	Stillbay		Angara culture	Sen-Doki
40,000 BP					Emirian		
50,000 BP	Mousterian (earliest graves)	Mousterian	Mousterian	Fauresmithian	Mousterian Mousterian	Soanian	Ngandong culture
80,000 BP latest glacial began (95,000 BP)	Micoquien		Micoquien	Mousteroid			Ordos culture
100,000 BP glacial ended (130,000 BP)	Upper Acheulean	Upper Acheulean		Sangoan		Acheulean Soanian	Fen Culture
200,000 BP glacial began (350,000 BP)			Acheulean	Acheulean			

	Tayacian				Acheulean		
300,000 BP	Middle Acheulean Clactonian	Middle Acheulean				Pre-Soanian	
500,000 BP	Lower Acheulean Worked pebbles	Lower Acheulean Worked pebbles	Lower Acheulean				Padjitanian
1,000,000 BP	Worked pebbles	Worked pebbles	Worked pebbles	Lower Acheulean Oldowan			Worked pebbles

Ecological/Cultural Timelines for Western Europe

See in the Reference Section

Movius Line Conundrum

When **H.**sapiens sapiens left Africa he took his modern Acheulean tools to Europe, the Middle East, Central Asia and East India (Movius Line), but not to the Far East, where only the older Oldovan tools were found

My suggestion: an earlier migration to China and a later one only up to India, supplanting the older generation of tools only up to the Movius Line

Notes regarding Sumeria: (ref. AK)

Assyrians and Babylonians = Semites
Sumerians = Indo-Europeans, "Black Heads", 1st of the High Cultures, language similar to Turanic = ancient Turkish

The 1st (more correctly: the so far oldest-known) human documentations by umerians of:
schools, mild corruption, youth delinquency, psycho war, political 2-chamber congress, historian, tax rebate, law codification, judicial precedent, medical prescription book, farmer's calendar, garden experiment, cosmological treatise, moral rules, "Hiob", proverbs, animal fables, philosophical hair splitting, paradise, "Noah", story of resurrection, "St.George", epical literature, love song, library catalog, "golden era of peace"
Other "firsts" are :cuneiform writing, dictionary, grammar, use of gold, step pyramids, ziggurats and generally, the precursors of the Babylonian/Assyrian culture
The Sumerian kings are recorded as "before the deluge" or "after the deluge"
Facial expressions of the Sumerian said to be found today in Afghanistan and Beluchistan up to the Indus Valley, where rectangular seal blocks were found, identical to Sumerian ones

f foods: **hunting/gathering/fishing, farming, cultivating crops, breeding animals**

1,8 Ma to 42,0 ka Lower Paleolithic Age

	Subject Ref.	Source Ref.	
1,78 **Ma**	d f	Q	**H.**erectus switches to being carnivore because of seasonal cold weather, Dmanisi, Georgia (1,9 + 1,44)
1,7	d,a f	S	**H.**erectus, 1 100cm^3 brain, used (but could not make) fire, hunted in teams, East Africa (1,6 Ma, 300 ka)
1,7	a,f	T	**H.**erectus female with deformed bones and growths due to hyper-vitaminosis, caused by eating the livers of carnivores, had been cared for, Lake Turkana, Kenya
1,44	d,f	W	Part of upper jaw with some teeth, skull of **H.**erectus, largely herbivore (Mrs.Leakey), Kenya (see 1,78 Ma)
164 **ka**	a,f	W	Oldest coastal habitation by **H.**sap.sap., shellfish, brilliant red hematite, Pinnacle Point, South Africa
140	m,f	AG	Start of 1st temporary occupation cycle by **H.**sap.sap., determined by Optically Stimulated Luminescence (OSL) and Thermo-Luminescence (TL), shell fishing, Blombos Cave, South Africa (see 70 ka)
70	f	7	**H.**sapiens.sapiens salt water fishing with spears, Blombos Cave, South Africa (see 140 ka)

42,0 ka to 10 ka Upper Paleolithic Age

	Subject Ref.	Source Ref.	
>30	f	H	Amerindians arrive in America, unlikely that they succeeded with their un-sophisticated weapons in eradicating many species of large animals (14, 11)
15	f	I	Grinding of gathered grain, Nile valley, Egypt
14	z,f	7 AG	Wolves domesticated to dogs, oldest dog bones in human remains, proving dogs were bred before humans settled (see 400 ka)
14	f	I	Start of large scale extinction of mammals, probably due to human activities, California (11 and 9,0 ka)
14	f	7	Big-game hunts, spear heads, "time barrier", Clovis, New Mexico, USA (see >30, 11 ka)
12	f	I	Plant cultivation, Hoabinhian culture (see 14 ka)
12	f	4	Temporary field camps, reaping knives to harvest wild wheat and barley, Levant uplands
12	f	7	Dog buried together with human (see 14 and 5,5 ka)
12	f,p	4	Natufian society, "complex" hunter-gatherers settled down, some become slaves, class structure, wars, Levant uplands

	Subject Ref.	Source Ref.	
11.3 **ka**	f	V	9 carbonized figs found with grains, acorns, tree species could not reproduce by pollination, only by planting branches, pushing back fruit cultivation by 5 000 years (? figs grow wild !), Palestine
11	z,f	L	"Pleistocene Overkill" by invading Clovis people, extermination of 57 species of large mammals incl. mammoth, glyptodont, elephant, mastodon, N.America (see >30, 14 and 9,0 ka)
11	m,f	H	Amerindians arrive in North America via Beringia, advancing 16km/a, with their sophisticated weapons they could have eliminated many species of the larger animals (see >30 ka)
11	f	4	Beans cultivated, Andes
11	f	W	30 beehives in a row, 80cm long, 40cm diameter loam and straw cylinders, Palestine
10,75	f	V	Start of local culture with diversified diet of seeds, fruits, small game, Guila Naquitz, Mexico (8,67 ka)
10,2	f	AC	Goats domesticated, Zagros, Iran
10	f	4	Hunter-gatherers disappear in Southern Europe

10,0 ka to 7,0 ka Mesolithic/Archaic Age

10,0	z,f	K	Aids virus theory: sick monkey eaten by chimpanzee (immune, but carry the virus), this eaten by Africans (see 5,0 Ma)
10,0	d,f	S	Khoi-San (Bushmen) split from Negroids, San people maintain hunter-gatherer style, Khoikhoi adopting pastoral ways, Southern Africa (see 25 ka)
10,0	f	N,W	Farming, goats, dogs, cake baked with mixture of various grains (oldest baked product), Jerf, Syria
10,0	f	7	Man's bones prove a marine diet, Alaskan coast
10,0	f	4	Incipient agriculture (cultivation of wild plants), 1st in Fertile Crescent: Iraq, Syria, Israel, then in SE Asia, Peru/Mexico, then neighboring areas (9,5 ka)
10,0	f	K	Sheep domesticated, Middle East
10,0	f	K	1st fishermen and farmers on isle of Ruegen, N.Germany
10,0	f	4	Bow and arrow, nets, snares, traps widely used
10,0	f	W	Capers found, Iran and Iraq
9,8	f	AC	Wheat, barley harvested, Turkey
9,5	f	4	Modern agriculture starts: breeding of plants and animals (see 10,0 ka)
9,5	f	K	Pigs domesticated, rice cultivated, China (7,0 ka)
9,2	f	4	Potato farming, Peru
9,0	z,f	W	Domestic cat established, Fertile Crescent (130 ka)
9,0	a,f p	4	Multi-roomed/storied houses as status symbols in mixed agricultural/trading villages, Middle East

	Subject Ref.	Source Ref.	
9,0 **ka**	f	O	Mattocks (primitive tools to break up soil without turning it), sledges, skis, rafts found at 190m² "factory", Star Carr, England
9,0	f	I	Peak of large scale extinction of mammals in California (by Amerindians ?) (see 14 and 11 ka)
9,0	f	W	Fenugreek (a herb) found, Tell Aswad, Syria
9,0	f	4	Paleo-Amerindian bison hunters, North America (11 ka)
9,0	f	K	Barley, beans, olives cultivated, Middle East
9,0	f	AG	Pistacia vera cultivated, Turkey
9,0	f	K,4	Bananas, sweet potatoes, sugar cane, New Guinea
9,0	f	4	Rice farming, India
9,0	f	4	Farming, herding, Eastern Sahara
9,0	f	4	Farming in the Balkans
8,67	f	V	End of local culture with diversified diet of seeds, fruits, small game, Guila Naquitz, Mexico (10,75 ka)
8,5	a,f	AC	End of Pre-Ceramic B, raising sheep and goats, Cyprus (see 9,4 ka)
8,5	f	W	Coriander found, Palestine
8,5	f	AC	Gathering of legumes, Western Europe
8,0	a,f	5	Oldest boat found, Black Sea (see 11 and 7,5 ka)
8,0	f	4	Farming of yams, taro, Thailand
8,0	f	4	Farming established incl. cebus and cotton, India
8,0	f	4	Farming in Italy and Spain
8,0	f	K	Cattle domesticated, Middle East
8,0	f	4	Plow starts to oust stone hoe only in Eurasia, because there are no draft beasts elsewhere (see 7,0 ka)
8,0	f	AB	Milk production additionally to meat as reason for husbandry of cows, sheep, goats, Marmara Sea, Turkey
8,0	f,p	4	Irrigation scheme by the ancestors of Sumerians, Iraq (see 6,3 and 5,1 ka)
7,9	f	4	Millet farming, Yellow River, China
7,8	f	4	Farming in Nile flood plain, Egypt
7,5	a,f	K	Boats are now built with planks, Middle East (8,0 ka)
7,5	f	I	Dogs the only domesticated animals, Iron Gate, Balkans
7,5	f	4	Horses domesticated, Russia (see 6,0 ka)
7,2	a,f	AC	Irrigated agriculture, ceramics, Cyprus (see 7,8 ka)
7,2	f	8	Proto-Chinese, Black Earth civilization, rice and probably silk farming (see 12 and 5,0 ka)
7,1	f	W	Wild chili peppers possibly 1st cultivated, Amazon Basin and Central America (see 6,1 ka)

7,0 ka to 5,0 ka Neolithic Age

7,0	f	AC	Stock rearing, Western Europe
7,0	f	K	Stone hoe, Hessia, Germany (see 8,0 ka)
7,0	f	4	Maize farming, Central America (see 5,5 ka)

	Subject Ref.	Source Ref.	
7,0 **ka**	f	4	Rice farming, Yangtze, China (see 9,5 and 6,0 ka)
7,0	f	K	Sorghum cultivated, Sahel, North Africa
7,0	f,p	K,P	Farming community erects globally oldest 75m diameter circular calendar structure to determine winter solstice, Goseck, Germany (see 6,25 ka)
6,8	f	5	Agriculture starts in the Cyclades, Aegean (9,5 ka)
6,5	f	4	Cultivation of yam, millet, sorghum at northern edge of West African rain forest
6,3	f,p	4	Civilization has to emerge to organize irrigation, Iraq, (see 8,0, 5,1 ka)
6,1	f	W	Cultivated chili peppers farmed, Amazon Basin and Central America (see 7,1 ka)
6,0	a,f	K	20 000 flint stone axes, adzes, saws found, hunters/ gatherers become farmers, Ruegen, North Germany
6,0	f	P	Neolithic farmers in Jutland, Denmark
6,0	f	4	Terraced rice paddies, villages abandoned when soils exhausted, re-occupied when recovered, China (7,0 ka)
6,0	f	K	Horses domesticated, Ukraine (see 7,5 ka)
5,5	f	K	Llamas, potatoes farmed, Andes, South America (5,1 ka)
5,5	f	K	Maize, turkeys in Central America (see 7,0 ka)
5,5	f	4	Farmers domesticate aurochs, pig, cultivate new strains of wheat, oat, barley, Britain, Scandinavia
5,5	f	7	Humans hunt with the help of dogs, Egypt (see 12 ka)
5.3	a,f	P,7	"Oetzi", hunter/gatherer buried in glacier, arrow head in his back, 1,6m tall, 46 years, charcoal tattoos, oldest copper axe found in Europe, flint dagger, unfinished longbow, tinder fungus and iron pyrites/ flints for sparks, tool to sharpen flint, bran of einkorn wheat, Eisack Valley, South Tyrol, Italy
5,2	f,p	AC	Enclosed villages, Western Europe
5,1	f	I	Evidence of agriculture, Peruvian highlands (5,5 ka)
5,1	f,p	4,G	Ancient dynastic civilization starts due to need of organizing irrigation, Egypt (see 8,0 and 6,3 ka)
5,0	a,f	Z	When Sahara rains stopped the people stayed, starting livestock farming, later oasis agriculture, (Garamantian civilization), rock engravings, Fezzan, Libya (see 70 ka)
5,0	a,f	Q	14 planked boats in mud-brick graves, oldest ever found, Abydos, Egypt
5,0	f	4	Farmers use Middle East cereals, Orkney Is., Scotland
5,0	f	C	Chinese princess Xi Ling Shi discovers silk thread (see 7,2 ka)

		Subject Ref.	Source Ref.	
5,0	**ka**	f	8	Horse, cow, sheep, pig, goat domesticated, Europe
5,0		f	W	Pepper is harvested in Calicut, India
5,0		f	W	Cultivation of onions, Palestine
5,0		f	W	"Antiseptic chewing gum" with teeth impressions, made of birch gum and carbolic acid, Finland
5,0		f	AB	Beer brewing, Spain

p political: civilizations, wars, empires, law codes, calendars

42,0 ka to 10 ka Upper Paleolithic Age

	Subject Ref.	Source Ref.	
25 **ka**	p	7	1st social stratification, Russia
20	p	7	Oldest settlement of Genezareth (Nazareth), Palestine (see 12,8 and 10,0 ka)
20	p	7	1st man found killed by others, Nile valley, Egypt (14)
15	a,p	AB	Earliest maps (cartography) (really ?) (see 8,2 ka)
14	p	7	1st systematic killing of men, women, children, Sudan (see 20 ka)
12,8	p	V	Founding of Jericho, Palestine (see 20 and 10,0 ka)
12	a,p	4	Permanent villages of several 1 000s, permanent stone and wood huts, mortars, grindstones, Levant uplands
12	f,p	4	Natufian society, "complex" hunter-gatherers settled down, some become slaves, class structure, wars, Levant uplands
10,8	p	AC	Founding of town of Asikh Hoeyuek, Turkey

10,0 ka to 7,0 ka Mesolithic/Archaic Age

10,0	p	4	Fortified towns: Jericho, Damascus (12,8 and 9,2 ka)
10,0	p	7	Bands/clans become tribes/nations, battles intensify since leaders are not anymore personally endangered, Fertile Crescent
10,0	p	7	Division of labor leads to hierarchies and armies, also to progress and higher living standards, Fertile Crescent
9,5	a,p	7	9km long coastal town: remains of 200m long building, 45m wide, near Surat, Gulf of Cambay, India (9,0 ka)
9,5	p	4	Class structures, wealth from surplus food, trade, chiefdoms, wars between cities start, Middle East
9,2	a,p	8	Jericho oldest fortified town, no pottery, mesolithic stone/bone tools, round huts, Palestine (10,0 + 8,0)
9,0	a,f p	4	Multi-roomed/storied houses as status symbols in mixed agricultural/trading villages, Middle East
9,0	p	W	Large villages, Indus valley (see 9,5 and 5,3 ka)
8,5	p	Q	Oldest traces of human presence, Athens, Greece (5,2)
8,2	p	W	Oldest village plan, with 3 270m volcano, Hassan Dao, Anatolia, Turkey (see 15 ka)
8,0	m,p	8	Hamites from Southern Arabia migrate to Egypt and Ethiopia, create 1st Egyptian empire (see 6,0 ka)
8,0	f,p	4	Irrigation scheme by the ancestors of Sumerians, Iraq (see 6,3 and 5,1 ka)
7,3	p	4	Iraq densely populated (see 6,5 and 6,0 ka)

7,0 ka to 5,0 ka Neolithic Age

	Subject Ref.	Source Ref.	
7,0 **ka**	f,p	K,P	Farming community erects globally oldest 75m diameter circular calendar structure to determine winter solstice, Goseck, Germany (see 6,25 ka)
7,0	p	K	1 000s of trees felled with stone axes to build "road" connecting several moor villages, Vechta, Germany
7,0	p	I	Important village at Tigris source, Cayonu, Turkey
7,0	p	I	Yangshao dynasty (mythical/historic ?), China (5,3 ka)
6,5	p	4	Eridu, Sumerian town of 5 000, Iraq (see 7,3 ka)
6,3	f,p	4	Civilization has to emerge to organize irrigation, Iraq (see 8,0, 5,1 ka)
6,3	p	M	Uruk, Sumerian city of 50 000, large public buildings of mud bricks on high kiln brick platforms, Uruk, Iraq
6,25	p	Q	365 day calendar in use, Egypt (see 7,0 and 5,5 ka)
6,0	p	4	Nile valley densely populated, Egypt (see 7,3 ka)
5,5	p	7	Major harbor city by pre-Canaanites, Ashkelon, Canaan
5,5	p	Q	Year of 12 months at 30 days each, plus 5 extra days, Egypt (see 6,25 ka)
5,3	p	7	Indus Valley civilization starts (see 9,0 ka)
5,3	p	I	Liangzhou dynasty (mythical/historic ?), China (7,0)
5,2	f,p	AC	Enclosed villages, Western Europe
5,2	p	I	Late Pre-dynasty starts, Egypt (see 6,0 and 5,6 ka)
5,2	p	Q	Oldest human settlement, Zagani Hill, Athens, Greece (see 8,5 ka)
5,1	a,p	K	Gold mines, golden treasures in royal graves, temple accountants used decimal and hexadecimal arithmetic, invented modern capitalism, credit, Ur, Sumer/Iraq (see 6,0 ka)
5,1	f,p	4,G	Ancient dynastic civilization starts due to need of organizing irrigation, Egypt (see 8,0 and 6,3 ka)
5,1	p	4,G	1st dynasty, 8 or 9 kings including Menes, 1st unification of Upper and Lower Egypt, capital Memphis (5,0)
5,0	p	4	Slavery, militarists, Iraq
5,0	p	4	Unification of Egypt by Narmer (see 5,1 ka)
5,0	p	O	Mycenae founded by Proto-Greeks, Greece
5,0	p	P	1st inhabitants, Hisarlik (later called Troy), Turkey
5,0	p	P	300m ring wall fortification, near Dresden, Germany

Leave a Review!

Thanks for reading *Parallel Developments: A Geophysical / Paleontological Timeline from Big Bang to 3000BC*! Your support makes it possible for this independent author to continue creating.

If you liked what you read, please leave an honest review wherever you bought this book! Your feedback is invaluable, and reviews help new readers discover my work.

About the Author

I am not a scientist but an amateur who is interested in the inter-linked relationship between geological, paleontological and environ-mental developments. Any criticism and additions (preferably with stated sources) are most welcome!

If you want to get in touch with me directly, use one of the various contact methods listed by BIOCOMM PRESS at hbteicher.wordpress.com/contact/

Website: hbteicher.wordpress.com/biocomm-press/

Made in the USA
San Bernardino, CA
19 July 2018